S0-BZV-217

WITH LOVE

A Caregiver's Journal

Marian E. Wright

Writers Club Press

San Jose New York Lincoln Shanghai

With Love
A Caregiver's Journal

All Rights Reserved © 2000 by Marian E. Wright

No part of this book may be reproduced or transmitted in any form or by any means, graphic, electronic, or mechanical, including photocopying, recording, taping, or by any information storage or retrieval system, without the permission in writing from the publisher.

Published by Writers Club Press
an imprint of iUniverse.com, Inc.

For information address:
iUniverse.com, Inc.
620 North 48th Street
Suite 201
Lincoln, NE 68504-3467
www.iuniverse.com

ISBN: 0-595-09179-2

Printed in the United States of America

Dedication

This book is dedicated with love and gratitude
to my mother, Verna I. Wright.

Acknowledgements

It is with honor, sincere appreciation, and deep gratitude that I acknowledge:

Grace Dukes for her artistry, expertise, and patience in molding the original manuscript; for her compassionate understanding and encouragement throughout the unfolding of this book, and for her unfaltering belief that this book would help other caregivers.

Zane Spencer for giving me the initial encouragement to write about my experience, for introducing me to Grace, and for always believing in this book, especially during my low moments of doubt.

Cris Platsis Chamis for sharing so much of the experience with me, for reading the original drafts, and for offering her insights and constructive feedback.

The Church of Today in Warren, Michigan for its weekly televised inspirational messages that not only kept me thinking positively, but helped me clearly see that my caregiving experience was an avenue toward my spiritual growth. There are no accidents!

Community Hospice and Home Care Services of Plymouth, Michigan for the competent and compassionate care given to my mother, for the understanding and help given to me, and for the love given to both of us. My gratitude knows no bounds!

All those wonderful friends and family members who believed this book had to be published, and who supported and encouraged me during its evolutionary process: Pat Austin, Elaine and Jim Cole, Josephine Daly, Karen Lucadam, Lois Rosen, Marcia Scarbrough, Carolyn and Jerry Shockley, Eleanor Spaven, and Joanne Sullenger.

Contents

The First Year

On the morning of July 23, 1990, without a warning, my comfortable, orderly world turned upside down.

I was enjoying my busy life of retirement in my home in Flint, Michigan, looking forward to a trip to Alaska, as well as the numerous projects and activities in which I was involved. My mother, healthy and active at the age of ninety-one, was enjoying her independent life in her apartment in Plymouth, Michigan. She was busy every day of the week with bowling, volunteering at her church and Schoolcraft College as a clerical aide, as well as knitting and crocheting countless lap robes and children's hats and mittens for charity.

Yesterday all was as usual. I had driven to Plymouth, a distance of sixty miles, to spend the weekend with Mother. We'd enjoyed our time together shopping for new shoes, having dinner at her favorite restaurant, and enjoying mother-daughter conversations—something we both treasured.

Then it happened.

It was 8:15 the morning of July 23rd. Mother didn't respond to my call that breakfast was ready. I went to her bedroom door to find out if she had heard me and what was detaining her. There she sat on the edge of her bed, half-dressed, and looking befuddled at the shoe she held in her hand.

She looked up at me. I saw the dazed look in her eyes. She put her hand on the side of her head, closed her eyes, and winced in pain. "My head," she moaned. "Oh, my head hurts so much."

Moments later I was on the phone, frantically describing her symptoms to the doctor. Yes, she was experiencing poor vision. Yes, she appeared to have poor coordination...her mouth drooped to one side...speech was slurred...pressure in the back of her head...noticeable weakness. As I responded to the doctor's questions, my panic mounted. This was my mother I was talking about.

"Take her immediately to emergency at Providence Hospital," the doctor urgently directed me.

There followed twelve interminable hours. Tests...more waiting...twelve hours of watching medical personnel come go...more waiting...facing an empty wall...staring at the parking lot below the window...trying to control the gremlins that ran around inside my body...inside my head...inside my heart. After the seemingly endless wait, the report was in.

Diagnosis: Stroke.

Prognosis: Good.

I could only pray they were right.

I stayed with Mother until I saw that she was resting comfortably in her hospital room. The nurses kindly assured me they would take good care of her. I kissed Mother good night with the promise I would see her in the morning.

As I walked the lonely halls of the hospital that night out to the parking lot, the shock of the last hours took its toll. I felt an overwhelming weakness in my knees and prayed that I could make it to my car without collapsing.

I was returning to Mother's apartment without her.

What was going to happen from here?

Stroke. What a frightening word. What did it imply?

Would she be able to maintain her independent life?

Would she be able to continue doing the volunteer work she loved so much and that gave such purpose to her life?

Would she be able to bowl, to drive her car?

If not, what were we going to do?

I was frightened. I feared what might be ahead. What would I do? I recalled a notation in my daily journal written just a week ago:

"I have a strange inner feeling that my life is going to change—perhaps by fall."

Little did I know.

One day at a time, Marian, just one day.

Tuesday, July 24

I was startled when I saw Mother this morning. She lay motionless in her bed with her eyes closed. Her face was flushed, and one side of her mouth drooped noticeably. She opened her eyes in response to my kiss and voice, giving me a weak smile of recognition. She whispered that the doctor had been in to see her and that she would have to stay a few more days. A tear trickled down her cheek. Her slurred speech was worse.

I panicked. *What has happened to my mother? She wasn't like this when I left her last night.* I should have stayed with her. I felt guilty.

As I stood by the bed controlling my impulse to throw back the covers to check her arms and legs to see if anything had happened, the doctor came in. He explained that her blood pressure had elevated to a level of concern during the brain scan they did late last night. He assured me, however, that it was under control now. The brain scan did not show that she'd had a stroke, but the presenting symptoms definitely did. The doctor said that was not unusual. Additional evaluations and tests were scheduled for the next two days.

LATER

I stayed with Mother the rest of the day, coaching her in doing the facial exercises the speech therapist had recommended, as well as engaging her in non-stop conversation. Having been a speech therapist, I understood the importance of that. As the day progressed, I saw a gradual improvement in her color and responsiveness. Her body was adjusting to the medication, and the effects of last night's trauma were subsiding.

By evening her speech showed a definite improvement. She noticed it, too. I mentioned that to her nurse. "Yes," the nurse said. "We all need to talk to her more. We sometimes forget."

The aide who brought in the dinner tray said nothing. When she left, Mother said, "She just comes in and doesn't say anything." Yes, Mother wants to talk!

Wednesday, July 25

Buoyed by the improvement Mother showed yesterday, I anticipated today to be even better. That hope was abruptly snatched away when I entered her hospital room and found the bed empty, appearing to be readied for a new patient.

I panicked.

"Could you tell me where my mother is?" I asked the nurse at the nursing station, in as controlled a voice as I could muster,

"She's in radiology."

I sighed a deep breath of relief. "How long…"

Before I could finish, the woman sitting next to the nurse looked up. "Are you Mrs. Wright's daughter? I'm Karen, the social worker. I need to talk with you. Let's go down to the room."

My heart did a triple beat. It had been doing a lot of that during the last hours. Numbly I followed Karen down the hall.

In a matter of moments, I, the reserved, outwardly calm and collected person I'd always prided myself in being, was pouring my soul out to her. I admitted being afraid to ask anyone about the pronounced droop on the left side of Mother's face and her slurred speech. Were these permanent impairments? I talked about my fear of being able to care for her, my fear of being alone with this responsibility, how I missed my brother, Bob. If he were here, he'd know exactly what to do. I still miss him so much, even after twenty-five years. Now I would have to carry on alone. Could I do it? I had no choice.

I couldn't stop talking. I had to say everything that had been preying on my mind for the past two days. Karen listened compassionately. I even confessed to praying desperately that Bob, Dad, Jack, my older brother who died just three years ago, would send strength to me. I knew this was another life experience for me; somehow, I would come through it. But right now I could deal only with this moment—and I was hurting. My heart and very soul were feeling such pain…confusion…shock. I was so scared, more so than I could ever remember.

Karen put her arm around me. "It's good for you to talk," she said softly. "Keep writing in your journal. I'll be back tomorrow."

Much to my relief, Mother seemed all right when she returned from the x-rays. She smiled when I mentioned that lunch was on the way. I could hear the rattle of the tray carts down the hall. I had filled out her menu sheet yesterday, not knowing what was ahead but doing it anyway. Laughingly, I told her if she didn't like her lunch she could blame me! She smiled and shook her head, indicating she'd never do that. She has always been so easy to please.

After she had finished lunch and I was assured that all was well, I kissed her goodbye, saying I would be back around dinner time. I headed for Flint and my hair appointment. Looking back, that seemed like an unfeeling thing to do. Yet, amidst the panic of these past days, it was suddenly necessary to have a semblance of order in my life.

That was the wisest thing I could have done. Lena, my beautician whom I'd known for several years, and I were alone in the salon. I was free to tell her all that had happened. She understood my tears. She was so kind, fussing with my hair and nails. I really needed that touching, that connection with someone who cared about me. I'm sure there are those who would think I had no compassion. Just a few days since Mother's stroke and here I was concerned about my hair? It was much more than that. Deep down inside I was lonely and very frightened.

Mother was awake and alert when I returned. She delighted in the roses that I had brought from my garden. I commented that I heard an improvement in her speech. She agreed that she was talking much better, even though she was very tired. Do I dare hope for a full recovery? It just has to be.

Mother and I talked about many things. It was so important to keep her talking. She even reminded me to water the plants in her apartment and not to forget the one on the table! I couldn't remember the name of the new resident who had been in to see her, but she did. "DeSoto, that's it!" she said proudly. That led to a conversation about the now-defunct DeSoto car. Mother mentioned those cars driven by sun power, a thought evoked by the recent solar car race. She even remembered that the University of Michigan won the race! Fantastic! She is coming back!

Thursday, July 26

"Don't be afraid of tomorrow. The Lord is already there." Those words appear on a plaque by the elevators at the hospital, calming the fears of the passerby. I know because they calmed me.

Mother looked great when I kissed her good morning. Her blue eyes sparkled when she saw me. "I'm going home today," she told me.

"That's great! Have you been up walking?" I inquired.

"No, maybe tomorrow." She smiled. "Oh, yes. The doctor wants to talk to you."

I left to check with the nurses.

Walking down the hall, I panicked. *Mother hasn't been out of bed. How could they think of sending her home? Would she have to go by ambulance? How was I going to handle her care?*

The nurse looked up at me.

"I'm Mrs. Wright's daughter." My voice started to break. "She says she's being discharged today…" I couldn't continue.

"Oh, no, not today," the nurse said. "She must have misunderstood. We need to get her up walking first. Also, the doctor wants her blood pressure stabilized."

She guided me into the lounge where I tearfully told her my fears: the death of my family, my aloneness, my panic. She said little; she didn't need to. I felt her strength, her support, and her understanding. Feeling calmer, I returned to Mother's room to explain that she would need to be up walking. She understood and was anxious to get started.

Later, the nurse mentioned placing Mother in a rehabilitation facility, explaining that the program would help her with self-care skills, such as dressing, feeding herself, and toileting.

Mother could do all that when I brought her in here. What has happened?

"Do I have a say in that?" I asked the nurse defiantly. She told me I did. "Knowing my mother, she will improve faster in her own home with me." There was no question. I would take care of my mother.

Saturday, July 28

I brought Mother home yesterday. She was so happy to return to her familiar surroundings. She picked up her crocheting, tried a few stitches, then quietly put it to one side. She couldn't do it. I said nothing, but my heart ached for her.

My niece, Marcia, called in the afternoon. She offered to help take care of my house in Flint. I was grateful to know that someone cared. I couldn't think of anything for her to do, but I have the sad feeling I'll need her help before this is all over.

As we talked this evening, Mother said she didn't know what she'd do without me or how she could ever repay me for my help. I put my arms around her and told her, with tears streaming down my cheeks, "Mother, I'll be here as long as you need me. I love you so very, very much."

"Oh, Marian!" she said. "I don't know what's going to happen."

"Neither do I, but the good Lord does," I assured her. "We have to trust in Him."

After I settled her in bed, I sat quietly on the couch in the living room—and faced my thoughts. I was sure that when death comes to Mother, it would be during the night hours. If so, what would I do? Did I make a mistake by not agreeing to the rehabilitation center? My brave words to the nurse about caring for Mother stared me in the face, and I became very frightened. The aloneness overwhelmed me.

In panic, I called Edith, a friend of Mother's, and sobbed out my fright. I really wanted someone with me, someone to put their arms around me and tell me that everything would be all right. But how could it be all right? My world had turned upside down, and now I was in a frightening world that I must face alone.

I listened all night for Mother to call me. I slept very little. Every hour, I checked to see if she was still breathing. Finally, I crawled in bed beside her.

Sunday, June 29

I telephoned Theo, my sister-in-law, this morning to ask if she could come over to see Mother and talk with me. I told her how frightened I was, how very alone I felt. She said she would be right there.

Theo suggested that a visiting nurse might be helpful, but I would need a referral from the doctor. I called Mother's doctor who agreed, especially when I told him about the blister that had broken on her buttocks. He assured me that the weakness she was experiencing was a normal reaction following a stroke. Hanging up the phone, I realized that I was coming to know the meaning of the word "normal" in quite a different way.

Theo brought a raised toilet seat with her, one she'd had for her mother. It helped Mother, and she readily accepted it. I was so grateful. By the time Theo left, my stomach was no longer in knots.

Theo and her husband came back later to install a bath chair, as well as a hand held shower. I was touched by their thoughtfulness. Mother wasn't too sure about the shower chair, though. She prefers tub baths, but right now she's too weak to get in and out of a tub safely.

Monday, June 30

I slept on a cot in Mother's room last night to be near her. I couldn't face the possibility of her falling on the way to the bathroom.

Mother admitted she was afraid to stay by herself now. Her concern, however, was that she didn't want to be a burden to me. I told her I planned to stay with her as long as she needed me; nothing else mattered. She offered to move to my home in Flint, but I knew that wasn't practical. There were four major advantages her own home had that Flint couldn't offer: her doctors, Theo (the only family member close by who could help), her friends, and the fact that the move would be too much for me. I assured her that it would be far easier for me to stay with her. Finally, she conceded by saying we'd think about it.

Mother didn't have the strength to dry the dishes tonight. After drying a few, she began breathing rapidly, felt weak, and had to sit down. She is so determined to resume her independent style of living that she pushes herself to help me and do the things she's always done for herself.

Tuesday, June 31

Joanne, the visiting nurse, called this morning to say she'd be here in a couple of hours. I was relieved, but when I told Mother, she started shaking and crying. She said she was afraid and didn't know what was going to happen. I sat on the footstool in front of her, holding her hands, taking her pulse (although I didn't know what I was feeling), telling her the simple things Joanne would do: take her blood pressure, listen to her heart. Gradually, her fears subsided, and calmness was restored.

Now we were ready for the next new adventure: trying out the shower chair! That experience so totally exhausted Mother that she slept soundly on the sofa until the visiting nurse arrived.

Joanne was amazed at Mother's rather insignificant medical history and the beautiful condition of her mind and body. The major effects of the stroke had manifested in a pronounced droop on the left side of her face, slurred speech, and difficulty in finding words to express herself. Her blood pressure was elevated as well. Joanne ordered the services of a speech therapist, as well as an aide for bathing and shampooing. A nurse will visit once a week. Knowing we will have that professional help, my worry fell away.

LATER

"Let's do the dishes," Mother said as we finished dinner.

"No way!" I quickly responded, recalling last night's experience.

Mother looked so dejected, though, I compromised. "Okay, but you must sit down." I allowed her to dry a few dishes before saying that was enough.

"I'm not tired," she tried to argue.

"Good!" I said. "I don't want you to get tired." As I turned to wash a few more dishes, she reached for a piece of silverware to dry. The little imp was going to have the last word! "Oh no you don't," I chastised teasingly.

Both of us laughed! I'm glad we can.

Later, while watching television, Mother picked up her crocheting. Within a few minutes, she became frustrated and put it away. We agreed that 9:00 in the evening was not the best time for handiwork. I assured her that her ability to crochet would come back, inwardly hoping I was right. She smiled and nodded her head. I'm not sure if that was a sign of agreement or resignation.

I called Shirley tonight, Mother's good church friend. She offered to stay with Mother tomorrow afternoon so I could run some errands. This is the first day I've been able to plan ahead. I feel more in control.

Wednesday, August 1

Mother slept until 9:30 this morning, very unusual for her. She said she felt so much better. Her voice was stronger, too. However, as the morning progressed, she seemed to get weaker and complained of being cold, even though the temperature in the apartment was a warm seventy-five degrees.

This has not not a good day for Mother. She isn't feeling as strong as she thinks she should, and that is discouraging her. We talked about the fact that there would be days like this.

I'm recalling the thought I had earlier in the spring that I was getting ready for a change. I didn't know what kind, but I think I'm finding out.

I do enjoy being with Mother and taking care of her. I treasure our intimate conversations about days gone by. At dinner tonight we recalled the memory trip we took last summer to visit the area in Canada where she was born and raised. I delighted in hearing her remembrances from childhood, driving the road that she walked to school, and seeing the farm where she grew up. That trip holds even greater significance now.

I consider it a privilege to take care of my mother, but I do worry so much. My faith is that God has a plan He is working out. If we don't fight it, our lives will be good—not free from pain or sorrow because they are a part of life—but more accepting, with less tension and stress.

Thursday, August 2

The shower procedure went more smoothly this morning. Mother felt so good to be "clean all over," and I was pleased that my newly discovered nursing skills were improving.

Diane, the speech therapist, made her evaluation this morning. She assured me that Mother was doing very well. Afterwards Diane and I talked, sharing our mutual professional background. I enjoyed that. I'm realizing how very important it is to give time to the caregiver, as well. Already, I have discovered how very lonely caregiving can be.

Marcia, my niece, came to stay while I made a quick trip to Flint this afternoon. Mother held my hand so tightly as I kissed her goodbye that I felt like a mother leaving her child with a sitter for the first time.

There were several cards and letters for Mother in today's mail. She was delighted to hear from Elaine and Carolyn, her two granddaughters who live out west. They offered to come and help. I appreciated their kind offers, but they have families to care for and full-time jobs. Mother's care will be long-term. Life, I realize sadly, is not going to return to the way it was.

Saturday, August 4

Mother is still sleeping. I'm taking the opportunity of the quiet morning solitude to write in this journal, my trusted companion. Later, I'll write to a couple of friends. Writing has helped me keep focused during these past two weeks. I find it is a comforting bridge to friends whom I love and who understand me, no matter how I feel.

Yesterday the doctor was absolutely amazed at Mother's recovery! He said she needed to push herself more, though, get back to crocheting, keep her mind stimulated and alert. Driving, however, was out of the question.

On the way home from the doctor's office, Mother was so depressed. She told me to sell her furniture and put her some place. She was giving up because the doctor told her she could no longer drive.

Later, we talked. I told her we had choices, although I didn't know what they were. "I'm looking forward to this as an adventure," I said optimistically. I sensed I was at the brink of the most beautiful part of my life being with her. We cried and hugged each other. It was a very tender moment.

At dinner, she talked again about selling the furniture. "But Mother," I said. "You're staying right here. You aren't going any place (like a nursing home, I thought but couldn't say it). I'm going to stay with you."

"Oh, no," she argued. "You can't give up your home."

I told her I had no intention of giving up my home. We would have two homes—hers and mine. That relieved her somewhat.

LATER

Being told that she could no longer drive is bothering Mother. "If I can't drive, it's not worth living," she told me. shaking her head dejectedly.

"Mother!" I said in utter disbelief. "Are you going to allow a car—a piece of metal—to control your life? Look at your life. Think of all the pleasures you've given others through the lap robes, hats, mittens, and hangers you've crocheted, through your smile, and all your volunteer work. And for you to say that that piece of metal out there is going to stop you from doing all those good things just doesn't make any sense." I told her that the two of us would be living together, and my car, which she likes, is all we would need.

Nothing more was mentioned about the car.

Sunday, August 5

I started to reread my journal entries this morning but soon stopped because it was just too painful. I think about the events of the past two weeks and can hardly believe it has been only two weeks, not two years. I don't want to relive the details. Only time will take away the sting.

Mother looked happy when she got up this morning, saying she felt good. She was able to dress herself and comb her hair for the first time in two weeks. I complimented her on how much more she'd been able to do today. She was pleased and encouraged that her strength was returning.

"I was going to have you fix your own breakfast this morning," I said jokingly, "but we'll save that for another day." She smiled and nodded her head gratefully. She felt stronger, but not that strong.

One step, one day at a time.

During our breakfast conversation, I mentioned going up to my home in Flint on Thursday and asked if she'd like to go with me. Did her face and eyes brighten up with that idea! "We have four days to get you strong," I said. "That means more activity, including the crocheting." Mother pursed her lips at that idea but nodded her head in reluctant agreement.

A half-hour later she was sitting in her chair crocheting! She was so happy that the skill she thought she'd lost had returned. She finished the cover for one coat hanger and even started another one. What progress! She has a goal now: going up to Flint with me on Thursday.

I feel relaxed and at peace tonight. My life will be devoted to making Mother's last years as happy and comfortable as possible and enjoying the time with her. When she passes on, I'll have beautiful memories and no regrets.

Monday, August 6

Mother continues to be more active. She even washed and dried the dishes last night! Showering, however, is still an exhausting activity for both of us. I'm glad the health aide is coming today.

Received two letters in today's mail from friends. I've reread each at least three times! That's the value of a letter.

Cris, a good friend who now lives in California, called tonight. She'd just returned from Alaska (a trip we'd talked about taking together) and was shocked to hear about this latest turn of events in my life. We talked non-stop for over an hour, crying and comforting each other. She suggested that Mother and I get out the family pictures taken over the years and make an album while we reminisce about those good times. That's a good idea. It would be a good project for both of us.

Tuesday, August 7

Mother isn't as alert today. I noticed some short-term memory loss, too. I hope it's just fatigue. I know there'll be down days. I hope I'll continue to understand them as such and not panic.

When Mother awakened from her afternoon rest, she looked at me so strangely. "I thought you'd gone away and left me," she said sadly.

My heart broke to think she thought I'd abandoned her. I hugged her, tenderly assuring her that I would never do that, that I'd been right there, and if I had gone to the store or some place, I would have told her before she went to sleep. Oh, how very fragile she is.

As I tucked Mother in bed tonight, she hugged and kissed me as if she didn't want to let me go. That was unusual. I wonder what it means. Is she realizing what has happened, afraid of what's ahead?

Wednesday, August 8

I pulled the afghan out of the bag, the one Mother had started the day of her stroke for her oldest granddaughter, Elaine. I couldn't believe the entangled mess it was. Mother's crocheting was always so perfect, stitches and patterns so even and exact. This looked like an awkward beginner's first attempts. Yes, the stroke was rendering its havoc long before we realized it. I reworked the pattern and then told Mother it was ready for her to continue. She showed no interest. In fact, she politely ignored me. I'll try to encourage her another day.

Thursday, August 9

I packed a picnic lunch, gathered the laundry and Mother's necessities, and we were off to Flint. Mother seemed to enjoy the ride but was very quiet. Nothing I pointed out looked familiar to her, even though she'd driven those roads for years. We stayed four hours which gave me time to run some necessary errands and cut the grass. Mother was anxious to return home. When she opened the door of her apartment, she gave a little sigh of relief. There's no place like home.

Saturday, August 11

I cleaned the apartment this morning. "I don't know how you can do so much," Mother commented awesomely as she watched me move furniture, vacuum, dust, and polish.

"What were you doing when you were fifty-five?" I asked, searching my memory bank to recall a significant happening in the summer of 1954. Then I remembered.

"Bob and Theo were married when you were my age, Mother! Remember that beautiful, periwinkle, formal dress you wore with a matching hat?" Mother shook her head.

I called Theo to ask if she could find the wedding pictures. She knew right where they were. She and Marcia were planning to come over later and would bring the albums.

The pictures were the hit of the day! The four of us poured over them, laughing at the happy memories they recalled. Mother noticed the twinkle in Bob's eyes, and Marcia commented how relieved her dad looked walking back up the aisle of the church. Theo remembered how nervous Bob was throughout the ceremony. Poor guy, he actually shook!

Sunday, August 12

Mother awakened feeling very rested after eight hours of uninterrupted sleep. Proudly she showed me how well she could walk.

The day was uneventful until evening when I noticed Mother shivering. I closed the windows and put an afghan around her. That helped. Later, while I helped her write a check that she wanted to put in the morning mail, she began shivering again. "I don't know what's happening to me," she lamented sadly, shaking her head. "I don't know."

I thought the check writing had something to do with her panicky feeling, so I put that away telling her calmly that we didn't have to do that now. After an hour of rest on the sofa and lots of TLC, she seemed more comfortable, but not well. Something is happening. I'll check with the doctor if this continues.

Monday, August 13

With my encouragement, Mother pulled the unfinished afghan from its bag. She began counting the stitches but had difficulty counting by two's. (She'd had difficulty earlier counting the money in her wallet, too.) I suggested counting out loud. That helped. Then, I read the directions while she slowly knit, guided by my instructions. It was exhausting work for her, and she needed frequent rests. She continued on her own while I checked on the laundry. That was a mistake. When I returned, the knitting was all mixed up and Mother was confused. Patiently, I ripped it back and reknit the rows. "It's like learning to knit all over again," Mother commented as she watched me. "If my memory would just come back, I'd feel better."

I kept my uneasy thoughts to myself.

Tuesday, August 14

In spite of nine hours of sleep, Mother dozed off while eating breakfast. Afterwards, she slept for two hours, and another two after lunch.

The doctor had no explanation for the two episodes of weakness. He said it wasn't the medication because it was time-released. He told me to call if there were any other questions or concerns.

Wednesday, August 15

This is a very special day. It's Mother's ninety-second birthday! The mailbox was filled with cards. The pleasure and joy she had from each one of them was most touching. "I do have friends, and they haven't forgotten me," she said, as she lovingly patted the stack of cards.

The grandchildren out west sent a balloon bouquet. Mother's eyes sparkled when the delivery person handed it to her! It was so festive in shades of blues and pinks with three special "Happy Birthday, Grandma!" balloons. Letting go of the string, Mother watched in awe as the balloons floated to the ceiling. She had never seen a bouquet like that. Another floral arrangement arrived later from Schoolcraft College where Mother had worked as a volunteer clerical aide in the English department for eighteen years. She was so pleased her friends remembered her. What a happy day!

Edith joined us for dinner at Mother's favorite restaurant where birthday dinners have been a tradition. She loves the chocolate cake that she is given and especially delights in knowing that with her birthday discount her dinner cost less than a dollar. "I'll get a free dinner when I'm a hundred!" she said gleefully. "Wonder what they'll do the next year. Guess they'll have to pay me!"

Theo and her husband called and sang a "Happy Birthday" duet, much to Mother's delight. That was her first phone conversation since her stroke. She has avoided the phone because of her uncertainty of speech. She did well tonight.

It was a heart warming day. I'm thankful and so very happy to see Mother smiling and laughing like herself once again.

Thursday, August 16

I'm amazed and pleased with the diligence Mother shows in working on that afghan. It upsets her, though, when she makes so many mistakes. I sit on the floor beside her chair, guiding her through the pattern and trying to prevent as many mistakes as possible. I told her we'd have to rename it the Rip-back Afghan. She laughed. In spite of all the delays, I have an idea she just might complete it.

We had a quiet time for an hour before Mother went to bed. I was feeling tired and just a little irritable for some unknown reason. I tried not to show my feelings.

"Let's talk about something nice," Mother suggested. "It's too sober."

"Okay," I answered with feigned cheerfulness. "What would you suggest?"

"Oh, I don't know," she said. "You choose."

"Well, how about yesterday?" I suggested.

Mother's eyes lit up and her face brightened with a big smile as she silently recalled the happy events. "That was such a nice birthday!" she commented.

We gazed up at the droopy-looking balloons and laughed.

Saturday, August 18

We drove up to Flint today. Unlike the last trip, Mother noticed familiar sights along the way. She worked on her knitting while I cut the grass. Big mistake! At lunch, she told me she was all mixed up. I asked which row she was on. She shook her head. "I can't remember."

I spent the next hour patiently ripping back and correcting the mistakes. I was discouraged. I had hoped that the knitting would come back so Mother could enjoy that productive activity once again.

Now and then, as I watch young people having fun and a good time, I think: Yes, Marian, you were like that at their ages, but now you are at a stage of life they have yet to experience. I'm so glad I did what I did in those younger years, especially traveling, and not wait until retirement. I view this time as just another stage in my life.

On the drive back to Plymouth, I asked Mother if she enjoyed her day. "I sir did," she answered enthusiastically. I smiled. Since the stroke, the initial sound of "sh" has been difficult for her to articulate.

Monday, August 20

After dinner Mother and I played double solitaire, a card game we enjoyed playing together years ago. At first she had difficulty remembering the sequence of dealing the cards, but soon caught on after a little help. It's important that I encourage her to do familiar things. I shudder at the thought of her in a nursing home. She would withdraw, wither up, and die. Her greatest fear has been to spend her final days in a nursing home. My prayer is that the good Lord will take her quietly in her sleep in her own home.

Wednesday, August 22

This was another special day. Mother's life-long friend, Mrs. Petrie, came over for lunch with her son, Don. She lives in a nursing home now, has impaired vision, and is confined to a wheelchair. Mother and Mrs. Petrie met as young brides and kept each other company while their husbands worked the night shift at the local newspaper. It was wonderful to see the two women sitting head to head, one with impaired vision and the other with impaired hearing, reminiscing about events they had shared during the sixty-seven years of their friendship. It was a memorable day.

Thursday, August 30

I took Mother to the rheumatologist who has been treating her arthritic knee. Having done all he could to relieve the pain, he referred us to an orthopedic surgeon. This may be a busy fall, but my attitude is positive.

Jill, our visiting nurse, was pleased to hear Mother talking so well today! Mother initiated the conversation, too, for the first time. Also, she has talked on the telephone four times during the past two days. That's significant progress because she has refused to have anything to do with the phone since the stroke. Last night, she called Edith and laughed just like she used to do. That was music to my ears.

Wednesday, September 12

We spent Labor Day weekend in Flint. Mother seemed more content this time which assures me that she'll be okay staying there this winter while I work at the tax preparation office.

Walking is becoming increasingly more difficult for Mother. Every step is agonizing because her knee no longer has a protective cushion of cartilage. She doesn't complain, but I see the suffering on her face. I'm anxious to hear the orthopedic surgeon's diagnosis in two weeks.

Friday, September 14

We did it! I mailed the afghan to Elaine this morning. Mother was so pleased to have it completed. That was a major project, believe me. It is not Mother's best work, but I know Elaine will understand. No doubt, that is the last afghan she will make. It will be a treasured piece.

Wednesday, September 19

Life has been routine this past week. Mother was able to return for a day of volunteer work at Schoolcraft College. She enjoyed working with her friends, but walking was too painful for her swollen knee. The pain is increasingly more intense. Tomorrow, we will find out what's ahead.

Thursday, September 20

The surgeon's diagnosis: knee replacement, without a doubt. After explaining the procedure and possible consequences, he told us to go home, talk about it, and call him with any questions.

During lunch Mother said she had made up her mind to have the surgery. The alternative was pretty bleak: continued pain and a wheelchair in the near future. That's certainly no life, especially if something better is possible. I called the surgeon's office and set the surgery date for October 1.

Tuesday, October 2

Mother has a new knee! Yesterday's surgery went fine. This hospital experience is so different from last summer's. First of all, I'm not making a living adjustment. My routine is established, and I feel in control. Also, this hospitalization is leading toward a better quality of life for Mother. Last summer I was so frightened, not knowing what was ahead and wondering if I could handle it. Now everything is upbeat.

Mother was sitting up in a chair today. I couldn't believe it! Yes, the pain was horrible when she got up, but it will decrease. The nurse said she will walk tomorrow. Miraculous! The surgeon tells us that each day will get better and better and better. I believe him!

Tuesday, October 9

This was homecoming day! Mother was so happy. It was a miserable rainy day, but that didn't dampen our spirits. This morning, the therapist showed Mother how to climb a step with her walker. Result: the four steps into the apartment presented no problem whatsoever.

Friday, October 12

I'm beginning to relax too much at night. The light Mother shines into the hallway doesn't awaken me, and neither does the bell she rings to call me to help her to the bathroom. I didn't hear her call last night and ended up doing laundry at two in the morning. She had dribbled on the carpeting, too, and, unfortunately, saw me cleaning it. That embarrassed her, even though I assured her it was okay. It must be humiliating to lose control of your body functions.

Tim, the physical therapist, came today. He was so gentle and kind that Mother liked him immediately. He was amazed at how well she was doing. He showed us the exercises she needs to do three times a day with me as her coach. I'm learning so much!

Saturday, October 13

This was a down day for Mother. She was experiencing pain from the exercises and felt as if she had taken a few steps backward. She likes continuous progress. "Sometimes it's necessary to take a step or two backward in order to move forward," I tried to reassure her. My encouragement helped because by mid-afternoon there was a marked improvement. Mother's smile reappeared, and her eyes looked brighter.

Friday, November 2

The past two weeks have been routine. I continue to coach Mother with her exercises three times each day. All of us are so pleased with her remarkable progress. She has exchanged the walker for a cane. When we walk outside, however, she prefers to use my arm for balance. I believe that is a matter of pride.

Tuesday, November 13

This afternoon was a down time. Mother and I took our usual fifteen minute walk around the apartment complex. For some reason, it tired her more today. She needed help getting up the single step to the apartment, and then collapsed into the chair just inside the door, totally exhausted. That distressed me.

Later, feeling the need for some brisk exercise, I walked two miles to the corner store for a newspaper. It was such a beautiful day, so bright, sunny, and crisp. I thought the fresh air and solitary walk would help to raise my spirits. My depressed feeling, however, continued to linger. I wanted to cry, but there was no place to be alone.

After Mother went to bed, I did shed some tears. Even though it felt good to release some of the emotion, I chastised myself for indulging in self-pity when I know there are others who have far greater burdens. I should be grateful.

Wednesday, November 14

Mother and her friend, Edith, went to Schoolcraft College this morning to do their volunteer work. I have some time alone for a little while. I really cherish that. It bothered me that Mother was so tired this morning. She said she shouldn't be going to Schoolcraft any more because she had to get up so early. I hope that is just a passing thought. She needs the activity and change of environment. And I need the break.

Writing certainly helps! It's like talking to a good friend. I guess I am my best friend. I'm always there, no matter what. Writing released tears for me today—relief I sorely needed. The stress needs to be released. The challenge is finding a time and a place.

Mother and I talked about the future this evening. It relieved me that she is willing to spend some time in Flint, especially during December and January. She figures that by February, when I'm in the busiest part of the tax season, she'll be able to stay alone down here. I'm not comfortable about that, but it's over two months away. It will work out.

Thursday, November 15

Inspired by rereading parts of M. Scott Peck's book, *The Road Less Traveled*[1] my awakening thought this morning was to think of difficulties or challenges as *learning opportunities* rather than problems. I like that thought. Instead of thinking, Oh no, here comes another problem, my thought will be, Great, here's another learning opportunity! That will certainly put a different light on the situation.

1   Peck, M. Scott. *The Road Less Traveled.* New York: Simon & Schuster, 1978.

LATER

This morning Mother said she dreamed about Dad last night. I asked what the dream was about. "Oh," she said smiling, a distant look in her eyes, "he came home from somewhere and crawled in bed with me." She paused. "But he wasn't there this morning."

Often when I sit in the rocking chair in the living room and look at the pictures of Dad, Bob, and Jack on the wall, I sense they are giving me encouragement, nodding their approval of what we've done, and assuring me that everything will be okay. That's comforting.

Since yesterday morning's reflection—thinking of writing as talking with a best friend—these poetic thoughts have emerged:

I am my own best friend.
That is not to say I don't have friends.
It is not to say that others don't care.
They call, they write, they share
their thoughts, feelings, concerns, joys.
But no one can be with me every second.
No one can reach inside my head and read the thoughts.
No one can see and feel the knots my stomach sometimes gets,
the tension I feel in my face, in my whole body.
No one can see or know the mental gymnastics of my mind
as I try to figure out solutions to challenges.
No one hears me when I retreat to the bathroom to muffle
my sobs in a towel,
or bury my face in the pillow
in the dark solitude of the night
to cry and release all the emotion I've suppressed.
No friend can be there during those times.
No friend could have that understanding.
In the final analysis,
I am my own best friend.

Tuesday, November 20

Went up to Flint alone and felt good about it. Mother enjoyed her day alone, too. She took her bath, called a couple of friends, and even went for a short walk! It proves we do need time away from each other in order to make our time together more meaningful.

I feel good when I think ahead to the upcoming tax season and the fact that Mother may be able to spend half the week without me. Other than not being able to drive, she's able to do most of what she used to. Edith will pick her up twice a week to do their volunteer work at Schoolcraft.

The car has to be sold before the cold weather begins. I'd like Mother to sell it herself. It's her car so it should be her decision.

Thursday, November 24

Today is Thanksgiving. Edith, Mother, and I enjoyed a delicious dinner at a local fine restaurant. It was good, providing not only a welcome change but a different way of celebrating the holiday.

Sunday, November 25

Mother sold her car today. I can only imagine how difficult it was for her to give it up. She told me she couldn't watch the new owner drive it away.

The tears have been coming on and off now for the past two days. Often I awaken before dawn with teeth and jaws aching from grinding my teeth. My emotion is centered around selling Mother's car. To have her give up driving, which was her independence, is a very real indication that the end of her life is coming. Each little awareness of her fragility makes that reality stronger. The tears come. Afterwards, the darkness lifts once again.

Today Mother said she'd be glad when "that chair is out of the tub," and she can take a bath again—a real bath! I heard her, loud and clear. She's in the tub tonight with bubble bath all over her, happy as a lark!

Now the question is: Will she be able to get out? "Don't worry," she told me, reading my thought. "When I make up my mind to do something, I usually do it."

And she did! That was a great accomplishment. Taking a bath alone was Mother's last step to say that she could live alone once again. We talked about that. She's concerned that she has worn me out. She knows I haven't been sleeping soundly. (Only a mother would know that.) It touched me to hear how much she cared. One of these days, I'll have no one who will care like that. But, as she and I agreed, we make adjustments in life; we don't give in or give up. What a model she's been for me! How much I've learned during these past five months!

It is difficult to contain my emotions. Sometimes I'm able to pull myself together with the thought that things could be worse. The pain, however, is still there, and it's very real. I need the release that tears afford. It's important that I understand why I'm feeling the way I do. I know now that my tears yesterday and today were from the significance of Mother selling her car.

Monday, November 26

I think about my life when Mother is no longer here. I think about funeral arrangements and my greatest worry: dealing with and controlling my emotions. It is frightening, a real fear of the unknown. I recognize the feelings of grievous pain: the tight knots in my stomach, the lump in my throat that won't go away no matter how many times I try to swallow, the numbing weakness in my legs. But I keep going.

Mother's death will be much more traumatic for me than Dad's, Jack's, or Bob's. I will be totally alone then. When Dad and Jack died, I was responsible for Mother. My own feelings were secondary. Bob's death was different. He and I were very close. He was my big brother.

LATER

Mother is so strong! She's walking straighter now—faster, too, with an air of confidence. She doesn't want anyone babying her, such as opening the car door for her or putting on her seat belt. Now is the time when I need to show my love by letting go and allowing her to be as independent as she chooses. My first night away next week will be a difficult one, but the good Lord will take care of both of us.

Monday, December 3

I drove back to Flint last night to avoid the predicted winter storm which did come early this morning. What a mess! Sure am glad I made the decision to return on dry roads.

I worked all day at the tax office. Mother phoned in the evening. All was well. She said she was a little lonely, missed having someone around to talk with, but had had quite a few phone calls. I felt better.

Friday, December 7

Mother is experiencing bladder incontinence. I bought a book on practical suggestions for incontinence and am encouraging her to read the chapter on bladder control exercises. It's worth a try, if she'll do it.

Saturday, December 8

Had a scare tonight. Mother could not get out of the tub. It was obvious she was frightened. Her unique way of getting in and out didn't work this time. Unable to get "in her groove," she called me for help. Thank goodness, I was able to assist.

I worried the rest of the evening, though, about how I would get her to accept the shower chair again. She might think she had lost ground which, in her mind, would be unacceptable.

Sunday, December 9

I calmly approached the "shower chair" subject at breakfast. Reluctantly, Mother agreed to using it—but only when I was away. That stipulation was made because she didn't want me to worry.

We went to church this morning. Mother was not acting like herself. She couldn't get up and down easily and complained on the way home about feeling a little light-headed. I prayed it was her body's reaction to discontinuing the blood pressure medication.

Wednesday, December 13

I awakened early this morning, feeling pressured and irritable. The commuting is getting to me. Mother doesn't want to leave home. I guess that means she doesn't want to go up to Flint between Christmas and New Year's. We didn't discuss it further.

I feel put upon, used, and a little selfish. I've given up so much of my personal life during the past five months that I wonder if I even have a life any more. I don't know how much longer I can continue living between two places. I feel as if I am the one making the total sacrifice.

I have my minimal belongings in a corner of Mother's bedroom and on a chair by the dining area table.

There's no room in this one-bedroom apartment and I feel cramped.

I've given up my life in Flint, but I'm hanging on to the tax preparation job, my only link to keeping my sanity.

What would I do, stuck in this apartment, the size of a postage stamp, for the next however long? Go crazy, that's what.

There are legions upon legions of caregivers going through this same personal struggle. Why do I feel so alone?

I'm not alone. Yet I am…so alone.

Thursday, December 14

Today I needed the personal therapy of having my hair and nails done. There was no time to make an appointment with Lena, so I called Mother's beauty salon and made an appointment for both of us. Mother was delighted! I looked forward to it, too, recalling the good feeling I always had when Lena fussed over me.

Mother's hair looked fine; mine was a disaster. The redo was just as bad. I recombed it when I got home, but it still looked like a mess. I cried for five minutes in the privacy of the bathroom. That helped, and slowly I began to regain control.

Why had the experience affected me so hard? I was anticipating Lena's gentleness—her tender stroking of my head, the gentle massage she always gave my arms hands while doing a manicure. But this wasn't Lena. I needed that physical touching today, but it didn't happen. I felt denied. Cheated. All the built-up irritations, the sacrifices I'd made, the denial of me as a person with needs—unmet needs—surfaced. Was it good that I felt this way? If so, will it bombard me again?

Friday, December 15

Sleeping on the sofa bed in the living room is beginning to bother my back. That mattress is so uncomfortable. The piece of sheepskin I placed on top helps a little. I'm only here for half the week, but can I put up with this discomfort as time goes on?

Mother began reading the book on incontinence and asked if I could detect any odor from her. I was honest and told her yes. That was upsetting to her because she didn't know what to do about it. She has always been so meticulously clean. Again, I explained that urine is strong smelling when it's concentrated. If she wanted to get rid of the odor, she'd have to drink more water. Evidently, what I said registered this time. She read more of the book and then tried the suggested exercises on her next trip to the bathroom. Later she drank a full cup of water! I complimented her and promptly filled a container for her to drink by dinnertime. She said she hadn't understood how important water was.

Monday, December 18

"The doctor was certainly pleased that you could bend your knee so far," I commented when Mother and I returned from the orthopedic surgeon's office, following the two-month evaluation of her knee replacement.

"Ha!" Mother said disgustedly. "If he had given me a little more time, I could have bent it farther!"

What spirit!

Monday, December 24

Christmas Eve! I'm most thankful that Mother is returning to good health again and that both of us are making the necessary adjustments. I feel like her big protector. I often think of Dad and how he protected Mother. Guess I have that role now.

Christmas Day

It was a quiet day—peaceful and relaxing. Mother and I opened our gifts from the grandchildren. Mother liked the sweater she received so much that she wore it all day!

Edith joined us at a local restaurant for a festive Christmas dinner with all the trimmings. It was a different experience, yet enjoyable. The family holiday dinners of past years are now just pleasant, happy memories. Life is one change after another. One must adjust and flow with the current.

Since the weather prediction was for snow showers, Mother and I agreed that I should return to Flint tonight. Tomorrow is a work day for me. As always, I hated to leave her. The roads were dry until I was fifteen miles from home. Then it hit—a blinding blizzard. The snow seemed to beat straight at the windshield, making visibility a minus zero. I was grateful for the pair of red taillights in front of me.

Interestingly, Mother asked me to call her when I got home. Last week, when I suggested I would do that, she said, "No, I know you'll get there." I'm not sure what prompted her this time, other than the inclement weather. I do recall my thought last week: Okay, Marian, you're on your own now. There's no one to care if you make it or not. This week, however, my thinking was the opposite. I know that I have to stay well and strong for Mother. She needs me and depends on me. I still need her, too.

Sunday, December 30

A snowy, icy, wintry day—a great day for reading. I'm learning from *The Road Less Traveled*[1] by M. Scott Peck that depression is normal and healthy when it precedes a period of growth. Giving up the familiarity of my comfortable home has created some anxiety, especially since I have no idea of how long or what is ahead. It concerns me that Mother seems depressed. To her, life is being useful and productive; she feels neither now. Making so many mistakes in her knitting bothers her. "I can't trust my memory any more," she tells me.

Life isn't always easy.

Monday, December 31

This is New Year's Eve. Sitting alone on the couch, I'm thinking about the year ahead. War is inevitable in the Middle East. The economy is in rough shape. The emotional barometer is that of gloom and anxiety. I will take it a day at a time. That's how God gives it to us anyway. He is so wise!

Tuesday, January 1, 1991

Happy New Year! This was my typical New Year's Day: wipe the slate clean, ready for a fresh start. I'm beginning with a brand-new journal, too. I know there will be times of joy and times of pain in the days ahead, but I will make it and learn from all of it. The experiences Mother and I have had during the past six months are only preparatory for what is to come. It is a toughening time. It also tells me that I can survive.

1   Peck, M. Scott. *The Road Less Traveled.* New York: Simon & Schuster, 1978.

One of the neighbors dropped in to wish us Happy New Year and to thank me for the loaf of Friendship Bread I'd baked and shared with her. As she hugged us goodbye, I had difficulty retaining my composure. The tears come so easily whenever anyone shows concern or understanding for me. I remember just six months ago, when Mother was in the hospital, how frightened I was, how I reached out for someone to hug me. I needed that physical touch so much. I did the same thing at my brother Jack's funeral, reaching out for anyone to put his or her arms around me. That's a real need for me. Maybe, being single, I've missed that.

I've always found it hard to say goodbye. The tears were always there. Dad and I were the emotional members of the family. We couldn't watch a sad movie without a box of tissues. Mother would laugh at us. She cried when she was hurt, but not often from emotion. She is not demonstrative, but her love is shown in many other ways. When I was caring for her last summer, I kissed her good night every night. Only once in a while did she respond with a kiss. Still, I knew she loved me.

Mother and I went out to eat tonight. As we sat enjoying our dinner, I watched older people coming into the restaurant, some with families, others alone. I wondered who, if anyone, would take care of them. They all looked so frail. I thought how fortunate I am that Dad is gone so I wouldn't have to care for him, too. I miss him, but I know he's happy where he is, experiencing a far greater happiness than I could ever imagine. If Bob and Jack were here, I'd still have the responsibility of Mother, but I'd have family with whom to share it.

Friday, January 4

Mother was not feeling well when I returned to Plymouth this afternoon. The muscle in her upper thigh was giving her a great deal of pain every time she raised her leg to take a step. She was using her cane to hobble around which told me that she was in distress. I'll call the doctor and make an appointment for Monday. It worries me.

Saturday, January 5

This was a down day. Mother still isn't feeling well. I put the heating pad on her leg. She said the heat felt good but didn't notice any difference in the pain when she tried to take a step. I fixed her breakfast, washed the dishes, made her bed—all tasks that she'd been doing. It seemed we were back to where we were last summer. That's why I was feeling so down.

I have some thoughts of anger, too. I'm angry with Mother that she is having a relapse after all we've been through. It certainly isn't her fault, though. I'm tired of commuting, of not having time for myself. I dislike living out of a suitcase, dislike not being in my own home. Those are real feelings. Now the tears are flowing so I guess I hit a raw nerve.

Let me sob. Let me cry. I like the release I'm feeling. Are those feelings I've stored up? Am I trying to deceive myself into thinking I've adjusted to this running back and forth? No! I haven't adjusted. All I'm doing is what I have to do.

Am I going to feel resentment toward Mother? I hope not. I know it's best for her to be in her own home. I know I'm the one who has to sacrifice. Am I being a martyr? No, but I don't like living this way. And yes, I am sacrificing for Mother. I just hope I don't have to give up the tax job. That seems to be the only part of my life I haven't given up. I've given up being with my friends and I've given up my home. But if Mother needs me, I'll give up everything.

Monday, January 7

Today's x-rays showed that Mother's left hip has practically no cartilage due to arthritis. The doctor said she may need a hip replacement.

I discussed that possibility with her tonight. She said she didn't want any more surgery. I understand that. We recalled people we knew who'd had knee or hip replacements and how well they are getting along now. Surgery is a better alternative than hobbling around with pain which will continue to wear her down.

LATER

The pain pills are giving Mother some relief. She has parked her cane, relying on the furniture for support—a real sign of improvement! She really resents using that cane.

Tuesday, January 8

Mother was feeling so much better tonight that she suggested going out for dinner. Both of us enjoyed the meal and the change.

I'm going to have to be more patient. I get so frustrated when I have to frequently repeat because Mother doesn't understand—or hear, in spite of the hearing aid—what I've said. I don't want to treat her like a child. After all, she's my mother.

We watched the news together tonight. I was pleased that Mother actually watched it, even initiating some discussion afterwards. I felt as if I had someone with whom I could share something. Maybe that's what's missing. I'll have to work on that one.

Saturday, January 12

Mother isn't much better today. I think she's waiting too long between pain pills. It's so difficult to see a loved one suffer.

I hate to leave Mother tomorrow to go back to Flint. I'd go crazy, though, staying in this small apartment with no space of my own. I do know I feel better, am calmer, and show more understanding when I return from a couple of days at home. Getting away is like a breath of fresh air. I know this will be a long haul. Somehow I must find a way to prepare for it emotionally and mentally.

Sunday, January 13

Mother showed improvement this afternoon. She was more alert, even able to walk without pain.

One of her friends called tonight. She had talked with Mother last week, while I was gone, and noticed the slurred speech. I believe it was the effect of the pain medication, but this friend told me it was because I wasn't there to talk with her. That upset me. I certainly don't want anyone putting a guilt trip on me. Of course, no one can unless I allow it. This underscores my thoughts that friends and family mean well, but they don't necessarily know or understand.

Wednesday, January 16

War began in the Middle East today. We attacked Iraq by air tonight. That fact sent scary chills through me. The fear is there'll be retaliation by terrorists. The possibility of that is truly frightening. If the activated warhead missiles are sent our way, there may be no tomorrow.

Sunday, January 19

I met two of my calligraphy buddies, Kathie and Marsha, for breakfast this morning. How I enjoyed it! It was fun to hear all about what they were learning in the watercolor workshop they'd come down to attend. What I appreciated most, though, was not being forgotten. There was no doubt about how much they cared.

Monday, January 20

Good news from Mother's doctor today! The diagnosis is Padget's disease. The good news is that a new drug has recently been released which will prevent the disease from damaging more bone tissue. It will also reduce those episodes of painful inflammation from occurring. Now we don't need to entertain the thought of a hip replacement. Wonderful!

Saturday, February 2

The groundhog saw his shadow this morning which means six more weeks of winter. I prefer to think of it as six weeks until spring.

Mother was happy to see me return, although she couldn't understand why I had to work on Sunday. We sat down and marked the calendar with my work schedule. That helped. I know how much she depends on me. Also, I know how much I need the break and challenge of working. I was more gentle and understanding today because I, too, have a life. How important and necessary that is.

Sunday, February 10

Mother couldn't make it to the bathroom during the night and had to use the commode beside her bed. My stomach felt queasy while I cleaned it. I'm not a good health aide. I know I must get used to doing those tasks.

I have decided to make the two-hour commute to Flint every day. By doing that, I can take care of Mother's needs in the morning, see that she takes her pain pill, and make sure she gets enough to eat. The daily commute will be tiring, but I can do it. This episode will pass and things will improve.

Mother is failing. I've accepted that, sad as it is. I hate to see her suffer pain, though. If only I could bear some of it for her. I feel alone, but I'm strong and capable. I'll do whatever I have to, one step, one day at a time.

Friday, February 15

I was able to leave the tax office early to drive down to Mother's. The pain in the hip area is really getting her down. She's having more difficulty with bladder control, too. Now she is unable to make it to the bathroom during the night or first thing in the morning, so uses the commode beside her bed. Tomorrow I'm going to call for a doctor's appointment. Maybe he'll have suggestions about the bladder problem, too. Or is this just something we'll have to learn to live with?

Mother is on my mind all the time. I see her failing and wonder how long. Last night a friend called to inquire about her. I said that she was fair. Her response was, "Well, she's had a good, long life." I believe the person meant well, but I was hurt. She's put my mother in her grave, I thought, and that's not fair.

Saturday, February 16

I'm in the basement doing the laundry, enjoying the solitude, and thinking about the Valentine's Day card Pat sent me. It spoke about friendship and how glad Pat is to be a part of my life. Why do I treasure its message so much? Is it because I feel so isolated, so alone? Is it because I have so little to hang on to?

Mother expressed her discouragement this morning. "It's hard," she said, "getting old and not being able to do things." It was the same thought I'd had many times as I watched her hobble around so slowly with her cane for support. This morning I looked at the picture of her receiving the honorary associate's degree from Schoolcraft College last May. That was one of her proudest moments. Receiving that honor, accompanied by an unprecedented standing ovation from the graduating class, was a memorable event for both of us. She knows her life is drawing to a close. She's ready and so am I. I'll miss Mother greatly. She's all I have. I don't want her to suffer.

I stopped at a local jeweler's today and bought a pair of earrings. That's a "Happy Valentine's Day" present to me! It's important to be nice to myself.

John Donne wrote: "No man is an island." I cry out against that. These days I think that everyone of us is an island, and the distance between my island and anyone else's is an awesome one.

Sunday, February 17

Mother showed her own discouragement this morning. "Why am I living?" she asked. "I'm such a care."

"Oh, Mother, why do you say that?" I put my arms around her and told her other people require far more assistance. Giving her a love squeeze, I added, "And they aren't half as nice as you!"

The role of parent/child is reversing. I'm beginning to accept it. Also, I'm bracing myself for the day when my mother is no longer here and I will be totally alone.

Monday, February 18

As usual, I hated to leave Mother this morning. She was sleeping so soundly that I didn't want to awaken her to kiss her goodbye. I left a note, instead. I think she'll just peacefully pass away in her sleep one of these mornings. That would be beautiful if it's God's plan. She was on my mind all day.

Mother sounded so up-beat when I called her tonight. "My, do I have good news!" she began. "I walked around all day without the cane!" She was so proud of her accomplishment. That was her goal: to walk without that cane. I didn't expect it to be achieved so soon.

Saturday, March 9

Many thoughts are racing through my mind today. One is that my house in Flint is too big for me. I'm not living there so it seems like excess baggage right now. I do need to put that in perspective, though. Contributing to that feeling is the spring cleaning fever that is beginning to hit now that the days are brighter and warmer.

Funerals are on my mind again, too. That's such a depressing thought. I guess, subconsciously, I'm always thinking about funerals, knowing I'll have to deal with it one of these days.

LATER

Mother surprised me today when she said she'd cleaned the bathroom while I was grocery shopping. Later, she put away the freshly laundered towels and linens. Being in control of those household tasks gives her a sense of purpose once again.

During our dinner conversation, Mother asked what I was going to do with her bowling trophies after she's gone. (She'd won ten trophies and prizes every one.) "What do you want me to do?" I asked.

She thought a moment. "They probably should be returned to the bowling alley."

The conversation was all very natural. Both of us know that her time on this planet is short. I'm so grateful that she is out of pain and is accepting the way things are.

Sunday, March 17

I watched this morning's inspirational telecast and liked the message:

It's not <u>what</u> is happening, but <u>how</u> you are responding.
In the face of adversity, you could be living the best part of your life.

The best part? That's a thought to remember.

Monday, March 25

It's a beautiful, warm spring day. I'm sitting outside on the patio, thoroughly enjoying the sun and the solitude while I write in my journal. I feel so relaxed. Mother and Edith have gone to Schoolcraft College this morning to do their volunteer work. Mother is doing so well! The only tasks I need to do for her are laundry, grocery shopping, meal preparation, chauffeuring, and heavy cleaning. She feels independent once again, and that has bolstered her self-esteem. All is well. The medication has done its work.

Thursday, March 28

Mother did her own laundry today, going down to the basement and using the machines. I couldn't believe it! I thought back to last summer when she couldn't bathe herself, couldn't walk without help, couldn't knit or crochet, and was dependent on me for almost everything. At that time,

I didn't think she'd live much longer, and that I'd have to give her twenty-four hour care—neither of which has become a reality, thank goodness.

Sunday, April 16

Enjoyed the telecast this morning. A few memorable quotes:

It's not the problem; it's your reaction.
Ask BIG! Dream BIG!
Pray for courage, strength, guidance—not miracles.

I'm glad those words are in my journal. I will need to be reminded of them many times.

Thursday, April 18

Mother is on my mind constantly. Often, when I awaken during the night, I have thoughts of her death and the funeral. Sometimes it is so real that I even have that sickening feeling of fear in my stomach. My feelings are so ambivalent, though. There are moments when I'm so afraid of what may be ahead, that I wish it were all over. But I don't want Mother gone.

Sunday, April 21

I felt so trapped in this apartment today. Nothing I did was right. Mother didn't like the aroma of my coffee brewing. She told me that the television program I was watching was silly and should be turned off. That upset me. Adding to my irritableness was my eye that bothered me so much I couldn't see clearly to read. That worried Mother. She said I was doing too much. I understand her concern. I'm her help and support. She doesn't want anything to happen to me. Feeling overwhelmed, I cried—in the privacy of the bathroom. It was good to release some of that suppressed emotion.

Monday, April 22

Mother and Edith are doing their volunteer work at Schoolcraft College this morning. It's good to be alone, enjoying a cup of coffee while I write. I have a sense of being in control once again.

My eye is clouding more. It's difficult to read the prices on the grocery store shelves, and driving is becoming a problem, too. I tried eye drops, but the vision remains blurry. I must face the fact that it's not going to get better, that I need to have it taken care of now while I'm in good health. Mother is okay, so I have the time to take care of myself.

Mother told me tonight that Wednesday would be her last day of volunteering at Schoolcraft. She got confused today when she was given some new work to do. That upset her. Maybe she'll change her mind by fall.

Friday, April 26

Today's appointment with the optometrist confirmed what my eye had been telling me: the cataract needs to be removed. I have an appointment with the ophthalmologist in two weeks.

Saturday, April 27

"I feel better when I can do things for myself," Mother said this morning. "I feel I'm getting back to being myself again when I can do the things I used to, like the laundry, cleaning, other things," she explained.

How important that is! We do harm when we take over and don't allow others to do what they are able to do for themselves.

Monday, April 29

Good news from the doctor! Mother is so improved that she no longer needs the medication. My, is she ever happy—and so am I! We stopped at the grocery store on the way home from the doctor's office. It pleased me that Mother was actually seeing things and thinking as she pushed the cart

down the aisles. She even spied a rack of day-old baked goods with her favorite bread. She certainly knows where to find a bargain!

Tuesday, April 30

I must get a Durable Power of Attorney for Mother. When she had to sign an insurance form at the doctor's office yesterday, I thought: What if she couldn't sign it? I'll call the lawyer for an appointment. Right now, I can't think beyond the next two weeks.

I took some time to reread my journal. That was good for me. The pages of the journal chronicled all that we'd been through, the strong emotions I'd had, and the outcome. It showed me the ups and downs of life and how things do work out eventually, although not always how I expected. I need to remember that.

Wednesday, May 1

Last night I started writing the Final Instructions for Mother's estate. It gave me a strange feeling, but it was something I needed to do. It's much easier to make that check-off list now while my mind is clear. My mind is so preoccupied with death. If I can get everything organized, including my own affairs, maybe I'll be more at ease.

Did some thorough house cleaning this morning. Mother wasn't able to help, but she did prepare lunch. She took great delight in serving me!

Mother's Day!

The message in this morning's telecast caught my attention. **"Seize the moment!"** the minister said. **"There is no magic station stop on this trip of Life after which all is happiness and bliss. Seize the moment! Life must be lived as we go along."**

LATER

Mother liked the blouse I gave her—a delicate shade of yellow that looks so nice on her. She wore it when we went out to dinner with her friend, Edith. Afterwards, I dug up the small garden beside the patio and planted flowers. That made her very happy.

Yes, we seized the moment!

Monday, May 13

I hooked up the hose so Mother could water her newly-planted flower garden. This morning, even before breakfast, she opened the sliding glass door to check on her flowers. A couple of weeks ago, I thought she'd given up the garden. It pleased me to observe her awakened interest. This afternoon she watered the plants, something she didn't do at all last summer. Just now, as she got up from a snooze, she mused, "Wonder how my plants are doing!" and wandered out to take a look.

Wednesday, May 15

Met with the lawyer today about setting up a trust for myself. What a relief to have started that procedure!

Mother is feeling so good. "I may be around longer than you think!" she said with a smile and a "just watch me" tone in her voice. There are some things she still can't do, like balancing her checkbook, but she shrugs that off saying, "That's okay, as long as I have Marian."

Thursday, May 16

I awakened this morning thinking about Edith's response when I told her how well Mother said she was feeling. "Marian," she said, "you had a lot to do with that. You have given so much of yourself. You have given up your home to be with your mother. Few children would do that."

Mother helped to take care of her parents. Grandpa died at our home. I recall the stories Mother told me of how Grandpa loved to wheel me up down the street in the buggy. Yesterday, Mother and I talked about caring for parents, recalling all the people we knew who had. The model for my caregiving role had been established years ago.

My feeling of fear and dread of this coming summer is beginning to dissipate. I still can't think beyond the next week, but that's okay. It leaves me free to lean into each day, unencumbered by preplanned activities.

Wednesday, May 22

My cousin, Doug, called from Canada to let me know that Uncle Harold, the youngest of Mother's family of thirteen, died yesterday. With tears in her eyes, Mother said, "I'm the only one left. I guess that's nothing to be proud of."

Being the sole survivor is not a matter of pride; it is a fact of life. I, too, will be in that position soon.

Friday, May 24

I'm adjusting to this new routine. I don't feel as frightened of the future as I did last summer. The only control I have is this moment. The past is gone, the future is unknown. NOW is all I have! However, I do think of the time when, once again, I'll be able to come go as I please. For a fleeting second, I thought it would be fun to go to Stratford to see a play or two when Pat visits in a couple of weeks. But I can't be away from Mother for that length of time. There will be other times. For the next couple of years or whatever, as long as Mother lives, I will be here for her.

Friday, May 31

I've had two very productive days at home, plus the enjoyment of having dinner with Alma and Laura, and breakfast with Jo. After dinner last evening, Laura I had a few brief moments of conversation. Since she'd cared for her mother, she was interested and concerned about how I was getting along. She asked if my mother wanted me with her more and more, whether she was becoming very dependent on me.

Mother likes my companionship and having me stay with her, but she doesn't demand it. I recognize what a frightening experience that stroke was for her, as well as her fear of another one. I remember she'd said that a couple of years before Dad died, he didn't want her to leave him. Maybe she's having those same feelings.

Sunday, June 2

This morning's telecast was directed right at me!

Faith and fear cannot occupy the same space.

What happens to me is not important; how I handle it is.

Nothing is good or bad, only thinking makes it so.

Wednesday, June 12

Mother sounded wonderful on the phone tonight. Her voice was clear, not gravel-like as it often has been lately. She proudly told me she did the laundry and ironing, finished crocheting a hat, covered one hanger and started another. "I want you to know I can do those things," she said.

I laughed. "You don't have to prove anything to me. You did far more than I did today!"

What a lady!

I feel wonderful tonight. Thank you, God!

Wednesday, June 26

Many thoughts fluttered through my mind as I drove up to Flint tonight. I recalled some of the events of this past year, reflecting on how it has been a growing year for me. A year ago, I was acutely aware that my life was going to change. Little did I know!

And this is only the beginning.

Friday, June 28

Got up early this morning for my pre-surgery appointment at the hospital. The cataract surgery is scheduled for Tuesday. Mother has accepted not going to the hospital with me.

"Did they want to know if someone would be staying with you at night?" she asked.

"Yes," I answered, "and you are that someone!"

Mother smiled. "Good! I can be of some use."

I agreed, secretly pleased that my "fabrication of the truth" worked.

Wednesday, July 3

I have a new eye! Yesterday's surgery was a "piece of cake", and now the patch has been removed. I can see!

I made plans to meet Kathy, one of my calligraphy buddies, for lunch in two weeks. That'll be something nice to look forward to.

Tuesday, July 9

Last night, while I sat at the dining room table writing a letter, Mother joined me to work on a word search puzzle. She loves those puzzles, but they drive me up a wall.

I finished the letter and picked up a book to read while Mother continued to work her puzzles. No words were spoken, but there was a definite feeling of closeness and love between us. The simplest moments can be the most beautiful.

Wednesday, July 10

Yesterday we drove over to the nursing home to see Mrs. Petrie, Mother's friend for seventy-five years. We had a wonderful visit! Mrs. Petrie is now ninety-eight years old. She is very alert, and her memory is better than mine! I admired her beautiful face, the softness and smoothness of her skin. Her impaired vision has prevented her from reading, an activity she always loved. That's so sad. The patients in the nursing home appear demented so she has no one with whom to carry on a conversation, except when family and friends visit. I marvel at how she has been able to maintain her sanity.

Several times today Mother mentioned Mrs. Petrie. Yesterday's visit is on her mind. She is so thankful to be in her own home. I just hope and pray she'll never have to leave here.

At the moment, my feeling is that of sadness. I gave up my life last summer for Mother. In fact, I told friends, "My life is on hold." I don't regret making that decision. Yes, there have been many difficult moments, but I realize that Mother would not be where she is now, nor feeling as well as she is, had I not devoted my life to her.

I sat out on the patio this evening, reading and enjoying a fresh cup of hot coffee. I paused to look at our flower garden. Everything is blossoming into a beautiful array of color. I recalled the scraggly plants I'd put into the ground two months ago. They looked as if they wouldn't survive the first rain, but with a lot of TLC they have flourished. Isn't that the way with all living things?

Sunday, July 14

Just finished reading *Recovering: A Journal* by May Sarton. I was impressed by the author's insightful reflections on pain, describing it as a "great teacher." Unlike the emotions of joy and happiness, "pain forces us to think, to make connections, to sort out what is what, and to discover what has been happening to cause it...."[2]

So true, so very true.

2   Sarton, May. *Recovering: A Journal*. New York: W.W.Norton & Co., 1980. p. 208.

The Second Year

Friday, July 19, 1991

Today marks the first anniversary of Mother's stroke. I probably shouldn't be thinking about that. If the next few months are stress free, we will be able to create new memories. I hope so.

I feel good and at peace, but I am anxious to get back down to Mother's. Often, while I'm in Flint, I think about the day I won't have a mother to see. It will be quite an adjustment for me. Life does go on, though. I must move forward with it and not look back, except for the happy memories.

Tuesday, July 23

Mother's neighbor won't be living here much longer. She requires increasing assistance, and since strangers rather than family (she has none) are providing for her needs, that won't last long. She'll be placed in a nursing home. That possibility has been on Mother's mind. She said to me this morning, "I've been thinking what would happen to me if I didn't have you."

Tuesday, July 30

I'm reading another of May Sarton's books this morning. Since I've enjoyed reading her published journals, I selected one of her novels,

Kinds of Love[3] I wasn't surprised that her thoughts on journaling were incorporated in her fictional writing, as well. Writing in her journal, Christina, one of the main characters in *Kinds of Love*[3] wonders if she's "a loon" to continue journaling, but admits she does it for herself. Making the analogy that journaling is like prayer because it "sets things in proportion again," she concludes that the purpose and importance of her journal is personal, whether or not it is even read after her death.

My journal has served as a medium for expressing thoughts and feelings that I wouldn't mention to anyone for fear of misinterpretation. Rereading some of the entries, I've discovered personal growth, and there's no greater incentive and sense of hope than that! Yes, like Christina, I will continue journaling because of what it does for me.

Monday, August 5

I was up earlier than usual this morning. It was laundry day. Mother wanted to do the laundry herself. I guess this was to prove that she is capable. I can't get over the change from a year ago when she could do so little for herself and had given up. I'm so thankful for all that she's able to do now. She did allow me to carry the laundry basket to the basement for her!

LATER

This evening Mother began the project of finishing an afghan a friend started but couldn't complete. She "fussed" about it because the colors were scattered randomly, not ordered in a repetitive pattern that she is accustomed to and likes. I told her that I would choose the colors if she would do the work. That resolved her dilemma and allowed her to begin. I thought back to a year ago when she couldn't remember how to crochet or knit, and I sat beside her, talking her through every stitch. I marvel at her comeback and am ever so thankful.

3   Sarton, May. *Kinds of Love:* A Novel . New York: W.W. Norton & Co., 1970. p. 31.

Wednesday, August 7

I was bothered all evening thinking how the neighbors are talking about my mother. They mean well, but it's like tattling. I was told that Mother walked across the street to the bank one day when I wasn't here. I assured the neighbor that Mother doesn't do anything unless she knows she can. What can I do?

It bothers me that the neighbors talk, but they will. I'm sure none of them would like to be put away in a nursing home. Sometimes people are so quick to make that judgment for others. Observing the slowing down process in older people isn't pleasant. It reminds us that we, too, are headed down that road someday—something we don't like to think about. Mother is doing fine. For now, our arrangement is working. If there is a change, we'll make the adjustment when the time comes.

Thursday, August 8

Pat, my friend from New Mexico, arrived this evening. It was so good to see her! Our weekly letters have kept us up-to-date on each other's activities, but there's nothing like face-to-face conversation. She'll be here for two weeks, making my home her base. During the days I need to be with Mother, she'll visit friends in the area. We'll have plenty of time to do things together, I know.

Thursday, August 15

Today is Mother's birthday—her ninety-third. What a change from a year ago! My cousin, Evelyn, who lives in British Columbia, Canada, called and Mother could talk with her this year. Theo and Chet dropped by in the afternoon with a "birthday pie"—a luscious rhubarb/strawberry pastry. Edith joined us for a birthday dinner celebration at Mother's favorite restaurant. Mother was thrilled to know that with her birthday discount, her meal cost less than a dollar! In addition, she was given her favorite chocolate birthday cake to take home!

The highlight of the day came when we listened to the broadcast of the Detroit Tigers baseball game. Ernie Harwell announced, "Happy Birthday to Verna Wright, who celebrates her ninety-third birthday today!"

Mother's mouth dropped open in surprise. "Now, who do you suppose did that?" she asked, laughing. I just smiled. "Oh, I bet Chet did!" she answered herself. She phoned Edith to find out if she had heard the announcement. Then, she called Chet to confirm her notion that he "did it" and enjoyed more good laughs. I listened, savoring every second. It was so good to hear Mother laughing again.

Wednesday, August 21

I had a "start" around 4:00 this morning. I thought I heard Mother call my name. It was so distinct that it caused me enough concern to get up and check. She was sleeping soundly. I must have been dreaming. She is constantly on my mind.

Friday, August 23

I'm fifty-six years old today. I asked Mother if she remembered the day I was born. Oh, yes she did! She said she called Dad home from work, but I didn't arrive until ten hours later in the hospital. It gives me a sense of connection to know and love the person who gave me birth. I can appreciate the need some adopted children have to search for their birth mothers.

Celebrated "my day" by going out to dinner with Mother and Edith. I recalled last year's birthday and marveled at the difference. Last night Mother mentioned how good she has felt all week. For the past six months she's had no set-back. We have much for which to be thankful.

Monday, August 26

The day began with a call from the apartment manager informing us that our neighbor across the hall had died. She'd been in a nursing facility for the past three weeks. The funeral was at the cemetery. It was so sad—only seven people, including the minister, were there. After a brief five minute service, her body was in the ground. That had been her life, too—one of seclusion.

I was concerned that the funeral had upset Mother. She was unusually quiet all day. I know she must have been thinking of her own demise, as well as the change that both of our lives have taken. She kept her thoughts to herself.

It was fun going through the accumulation of mail tonight—all the birthday cards friends had sent! I enjoyed opening each one and reading the message, laughing at the humorous ones and savoring the personal notes that friends had taken the time to write.

Sunday, September 15

Mother's volunteer work at Schoolcraft College has ended. She has decided not to return this fall. She's very content to stay home and occupy her time with knitting, crocheting, puzzles, reading, and whatever else she chooses to do. At the age of ninety-three, she doesn't need to be pushed into anything she doesn't care to do. After all those years of living, she has certainly earned the right to do what she wants.

Sunday, September 22

I put my life "on hold" last year. When I look back, however, what I had put on hold was not really my life. I continued staying in touch with friends, caring for Mother, taking the tax course, working in the tax office. But something else happened. As the "busyness" of my days ebbed, I began taking the time to look inward. I discovered that the spiritual part of my life had been missing. And that's the most important part, without which nothing else is possible. Yes, it has been a growing year for me! It will continue.

Mother is doing so well! We walked this morning and I was pleased that she walked faster and more confidently. What I really noticed, however, was her alertness and return of control over her life. She's aware of it, too. She told me that I didn't need to come down as often if I had things to do in Flint. "Don't baby me," she said.

Tuesday, September 24

This is my third journal in the past year and a half. The gains and rewards of journaling have been immeasurable. Not only has it served as a safe place to write my innermost thoughts and feelings, but it's a memory book to put clippings or notes I want to save. I have taped this quote to the inside cover for easy reference at those times when fear seems to have control.

> **"You gain strength, courage, and confidence by every experience in which you really stop to look fear in the face...You must do the thing you think you cannot do."**
> *Eleanor Roosevelt*

Tuesday, October 1

This morning I looked at the impatiens "slips" Mother has planted to "winter over." One plant looked very dead yesterday, and I was sure it wouldn't survive. This morning I couldn't believe my eyes! It had taken on new life overnight, looking strong and very much alive. Mother just smiled. "You have to give them time to take root," she said.

How poignant that is to everything in life. In order for me to achieve the new, higher level of thinking I'm eager to experience, it will take time to set down new roots. Perhaps, like the impatiens plant, I'll awaken some morning and be so alive, so strong, and so full of life!

Thursday, October 17

Mother sounded happy when I called her tonight. In preparation for winter, she'd pulled out all the flowers from the garden, even the big poinsettia whose roots were so deep that she had to use the big spading fork.

Imagine a little ninety-three year old woman digging with a big ol' spading fork! When Mother makes up her mind to do something, she does it!

I'm beginning to see my own age. When I look in the mirror, I see an older face—more wrinkles and creases, evidence of wear and tear. I really don't feel older, otherwise. There's an easy solution for that: Don't look in the mirror!

Monday, October 28

Mother and I walked over to the bank this morning. All was well until the return trip home. As we stepped out to cross the street, Mother toppled over. She had hold of my arm but lost her balance so suddenly that I couldn't catch her. Two people stopped to help us. Mother was surprised that she fell; she had no warning. Thank goodness, she wasn't hurt and was able to walk home with no difficulty. That experience made me realize never to take even one moment for granted. The next moment is not ours until God gives it to us.

Monday, November 4

I was startled out of bed this morning by a crash. I bolted into Mother's bedroom. There she was, sitting on the floor between the bed and the dresser, looking bewildered. She'd lost her balance while putting on her slacks. I was able to help lift her up with no difficulty. Other than a sore spot on her back where she had hit the dresser or the bed, she seemed okay.

It would be so easy for me to be fearful of leaving her—after two falls within a week. I will continue to trust in God to guide and protect us. Without that trusting faith, I'd be a basket case.

Tuesday, November 5

It bothered me this morning when Mother said. "Don't get cross with me." I apologized, and tried to explain that I wasn't "cross" but frustrated.

It upsets me when I talk to her and she gives me a blank stare, only to discover she hasn't turned on her hearing aid.

Mother says she's not herself. When I asked what she meant, she described incidents of forgetfulness, like not turning on her hearing aid. I need to change my thinking and take a more humorous approach. I'm beginning to get down on myself, to feel self-pity. That cannot be allowed. I'll try adding a little levity once in a while.

Saturday, November 9

Mother appears to have declined this week. That fall last Monday shook her up. She has a bruise on her back which has given her discomfort all week. She didn't go out the days I was in Flint for fear of falling. I think my "almost decision" not to work this coming tax season might be a good one. Mother feels safer and more secure when I'm here.

Monday, November 11

I'm out-of-sorts this morning. I'm into negative thinking and want to yell at the world and all therein. I know I'm the only one who can change my thinking, but it sure is a struggle this morning. I have that awful trapped feeling again, that my life has come to a standstill, and I can't do anything.

After much thought, I've given up the idea of returning to the tax office this coming tax season. That's making me feel angry, so what's the fear? The fear is of being trapped, of not doing anything, of feeling useless. I am what I think. If that's how I'm thinking, that's the way I'll be.

Change your thinking, Marian!

Onward to this day! The sun is shining, the coffee is perking, all is well.

Wednesday, November 13

When I returned to my Flint home today, the phone was ringing. It was my good tax buddy, Denna. "Marian," she said, "I'm going back to work and you'd better, too!" Denna never beats around the bush, and I love her for it. It wasn't long before I had been persuaded to return to the tax office this coming season. I couldn't believe how relieved I felt! I really do need to be useful and productive, to be challenged, and work with "fun" people.

Mother called. When I told her about returning to the tax office next month, she supported and encouraged it. She said that if I worked, she'd think she was better. When I hover too close I must give her the feeling that she isn't well.

Friday, November 15

I checked out some large-print books for Mother from the library. She is getting bored with knitting and puzzles. Who wouldn't be? Maybe these books will rekindle her interest in reading.

Sunday, November 17

There was an obituary in today's paper about a ninety-two year old woman who died from complications from a fall in her apartment. That caused me to think about Mother and her latest experiences. I was right there and she still fell. I just hope and pray it doesn't happen again. What can I do about it? Quit worrying and give it over to God, that's what.

Monday, November 18

I'm becoming concerned about the odor of Mother's urine. Today I detected a strong odor in the bathroom. I cleaned and aired out the room, but the odor remained. Then I discovered the source: the underwear hanging on the towel bar that Mother had rinsed out, but not well enough. I don't want her to be embarrassed, but I do need to check her clothing more often, as well as do the laundry. She is unaware of the odor. I'll buy some plastic covers for the seats of the chairs she sits in, too. My responsibilities are increasing.

Tuesday, November 19

I didn't sleep well last night, thinking about Mother and how I was going to handle the odor challenge. I was relieved this morning that the chairs were smelling fresher after my scrub job last night. I talked with Mother about laundering and offered to do it. Much to my surprise, she didn't object. In fact, she seemed relieved. I pulled out the book on incontinence again. Mother listened while I read some of the pertinent points. As she said, growing old isn't pleasant. She doesn't know why they call these the "golden years."

LATER

The apartment is odor free once again. I put plastic covers on the chairs. Mother accepted that, thank goodness.

I was upset when I detected a urine odor in the car this morning. It quickly disappeared, though, when I scrubbed the seat Mother sat in yesterday. She can't help it, and she is trying to control it. I'll put a piece of plastic on the car seat to prevent any future problems.

It's strange. As I wrote the last paragraph, tears began to well up, but they never developed when I thought: It's called self pity, Marian, and that doesn't help. It's been over five months since I remember crying. Even sad movies don't bring tears any more. Sometimes I feel as if I'm removed, that I'm looking at life from the sidelines or from above. Or is it myself I'm watching?

Monday, November 25

Mother had to change clothes only once today, compared to the usual three or four. Her worst time is early afternoon. We'll have to figure out what to do about that. I'm glad she's not teary-eyed and hand-wringing about this change in her body. Her attitude is really good, except she doesn't seem to acknowledge the need to change her clothes.

It isn't easy to "parent" one's mother. Today she said, "I bet you didn't know you'd have to care for a baby." She's uncomfortable about all this. Who wouldn't be? The best I can do is help her and keep a sense of humor.

Wednesday, November 27

I bought a package of incontinence undergarments for Mother so that she'd be more comfortable tomorrow—Thanksgiving. While I demonstrated how they fit, Mother watched quietly. I think she'll accept this change. As she said, "It's no fun." I agreed, but said it's a change we'd adjust to.

Thanksgiving Day

This was truly a day of thanksgiving! Edith joined us for dinner. It was a wonderful afternoon. The delicious aroma of the turkey roasting in the oven filled the apartment, giving a feeling of warmth, comfort, and happiness. The greatest gift, however, was that Mother was dry *all* day!

Saturday, November 30

Mother rode up to Flint with me this afternoon to have, as she said, "a few days vacation." Evidently the trip interrupted her bathroom schedule. The towel I'd put on her favorite chair was wet. I know she's embarrassed about this, but we are going to have to deal with it.

Wednesday, December 4

Mother's clothes stayed dry today! Making regular trips to the bathroom must be helping. I hope so.

She even shoveled snow off the driveway. Imagine doing that at her age! She said she wanted the exercise and fresh air. Today I felt that all was well, and I would be able to finish this tax season.

Tuesday, December 10

My attitude of gratitude will make wonderful things happen to me.
It's not what happens, but how I respond. That's the key. I'll begin by
being thankful for—

> a good night's rest last night.
> feeling so good this morning.
> Mother's good health.
> Mother's good attitude toward the infirmities
> of being ninety-three years old.
> a car that runs well, so I can make the trips between
> Plymouth and Flint worry-free.
> so many supportive, encouraging friends.
> being able to grow spiritually.
> my excellent health.
> being able to think, to have a mind that wants
> to learn and grow.
> knowing I can meet every experience with courage
> and confidence because God is with me.

LATER

I had a couple of stomach pangs today, similar to what I imagine parents must feel when they realize that their children are no longer dependent upon them. That feeling came when I observed how much Mother
had taken control. She even decided what we'd have for dinner—meat-
loaf!—and had taken it out of the freezer. Taking charge of simple tasks
makes her feel more independent. I'm happy about it. What I don't know
is how long it will last.

Wednesday, December 25

MERRY CHRISTMAS!

It's a quiet morning. No change in our routine. In a little while, Mother and I will enjoy opening our gifts. Edith has invited us to join her for dinner at a fine restaurant nearby. I'm ready for their specialty—prime rib!

Sunday, December 29

We had a wonderful visit today with two of Mother's granddaughters, their husbands, and children. Carolyn and Jerry, Elaine, Jim, Lauren, and John had flown in for the weekend from their respective homes in California and Idaho. We went to Mother's favorite restaurant and enjoyed a good dinner and conversation. It was touching to watch Lauren and John Patrick gently take their great-grandmother's hands and assist her walking in and out of the restaurant. Mother loved it!

Earlier, while thinking about transportation to the restaurant, it was decided to divide our little band into "girls" and "boys", as sexist as that sounds. John Patrick made the designations, pointing to each individual and stating the gender. He had no problem until he came to Grandma. Pausing for a second, he looked up at his dad in puzzlement. "Is her a girl?" he asked with all the innocence of a four- year old. Our uproarious laughter in response to his very serious question perplexed him, I'm sure.

Tuesday, December 31

Sometimes I get so exasperated with this mother of mine. This morning she put on a pair of slacks that needed to be laundered. She couldn't understand how there could be an odor because she'd "only worn them once." When I explained, and not so patiently, she took it well.

Later I told her I hoped she wasn't upset with me, but I'm probably the only one who would tell her. She said she was glad I did. This must be so difficult for her.

LATER

The appointment with the urologist was well worth the trip. He prescribed medication to control the incontinence problem. Mother was pleased. "I guess I'm not hopeless," she told me on the way home.

Wednesday, January 1, 1992

HAPPY NEW YEAR!

I'm looking forward to this year. Mother seems to be doing better today with bladder control. She was able to go for four hours with no leakage. I told her that when the pills take full effect she may not have to wear the protective undergarments around home. Oh my, did she brighten up with that thought!

Monday, January 6

I took Mother to the ophthalmologist this afternoon. The news was good and bad. The "bad" is that she has macular degeneration which, in her case, is incurable. The "good" news is that she won't be blind. Her central vision will be affected, but her peripheral vision will remain unchanged. Eventually she won't be able to read, watch television, recognize faces, or do any close work. Her peripheral vision, however, will allow her to walk around and see where she's going.

Understandably, Mother was very discouraged about this latest change. I did some fast talking about positive thinking, focusing on everything she can do. She wanted to know what those were. I began listing them, and she added a few of her own: eat, dress, launder, bathe, cook, think, read, knit, crochet, write, plus having me around to help out.

It worked! Her attitude changed instantaneously!

Saturday, January 11

Mother tries not to wear a protective pad, but it's not working. I was upset tonight when she knew she was wet, had wet the towel on the chair, but put it on the floor and moved to another chair—without changing her clothes. I just couldn't understand that and told her so. "Maybe you will," she told me. "Wait until you're my age." I felt terrible and apologized while I helped her rinse out the clothes and put on clean ones.

Sunday, January 12

I realized today that it's the "little things" in life that cause us to break. For instance, it's difficult to sit at the table with Mother in the morning and listen to her "slurp" her oatmeal. The sound is so irritating to me. Sometimes I just grit my teeth and try not to hear it. Other times I have to get up and do something else so it doesn't bother me. I don't want to mention it to Mother any more. She can't help it. Bringing it to her attention only makes her feel bad. Instead, I need to focus on all the things she can do well.

It was incredibly difficult for me to write that last paragraph. In my mind I want to be the perfect daughter, but I do get irritated at times. It's so difficult to watch my own mother become frail and dependent, this person who was always strong and independent. I know this is a part of life. I understand, too, there is no achievement without adversity.

I will learn from this opportunity.

Monday, January 13

I looked in the mirror this morning and saw that my face no longer had the "look of youth." The stress of the past year and a half is taking its toll. Oh well, so be it. I trust God to put me in the right place at the right time, to be there when Mother needs me. He hasn't failed me yet—and won't.

Saturday, January 18

Mother was more "together" today. She changed and rinsed her clothes as necessary without any reminders from me. Tonight she walked around the inside of the apartment twenty times for exercise. This new routine was her idea. I counted out twenty buttons, placed them on a table with a cup in which she deposited a button every time she passed it. She liked that game-like idea. It gave her some incentive, in addition to helping her keep score.

Sunday, January 19

Mother's eyesight was so poor this evening that she had difficulty reading the large-print books. I offered the magnifying glass. That helped. I'll check into an "around the neck" magnifier which would allow her hands to be free to knit or crochet. Thank goodness, these problems (Oops! Change that to learning opportunities!) come one at a time. I'm so thankful that she can walk, talk, think, and laugh.

Friday, January 31

The tax season is in full swing now. I'm grateful Mother is doing well enough that I'm able to leave her alone a couple of days so I can work. Our daily phone calls assure me she is okay. Every evening she walks around the apartment twenty times. She says walking helps her sleep better.

Sunday, February 9

Just reread the letter I received this week from my good friend, Cris. Evidently I do show what I've been striving for, but I know I'm not there yet. Cris wrote:

> *"You have had the discipline, determination, and inner drive to make your life meaningful and productive. The happiness is in today and the doing is now. Keep up that great attitude and enviable ability...."*

LATER

Mother and I have had a wonderful weekend. I was relaxed, patient, and we enjoyed some good conversation. I prepared something different for dinner today—cranberry glazed chicken with stuffing. This was a recipe I'd found in the newspaper. I plan to try a new recipe at least once a month to add a little zest to our lives.

Friday, February 14

Valentine's Day! We celebrated by driving up to Flint for hair appointments. Mother had a perm and is so pleased with it! The day was without incident, except Mother didn't use the bathroom as often as she should have; consequently, an "accident." It didn't bother me as much as it has in the past. I'm beginning to learn, adjust, and gradually accept.

Monday, February 24

This was included in a newsletter I received in today's mail. I've read it several times. It gives me something to strive for.

SYMPTOMS OF INNER PEACE

An unmistakable ability to enjoy each moment.

A loss of the ability to worry.

Frequent, overwhelming episodes of appreciation.

Contented feelings of connectedness with others and nature.

Frequent attacks of smiling.

An increasing tendency to let things happen, rather than make them happen.

An increased susceptibility to the love extended by others as well as the uncontrollable urge to extend it.

Saturday, February 29

Wow! An extra day this year! How wonderful that it's a beautiful one with an abundance of bright sunshine, blue sky, and crisp air.

I bought a puzzle book to give Mother something different to do. Her days tend to be long since she's unable to fill them with all the activities she used to enjoy so much. Her vision continues to deteriorate. She doesn't complain, though. I'm truly thankful for that. I'd have a difficult time deal-ing with this situation if Mother whined and complained.

Monday, March 2

Mother needed something to do and thought she could see well enough to crochet covers for hangers. She'd crocheted so many of those over the years, I'm sure she could do it in her sleep. I bought six skeins of yarn this afternoon for that project, much to her delight!

Sometimes she gets so discouraged. I remember Dad saying that when Mother was "down" she was *really* down. Usually I'm able to boost her spirits. I hope that will continue in the days ahead.

Mother hugged me as I was leaving tonight to return to Flint for a cou-ple of days. I don't recall her doing that since the stroke. I always hug and kiss her goodbye when I leave, but tonight I was able to respond to the warmth of her hug and kiss. It felt so good!

Wednesday, March 11

Mother has been busy this past week crocheting hanger covers. I gave a few to Jackie, one of my neighbors in Flint. Jackie was delighted, saying they looked like Easter eggs, all the beautiful pastel colors grouped together. Mother was so pleased when I told her about Jackie's enthusias-tic response. Knowing that she made someone happy, she will sleep very well tonight—with a smile on her face.

Monday, March 16

Today was my brother Bob's birthday. Bob was so kind and generous. I recall the time he took the bag of dirty camp laundry out of my car, unbeknown to me, and laundered it all so I would be free to do other things on my day off from a summer camp counseling position. What a brother! I really miss him.

Mother applied for her first-ever library card today! Now I can check out large-print books for her at the library in Plymouth, rather than Flint. They have a good collection, so she will have a variety to read. I'm thankful she enjoys reading. And I'm especially grateful to the publishers of large-print books.

Saturday, March 21

I'm thinking about the span of Mother's lifetime and what she has experienced:

She went to school in a horse and buggy—and now (up until the stroke) drives her own car and has traveled by air.

She taught herself to drive—on her own initiative—sixty years ago, long before "women's lib."

She learned to cook on a wood stove—and now uses a microwave, as well as a telephone and a television.

Yes, the twentieth century has been one of rapid technological growth and progress. It's an awesome thought to know that my mother has seen it all happen!

Monday, March 23

What a beautiful morning! While I was immersed in reading a new book today, Mother interrupted me three times to rethread her sewing machine. It didn't upset me.

"I don't know what I'd do without you," she said each time I rethreaded the machine.

I asked why. "I know," I chuckled, answering my own question. "You need me to thread the sewing machine!"

"Oh, no," Mother responded. "You do so many things for me."

Later, she peeked around the corner for the third time. "I need you again. This is the last time."

"I hope not," I said as I walked back to the sewing machine with her, my arm around her shoulder.

LATER

While looking for something else today, I discovered the following quote by Edward Bulwer-Lytton, an English 19th century novelist:

> **"We are born for a higher destiny than that of earth.**
> **There is a realm where the rainbow never fades, where**
> **the stars will be spread out before us like islands that**
> **slumber on the ocean, and where the beings that now**
> **pass before us, like shadows, will stay in our presence forever."**

Good thoughts to ponder.

Friday, March 27

Enjoyed breakfast this morning with my friend Jo. Hearing all about her wonderful six-week trip to Nassau, Washington, DC, and New York, gave me the urge to travel again.

I need a creative challenge. I'm restless. I have a gnawing feeling of wanting and needing some intellectual or creative stimulation. My life has not lacked this until now.

Tuesday, March 31

This was a "feel sorry for me" night. I know I give the picture of having everything under control. I do, but that doesn't mean I don't need support. I've had support from my true friends, but I also expected something from others, too. Is this the way life is for other caregivers, too? Maybe I shouldn't expect anything; then I wouldn't be disappointed.

Friday, April 10

Mother met John Robert, her newest great-grandchild! I'm so glad that my nephew Bob and his wife Donna were able to make the trip from their home in California to give Mother that moment of joy. I know it meant a lot to her.

Wednesday, April 15

Yea! The tax season is over. Am I glad! I'm weary tonight, some of which is the thought of having to switch gears again for another change in the routine of my life. I wonder what challenging adventures are ahead. I wonder, but I don't want to know.

Monday, April 20

It's a dreary, rainy Monday morning, a great time for writing, reading, and thinking. It's very important for me to have quiet time alone. Thank goodness, Mother is quiet and not constantly demanding my attention. I cherish time alone—like now—when I can sit and think and write. Is that being selfish? If so, so be it. It's my choice. There is a saying that if you can't live with yourself, you can live with no one. That's another way of saying, "Know yourself!" I still don't know myself, but I'm working on it.

Saturday, April 25

I was disturbed to see a big sore on Mother's elbow and learn that she'd fallen while walking alone when I was gone. She thought nothing about it, casually telling me that a man helped her up and she continued on her walk. Once she's set her mind to do something, she doesn't stop. I can't be with her every moment.

Monday, April 27

I cleaned Mother's bedroom because I had to do something physical. I was so upset with her. She had sneezed two or three times, leaking urine each time. I could smell it and told her she needed to change her pad. Instead of doing that, she sat down in her rocking chair and crocheted a hanger cover. When she got up, the towel protecting the chair was wet and so was she. I couldn't hold my tongue. "Why do you do that?" I demanded. She said she wanted to finish the hanger. I told her that could have waited, but changing that pad couldn't. That is so upsetting to me.

I can't say I feel much better now. This is an awful thought, but some-times I wish Mother would die and end all this. I see her able to do less and less. I need to get myself out of this thinking pattern. My problems are made heavier by thinking about tomorrow, an unknown about which I can do nothing. What I have is this moment. I need to make the most of it.

Tuesday, April 28

I took Mother and Edith to a luncheon honoring volunteers. I didn't enjoy myself. The reverberating echo of dishes clanging and chatter in that cavernous hall seemed to set every nerve in my body on edge. To top it off, I was embarrassed when Mother tried to put a butter pat in her purse. I guess her saving nature got the upper hand, but all I could envision was a greasy mess. I need to get away.

Wednesday, April 29

I've been crying a lot yesterday and today. I cried all the way on the drive to Flint. The tears didn't stop when I walked in the house. I started to go upstairs, but collapsed halfway and sobbed and sobbed. It really didn't make me feel any better. I could have cried the rest of the day, but decided that wasn't going to resolve anything. I cut the grass, instead.

Having dinner with the calligraphy group tonight helped. I realized how starved I was for good conversation and the company of friends.

Thursday, April 30

Alma called to suggest eating out tonight. That was a good idea. I met one of my former principals at the restaurant and stopped to chat with her for a few minutes. She is looking after her father, who is a year or two older than Mother. "It's not easy, is it?" she said compassionately.

I didn't realize until just now, as I write and reflect, how supportive her words were and how much I needed to hear them from someone who actually knew. Alma gave me a boost of support, too. I was able to talk about how upset I get sometimes. She assured me that was okay.

How important those two conversations were! Thinking back to the beginning of this week, my real frustration was because I felt no one understood. I had been looking for support from Mother's friends. Now I realize they can't help me, but my friends can.

Saturday, May 9

I began reading *Dare to Connect*[4] by Susan Jeffers this morning. What she said about becoming a "giving" rather than a "getting" person in a relationship makes sense. If I give unconditionally with no expectation of a return, there will be no disappointment and no rejection. Those are two of my fears. I need to think about giving with no strings attached. But can I do it on the days when getting is what I need so badly?

Mother's Day

I gave Mother her card and gift. As I expected, she had trouble accepting it. (It has always been easier for her to give than to receive.) She took the lid off the box, saw it was a blouse, and promptly replaced the lid. I could have been hurt, but I chose not to be. My gift was just that—a gift selected with loving care and given from my heart. I continued doing what I needed to do: shampooing and setting her hair, going out to buy a newspaper, coming back and reading it while enjoying a hot cup of coffee on the patio. Meanwhile, Mother fixed her breakfast. She read the card while she ate. "That's a lovely card!" she said. The box, however, was left unopened.

A few minutes later, I opened it and put the blouse up to Mother's shoulders, remarking how beautiful that shade of green looked on her. "Wonder which of your slacks this will go with," I mused aloud. I checked her closet and returned with an armful of slacks that would complement

4   Jeffers, Susan. *Dare to Connect*. New York: Ballantine Books, 1992.

the blouse. Mother just looked, but didn't respond. I desperately wanted to help her accept the gift. I know she thinks I've done more for her than she could repay, but that's not the point. I just wanted her to accept my symbol of tribute to her.

We were taking Edith out for dinner. "I think I'll wear the new blouse you gave me," Mother said. I smiled.

While helping her get dressed, I spotted a medallion necklace in her jewelry box that had the color of the blouse. "Try this!" I suggested.

Mother looked at it and was so surprised. "I made that necklace!" she exclaimed with joy and pride. And she had, many years ago.

Edith remarked how lovely Mother looked. She responded with one of her beautiful "thank you" smiles. It was a very good day!

Wednesday, May 20

Some thoughts this morning:

> *Why* isn't it easy to just let go and let God handle it all?
> *Why* struggle against the current, which is a losing battle?
> *Why* not put my energy, my focus on what is already planned
> for me—and thus gain all the power and energy I'll ever need to
> do what I need to do?
> It's so simple.
> *Why* is it so difficult?

Sunday, May 24

During the past months, there have been many times I've felt resentment and anger. It hasn't been easy to give up my freedom. I have no idea how long Mother will live, nor do I know what may be ahead for us. But this much I do know: I'll have no regrets.

LATER

Mother got up from her chair at dinner with wet slacks—again. After I rinsed out everything and found fresh clothes, I told her—for the umpteenth time—that she simply can't wear one pad all day. I asked when she'd put that one on. "Why, this morning," she said, as if that wasn't very long ago. She has never wanted to make extra work for anyone, but it certainly is happening now. For some reason or other, that fact doesn't cause her to change her ways. Maybe she doesn't see it. I'm at my wit's end.

Wednesday, May 27

The sheet on Mother's bed was wet this morning, even though she did wear a protective pad. The medication isn't as effective as it was. I'm ready to call the urologist for an appointment. Mother doesn't want me to. She thinks this will pass.

LATER

I finally got through to Mother. Reluctantly, she told me it was okay to call for an appointment. This was a compromise, however, not a change in her attitude. She didn't want me to be upset.

Tuesday, June 2

The appointment with the urologist was well worth the forty mile round trip, the physical effort to get a wheelchair for Mother, and the challenge of maneuvering around that large office building up to the twelfth floor. The doctor recommended increasing the medication. If that doesn't work, he'll prescribe a different one. I can only hope that means more harmonious days for both of us.

Sunday, June 7

Sadly, Mother is reverting to childlike behavior. Because she doesn't sit up to the table, she spills food on her clothes. (How many times do I remember being told that as a child!) When we were walking out of K-Mart today, she stopped right in the middle of the automatic door with someone directly behind her, to pick up something she thought was a coin.

When she went to the grocery store with me, she steered the cart too close to the shelves and shoppers, totally unaware of what she doing and the consequences. This was not like my mother who has always been thoughtful of others. I was embarrassed as I apologized to the other customers. Then, she walked so slowly coming out of the store that I had to encourage her, like one would a child, saying, "Come on, come on." I recalled the numerous times during my childhood she'd said that to me when I dawdled.

It is a release to write all this. I realize that my irritation was embarrassment because I haven't accepted the role reversal yet. This is my mother, not my child. Her increasing dependency worries me.

Monday, June 8

Mother says the new prescription has helped. I'll call the urologist in the morning with the good news. Today was a better day. I need to relax a little more, to lighten up, and trust that the plan for my life is working out exactly the way it's supposed to.

Wednesday, June 24

While cleaning out a drawer today, I found a picture of Mother proudly holding her bowling ball. She loved to bowl and was a very good bowler, too. When I showed her the picture, her eyes just sparkled! I held the picture in my hands for a few minutes, reflecting on how active and happy Mother was at that time. That's how I want to remember her.

Saturday, June 27

We talked about death for a few minutes this evening. Mother said I'd probably be glad when she's not here so that I won't have so much running to do. I told her that what I want is for her to be well and content.

I wonder if this two-year period was meant to prepare me for something. I wonder, but I really don't want to know what it is.

I wasn't as irritated with Mother's behavior today. When something did begin to jar at me, I asked myself: What difference does it make? That helped.

I'm beginning to accept things as they are. I hope this new-found sense of peace continues.

Monday, June 29

I remember this day twenty-two years ago so well. Jack called to tell me that Dad had died unexpectedly from a massive heart attack. Mother was so distraught that whole summer. I couldn't leave her alone. We spent most of the summer at the cottage, allowing the healing effects of nature to work their wonders on our bodies and minds. A week after the funeral, while quietly sitting in the yard one morning, Mother had a vision of Dad. "Don't grieve for me," he told her. "I'm happy. I'm not out there." (We interpreted "out there" to mean the cemetery.) Although the effect of that vision comforted Mother, she remained deeply engulfed in her grief.

By August, when she still could not even open her mail, I worried. What was I going to do when I had to return to my teaching position in Flint? We didn't talk about it, but Mother had the same concern. By the end of August, she pulled herself together and knew that she had to make a life for herself without Dad. That fall, she busied herself with bowling and volunteer work. Her days were filled with productive activity and positive people. She missed Dad terribly. She told me she used to look out the kitchen window, see the car in the parking lot, and wonder why he hadn't come in the apartment and what was taking him so long.

Saturday, July 4

I'm bored right now. I'm fighting to keep my sanity. I'm sleeping a lot, too, which I know is nothing more than an escape. That's frightening. I'm realizing that Mother is getting worse. She can't walk as well now and is becoming increasingly more feeble in many ways. Will I be able to handle it? I see myself being in Plymouth more next year. I'm down here four

and a half days a week now, but I believe that'll be increasing next year—
or sooner.

Wednesday, July 8

Cris, my friend who now lives in California, arrived this afternoon for
a short visit with friends and family in Michigan. She has made my house
her home base. I was happy we could spend some time together.

We picked up our conversation without missing a beat and talked non-
stop. It seemed as if we'd seen each other just yesterday! Our conversation
centered around my feelings. It was easy to talk with Cris because she listened and understood. She assured me that it was okay to feel anger at
being trapped, and that occasional self-pity was normal. We talked about
what people often say at the time of a funeral: *She lived a long time....the
suffering is over....now you can get on with your life.* Although said with
good intentions to make the one who is grieving feel better, those com-
ments need to be said *by* the grieving person, not *for* that person.

After dinner, Cris shared the comment that a mutual acquaintance of
ours had made after her mother died. She said she felt at peace because
she'd done everything she knew to do for her mother to make her feel
comfortable and her days pleasant. I want to feel the same way and for the
same reasons.

Cris left at noon. I cried as I hugged her goodbye. I wonder when I'll
see her again. It was so good to have someone I could talk with so freely.
I miss that more than I admit.

Monday, July 13

A note in my journal: **With God's help, I am able to see things differently, and that gives me hope.**

I do need to see things in a new way. I need to get out of this "couch
potato" pattern of thinking.

LATER

I took Mother to the ophthalmologist today. Her vision has definitely decreased. The doctor referred us to a low-vision clinic to see if there is any magnifying equipment that could help. There is hope. I want Mother to have quality in the final years of her life.

"I'm such a burden for you," Mother commented sadly during the drive home from the doctor's office. She is a strong, independent woman who has never wanted to be a burden on her children. The roles have been reversed now. Mother was always there for me when I was growing up. Now it's my turn to be there for her.

The Third Year

Saturday, July 18, 1992

Today's thought from my journal: **I am strong and have no fear because I know God is with me.**

Keeping that in mind, onward to this day. This begins the third year of caring for Mother. I wonder what it will bring.

Thursday, July 23

Mother sounded like herself tonight when I called. Her bothersome eye is much better, not watering as much. Then she told me her latest good news: a covered hanger business! She was so excited telling me that Polly, one of her friends, is going to give her some hangers to cover and will solicit orders. Once again, Mother has a purpose, a reason to get up in the morning. How very important that is!

Saturday, July 25

I'm recalling the conversation I overheard yesterday in the beauty salon. A lady was telling the beautician about her eighty-three year old mother, describing how very set she was in her ways. The daughter didn't approve of her mother's hairstyle, but the mother wouldn't spend money on having it done professionally. She was saving her money to pay someone to take care of her in her own home so she wouldn't have to go into a nursing home. That was her greatest fear. The daughter was disgusted with her mother's attitude. The beautician listened and recognized that there was no point in the daughter fighting her mother, trying to change her.

Yes, older people do get set in their ways. Will I, too, one of these days?

Sunday, July 26

I'm contemplating whether or not to work during the next tax season. The company is changing to a computer system. That will mean additional training time to learn the new program and all the changes involved. I don't need more stress in my life. Volunteering to prepare tax returns at the senior center in Plymouth may be far more rewarding. I'll look into that.

Monday, July 27

This is the second consecutive day that Mother has wet her clothes. I detected the odor when she came to the table for dinner. I mentioned it, but she ignored me. I kept still. When she left her chair after dinner, the odor was very strong and her slacks were damp. I told her. She went to the bathroom to change, but returned wearing the same pair of slacks. When I said she needed to put on clean slacks, she mumbled something about "being tired of me always mentioning this." I felt bad. Finally, she did change, and I offered to rinse out the slacks for her. I don't know what I'm going to do. The problem threatens to get worse.

Tuesday, July 28

Shirley, a friend from Mother's church, visited this afternoon. That did wonders to bolster Mother's spirits!

Polly stopped by with more hanger orders. She was thrilled with the four hangers Mother had finished for her. Mother beamed! This mini-business that the two of them have initiated will keep Mother busy and happy. I am pleased. It has taken some of the pressure off me.

We played backgammon tonight. I was surprised to see how well Mother remembered the game. It provided good mental activity for her, but two games were enough. She was tired.

Monday, August 3

I prepared a delicious chicken dinner, complete with a fresh fruit compote for dessert. Mother enjoyed it! She does like to eat, especially when someone else prepares the meal. I baked chocolate chip cookies for an evening activity and snack. Mother took a plate of the warm cookies to Norm, our neighbor across the hall. He was delighted with the surprise treat, and Mother was pleased she'd helped to make someone happy!

Tuesday, August 4

My aching back awakened me early this morning. I spent most of the morning on the heating pad. Now it's time to take Mother to the foot doctor. I get so tired, but I must keep going. I'm sure this tiredness is all due to stress. What can I do?

Today's journal thought is one I'm going have to think about: **I have nothing but energy, enthusiasm, and optimism!** Wow! I'm going to have to really work on that one. Right now, I'm feeling the opposite. Depressed. Pessimistic.

Mother's incontinence problem seems to be under control once again. There've been no major accidents—a definite improvement from last week.

I hope this continues, but I must be realistic. This may be just a reprieve.

Wednesday, August 5

I used a pillow under my lower back last night to relieve the pressure. I'm so tired of living out of two bags and running back and forth between Flint and Plymouth. It could be worse, Marian—a lot worse. I have to keep reminding myself of that fact.

Mother gave Polly several finished hangers today. Polly's friends are buying them—three for a dollar! Mother is absolutely exuberant about being an entrepreneur. That's quite a feat at the age of ninety-four!

Saturday, August 8

It is so pleasant to be in my own home, sitting at the dining room table in the quiet of this morning, sipping a hot cup of coffee, gazing out over the beautiful new deck and beyond to the majestic maple tree…listening to the rustle of its leaves and the soft sound of the wind chimes…feeling the soft caress of the cool breeze coming through the patio door…thinking, appreciating, and being thankful. I really love my home and enjoy the times I'm able to be here.

Monday, August 10

I was frustrated with Mother today because she couldn't hear me. The hearing aid battery was dead. She claims she just replaced it—and she might have, but she forgets and leaves the darn thing on all night. Guess I'll need to check that every night now.

I need to be more patient with Mother and praise her more. Her feeling of self-worth is diminishing. Sometimes, though, she acts so much like a helpless child that I get upset. In my mind, my mother is supposed to be strong, the person I can lean on. That isn't reality any more. Is there any daughter who would willingly change places with the mother who raised her?

Tuesday, August 11

Today's journal thought is a good one: **I am being guided.** That tells me I'm not alone, an image I need to keep at the forefront of my mind.

Called Cris. We had our usual wonderful conversation with some hearty laughs. What a panacea that was for this weary spirit!

Saturday, August 15

Today is Mother's ninety-fourth birthday! She's had her bath, back scrubbing, and shampoo. She's squeaky clean all over, ready to celebrate this special day. I was so tired afterwards that I took two naps to try to revive myself.

LATER

Edith joined us for a birthday dinner at Mother's favorite restaurant. Mother delighted in getting ninety-four per cent off the cost of her dinner—plus her favorite chocolate cake!

She had been looking forward to her birthday for the past month. Tonight she said it was all she'd hoped for. I'm so glad! I can't help but wonder if it will be her last. She looked older today, definitely more frail. She has shrunk in height, too, and is much more bent over. But her voice is strong, she's mentally alert, and her health is good. What more can I ask?

Monday, August 17

Today's journal thought is a hard one to believe because I feel so trapped. **I am free to enjoy all the wonderful things life offers!** Free? I certainly don't feel it. Am I limited by my thinking? I get so uptight when I start making comparisons between this apartment and my home in Flint. Even taking a shower down here is a task because Mother's shower chair takes up so much space, leaving no room to turn around. I live out of a suitcase four to five days a week now.

This is the third year, and the stress is beginning to take its toll. What can I do about it? I decided not to work at the tax office this year. Maybe working as a tax volunteer down here will give me a break. At least if I'm here, I won't worry about Mother as much. We'll see what happens.

LATER

I'm sitting in my car in the K-Mart parking lot trying to sort out my feelings. I needed peace and quiet and solitude. This was the only spot I could think of to get it.

I'm angry. I don't know if it's because all the attention has been on Mother this weekend—which it should have been for her birthday—with no acknowledgement of my help in making it possible for her to have lived happily these recent years in good health and in her own home. I feel nobody realizes that, or even cares about my sacrifice. (Wow! Writing that really triggered some *hard* tears—even a cry of pain.)

This is one month into the third year now. Can I do it indefinitely? If I don't take care of Mother, what will happen? There is no one else. I am all the immediate family she has. Placement in a nursing home would kill her. That's her biggest fear—and mine, too. A foster home is an option, but she'd feel I had abandoned her. I couldn't live with that guilt.

The best place for Mother is right here in her own home, right where she is. But will I able to manage? I have needs, too; needs which aren't being met or I wouldn't feel so miserable. What are my needs?

I need

> some time and space each day for me.
>
> someone who understands, who cares about me and my needs.
>
> mental stimulation.
>
> to express my feelings without hurting someone.
>
> to feel productive, to justify my life.
>
> to have some fun.
>
> to feel good about myself.

If some of those are not fulfilled, how will I ever be able to carry on?

Tuesday, August 18

I still feel miserable. I was upset with Mother tonight because she wouldn't change her slacks, claiming the urine doesn't go through her slacks when she wets the towel she's sitting on. I have no idea how she figures it bypasses her slacks. Those slacks stink, but she can't smell it. I've given up. I told her if other people smell her, that'll be her problem. I'm no longer responsible.

I went into the bathroom tonight and cried and cried. It was a cry of frustration—and a desperate cry for help. Am I trying to do too much? Mother is becoming too dependent on me. I think I have to do everything. I'm beginning to not care—not care about my personal appearance, not care about what I do or say. I know that translates into low self-esteem and depression.

I don't know what to do.

Wednesday, August 19

The foam egg-crate mattress worked! I need two, though. The sofa bed mattress was killing my back.

I'm tired of everything. I thought I'd accepted this caregiving responsibility as my role in life at this point. Is this what I need to learn from this experience: acceptance of those things I cannot change?

LATER

One more episode of wet clothes not being changed. I ended up tearfully telling Mother how it upsets me because I'm trying to keep everything clean and fresh-smelling, the way she wants it, too. She seemed to understand.

Inwardly, I am relieved to return to Flint for a couple of days. I must figure out a way to handle all of this, though. These past five days have been the most frustrating I've had with Mother. As I was leaving tonight, I told her I thought she'd be glad to have me leave so she could do as she pleased. "I do as I please, anyway!" she politely informed me.

LATER

It feels wonderful to be home! Peace…quiet…space…comfort…and privacy. I love it here. During the past five days, I mentally saw myself here several times, walking into each room and wishing I could be there.

Thursday, August 20

I treated myself to a massage this afternoon and then soaked in a hot tub at home, relaxing those tense muscles even more. It was difficult getting out of the tub, though, so I used Mother's technique of getting on my knees first. It worked! She's still teaching me.

Saturday, August 22

Notes from my reading of Susan Jeffers' book, *Feel the Fear and Do It Anyway:*[5]

> Every time I take a step into an unknown, I will feel fear.
> Pushing through fear is easier than living with the helplessness.
> This, too, shall pass!

This, too, shall pass! Yes! The situation I'm in now will not last forever. It will pass. Meanwhile, I can't just exist. I need to learn from this experience. The question is *what?*

Sunday, August 23

HAPPY BIRTHDAY to me—my fifty-seventh! Mother and I had dinner at the usual restaurant. I so enjoyed not having to cook that I ate far too much! My sister-in-law, Theo, and her husband came over in the evening to enjoy cake and ice cream with us. They are off to Chicago on Tuesday for a harmonica convention. I felt a slight twinge of envy.

---

5   Jeffers, Susan. *Feel the Fear and Do It Anyway.* New York: Ballentine Books, 1987.

Monday, August 24

I see Mother becoming more feeble. As I observed her walking back from visiting a neighbor last night, I saw how very bent over she is, almost at a forty-five degree angle. Her blouses hang down further in the front now, too.

I need to reread this journal and discover where I am. I need to see evidence of growth. It's there. I just don't see it until I look back.

Wednesday, August 26

Started the tax class today, just in case I do decide to work this season. After class, Katie and Denna surprised me with a birthday lunch at the Fenton Hotel. Being together with friends, with whom I can laugh and have a good time, certainly does wonders to lift dragging spirits!

Saturday, August 29

I didn't awaken until 7:30 this morning. Mother was in the bathroom. That was okay until I heard her start running the bath water. This was "shampoo her hair" morning; I knew I had to get up. No quiet time this morning. I thought she was manipulating me in a subtle way. I kept asking myself: Okay kid, what are you going to do about it?

There was nothing I could do but help Mother with her bath and shampoo. When I finished setting her hair, I told her I thought it was inconsiderate to expect me to do what I did before I had a chance to get up, get dressed, and have breakfast. All last week she didn't get up until mid-morning. Why did she have to get up at 7:30 this morning?

"I just woke up, so I got up," she told me.

"Well," I declared, "next time you'll need to make an appointment with me to do your hair!" She's not going to manipulate me like that.

Whew! It feels good to have released those pent-up feelings. I just can't keep suppressing them.

Now, on to this beautiful day.

Sunday, August 30

I slept well last night, but Mother said she didn't. I asked if she had something on her mind. "Yes!" she said. "You!"

That startled me, but I didn't pursue it. I was feeling good and on my way out for a walk.

Later, Mother surprised me by saying she didn't want me to drive down to Plymouth so often, that she'd be fine if I stayed in Flint all week. One part of me said, *Accept it. She's thinking about you.* Another part of me said, *No, you have a responsibility to be here.*

LATER

I felt good all day and was more patient with Mother. It didn't upset me when she had an "accident," and I ended up with the usual washing and mopping. That's real progress.

It's been difficult, but the relationship Mother and I have now is much closer. She realizes that my needs are important, too. I have learned that it is okay to express my feelings and to expect her to assume responsibility for what she can do. She had to know that she was wearing me down.

Marian, you are learning!

Sunday, September 6

It's okay for me to be away from Mother for three or four days. She is capable of functioning alone as long as there are some quick-fix meals that she can pop in the microwave. I think I'm trying to do too much. I need to conserve my strength for whatever may be ahead.

Thursday, September 10

This was my day! I treated myself to a massage, a pedicure, and a new hair style. The pampering felt wonderful! I deserve it.

Monday, September 21

Mother and I had differences today over an old patched-up and torn bed sheet. I told her she had plenty of good sheets in the linen closet to use. She claimed she didn't.

Later, there I sat mending her threadbare pajama top. I was disgusted. "Why don't you wear the good pajamas that are in your bottom dresser drawer?"

"I like these better," she explained. "They're softer."

So be it. *Patience, patience, patience.*

I told her I'd have to learn to be more patient. "I should say so!" she replied, adding that she's afraid to ask me anything because I "fly off the handle" so easily.

As I kissed Mother goodbye tonight before leaving for Flint, I asked her to forgive me. "I still love you very much," I assured her. She said she needed me.

Oh, Marian, you have so much to learn.

Sunday, September 27

I had an unexpected surprise today. On my way back from buying a newspaper, I was delayed because the road was blocked off at the railroad track. The President's campaign train was about to pass through, and my car was the first in line at the track. I had a close-up view of President and Mrs. Bush waving from the platform of the caboose. What a memorable experience!

Monday, September 28

It was a miserable night. I was so uncomfortable. All night long I felt the hard, inflexible floor in spite of two foam mattresses. I need to figure out an alternative. Maybe an air mattress, like I used for camping, would work.

LATER

I bought an air mattress, hoping it will resolve my sleeping problem. I'm sure it will. I don't know what my next step would be.

Tuesday, September 29

The air mattress worked, thank goodness. Farewell and good riddance, sofa bed!

Today's thought: **Life just keeps getting better and better each day.** My conscious mind doesn't believe this yet, but I will keep saying it anyway.

Monday, October 5

Mother recalled a dream she'd had last night. She was packing her dishes, preparing to move. She didn't see me in the dream, but knew I was there because I'd hired a young man to help. She said she was a lot more spry in the dream than in real life. Could this be a hint of changes to come, or am I reading too much into it?

Saturday, October 10

Baked a cake today which Mother enjoyed sharing with the neighbors. My sister-in-law, Theo, dropped in for a visit this evening with her two daughters, Kathy and Marcia. Mother enjoyed hearing all about her granddaughters' activities and even participated in the conversation!

Mother has changed. She is more alert and her face has a healthy glow. The medication has helped the incontinence problem. The fact that she entered into the conversation tonight was something I hadn't observed for a long time. Maybe this "hanger business" she has with Polly has been a real self-esteem booster. She told the girls that she's earned about seventy dollars. They were impressed to think that Grandma, at the age of ninety-four, is still working!

Sunday, October 18

I am what I think. I really believe that! I know how powerful a thought is. My life reflects my thinking. Nothing will change for me until I change my thinking.

When I think about the pressures of the coming tax season, my stomach and shoulders tense. I need to be free to do whatever is necessary for Mother's care. It's time to devote my full attention to that.

Sunday, October 25

I'm concerned about giving up the tax job. It's time, but I do have some fear that I'm giving up security. That's ridiculous. There isn't any security with that job. Who am I kidding? Be honest, Marian. That tax job is a way to satisfy your need to be productive. True, but I want some new experiences. I don't know what, though. What I do know is that I need to get out of this rut I'm in.

I dread the upcoming holidays. I fear the winter, too. Not working frees me, but it's frightening. I think I'll be bored. Well, if I am, it's my choice. Change your thinking, Marian. Okay! I need to do something right now. Guess I'll go over and wash the car for some exercise. That'll get me out of this apartment, at least.

Tuesday, October 27

What an experience last night! I awakened in the middle of the night, thinking and feeling as if I were drowning and suffocating. I was! The plug had come out of the air mattress! Pumping it up in the middle of the night reminded me of my camping days. There is some humor in all of this, if I look for it.

Friday, October 30

I'm so glad I made it official to not work this tax season. Letting go of the tax job will give me lots of free time which I may need. I sense another change is coming.

Tuesday, November 10

Adele's mother died. During the past few months that Adele has been my massage therapist, she has shared some of the experiences she's had in caring for her mother over the past five years. I wanted to show my support in some way, so I visited with her at the funeral home. She was pleased.

I've been very uptight ever since. While driving home, my left arm numbed up again and my tense shoulders were almost touching my ears. I tried all the exercises Adele had taught me, but the tension remained without relief. I know why. One of these days I'll have to experience my own mother's funeral.

Thursday, November 12

Just looked out the patio door of my home on to the deck. I was awe-struck by the incredible beauty! The rain, peltering on the deck, appeared to renew the cedar to its original soft tone of harvest gold. The red leaves on the maple tree in the foreground exuded an exceptional brilliance, enhanced by the background of luminous yellow leaves from the larger maples next to the redwood fence. Cast against the luscious dark green lawn beneath and the opaque, ominous clouds overhead, the autumn beauty was dazzling.

I stood in awe.

Life offers many gifts. That was one.

Saturday, November 14

There was a blanket of snow on the ground this morning. Winter has arrived! I looked out at the barren, gray trees and envisioned that in another six months all will be in full bloom and green with life. That's the miraculous cycle of life: a time for renewal, a time for growth.

This is the "winter" in my life, a time when I can gain some understanding of why I'm here. I have always known that my life had purpose.

Often, I thought I knew that purpose to be exactly what I was doing at the time. That's true. I am doing exactly what I should be—but there are more lessons to be learned, many more.

Thanksgiving Day

It was a quiet day in Flint. The house was filled with the aroma of the turkey roasting and all the other good foods that are a part of a traditional Thanksgiving dinner. A friend joined us to share the feast. Mother seemed content, sitting in the rocking chair busily crocheting hanger covers.

The three of us played a simple card game after dinner. Mother wasn't as sharp as she used to be in playing the game. I began to get uptight when I had to keep explaining it to her. Part of my impatience these days is seeing my mother losing ground. This isn't just a temporary condition. That's what is so difficult to accept.

Tuesday, December 1

While I was out today, Mother tried to clean up after a wetting accident. She'd rinsed out the protective towel on her chair, but was still wearing the same pair of slacks. I said nothing.

Later, she wandered out to the kitchen to see what I was preparing for dinner. "Mother," I said softly and confidentially. "I hate to say this, but I can smell your slacks." She denied it.

She went back into the living room and sat in a chair that was not protected. Quickly, I put a towel on the chair and mumbled something about being "worse than a baby." Unfortunately, Mother heard it. She told me that I'd better think of putting her some place.

"Where?" I asked, knowing full-well she meant a nursing home.

She said she didn't know. I put my arm around her shoulders. "That's ridiculous," I said. "You're fine right where you are. I'm sorry I said that."

The incident showed me how sensitive Mother is about her increasing inadequacy. When I show my dislike for being in this apartment, she thinks she's too much trouble for me. How would I feel in her place? I need to continue to allow her to do what she can do and support her in that. I am so torn. How do I care for her and still take care of my own needs?

Wednesday, December 9

When I try to think ahead, I have an overwhelming, almost terrifying feeling. The key must be that it is fine and good to plan ahead, but all I can actually do is what I need to at the moment. I must remember that. God gives me only one day at a time. I do well to live it.

Sunday, December 13

Writing what I'm thinking and experiencing has helped me to put things in perspective and work out frustrations. A long time ago, I said this journal was my best friend. I believe it even more now.

Sometimes, friends disappoint me. I'm learning that I can't depend on any one person for everything. Each of us is on a solo journey. I cannot ask anyone to live my life with me, as much as I'd like to share my experiences. Also, I'm learning to give to others without expecting anything in return. Unfulfilled expectations cause disappointment, frustration, and resentment. I want to avoid as much of that as possible.

Saturday, December 19

I'm more aware of the number of women my age taking care of their elderly mothers. Yesterday I saw two at the grocery store. One lady was at the check-out counter and had to get the money out of her mother's wallet for her. I've done that, too. Then, as I was pushing my cart out to the car, I saw another woman walking into the store with her mother leaning on her arm, just the way Mother holds on to mine. I suppose I'll be more aware of this now and in the days to come.

Monday, December 21

Mother is sitting in her chair, staring out the window at nothing. I don't feel obligated to provide activities for her. I always had to entertain myself when I was growing up. (Early on, I learned not to whine about having nothing to do. If I did, Mother always gave me something distasteful to do, like dusting or polishing the silverware.) I have to find things to do in this apartment; she'll have to do the same. If this is called retaliation, so be it. She's depending on me too much.

I've stayed in this apartment all day, except for the minutes I went out to buy a newspaper. That's no life. I have to get out of here. The apartment walls close in on me more and more.

Tuesday, December 22

I can't believe I'm going home and will sleep twelve whole nights in my own bed! That'll be the longest stretch of time at home in over two years. I'm really looking forward to it. When Mother and I discussed our holiday plans earlier, she was reluctant to be away for more than just a few days. Yesterday, she agreed to stay a little longer. I didn't ask what caused her to change her mind; I'm just glad she did. We'll leave tomorrow.

Wednesday, December 23

I'm *so* happy to be home and, especially, to know that I'll be here for twelve wonderful nights! I'm thankful Mother seems content, too. I've put plastic mats on the hall and bathroom carpets for protection against accidental dribbles and placed the commode in her bedroom. She didn't use it when she was here at Thanksgiving. Still, one never knows.

The little Christmas tree is all decorated with gifts beneath, making the house look festive. Tomorrow I'll put the holiday tablecloth on the dining room table. That'll help put us in the spirit of the season!

Thursday, December 24

Oh, it felt so good to sleep in my own bed last night. I slept for almost eight hours without awakening! I'm excited about trying a couple of new recipes today. It's important for me to have a challenge.

LATER

Mother was exhausted after a trip to Lena's beauty salon, however, a two-hour nap and a good dinner revived her. Afterwards, I showed her the directions for making a crocheted dishcloth. She seemed anxious to try it, saying it would give her something different to do. She couldn't see the directions well enough, so I rewrote them on the computer, using large, boldface type. That resolved the problem and Mother was pleased. She thinks she might start the dishcloth tomorrow. It encourages her to have something to look forward to, a reason to get up in the morning.

Christmas Day

What a wonderful day! Mother *loved* the new slack outfit I gave her. The red-violet slacks with a matching tapestry print top complimented her snow-white hair beautifully. "Oh, good!" she said as she opened the box. "Now I'll have something to wear to Mrs. Petrie's party next month!" We've been invited to help celebrate her one hundredth birthday.

Remarking how comfortable and warm the new outfit was, Mother wore it the rest of the day—until she had a wetting accident. The slacks laundered well, though. Surprisingly, the episode didn't upset me. That's progress!

Dinner turned out *magnifico*! We feasted on a pork loin roast with cinnamon apples, baked potatoes, yams, green bean casserole, banana-bran muffins, and key lime pie. Mother really enjoyed it, as did Virginia, a friend I'd invited to join us. I'm so happy to be home! I even sang while preparing dinner, a true sign of my contentment.

Wednesday, December 30

Today I talked with Jean and Don, friends of many years. Don is very ill, and the prognosis is not good. Jean said he is extremely weak and becoming more so. I'll call tomorrow morning and, perhaps, stop by for a short visit. Jean was pleased.

Five minutes later Jean called back, tearfully asking how I cope. I realized this was a cry for help. I told her about my need to be alone and how I managed that by using the basement, going out for a drive, or sometimes just sitting in the car at a shopping mall parking lot.

I talked about my journal writing, mentioning how it worked for me as a friend who was always there. She was interested, saying that if it helped me through the difficult times, it might do the same for her.

Thursday, December 31

Jean called at 8:30 this morning. Don had died two hours ago.

I visited her this afternoon, taking a lemon cake I'd baked earlier. Our short visit was a very emotional experience. It's difficult to lose a good friend, to see and feel the painful grief of those left behind. Some of my emotion stemmed from knowing that the funeral experience is ahead for me, too.

I needed to be alone when I returned home. Mother's questions irritated me. Finally, after dinner I went upstairs and stretched out on my bed. That helped. My sorrow is for Jean and the lonesomeness she'll experience. There's learning in that, too, difficult as it will be. This business of living is a mighty tough one.

Friday, January 1, 1993

HAPPY NEW YEAR! It's a quiet, very cold morning—a typical New Year's Day in Michigan.

Today's thought: **As a brand-new year begins, I totally release the past and live each day—now!** Staying in the present moment will be one of my goals this year. That will take a lot of practice!

Saturday, January 2

Mother is knitting her sixth dishcloth! Her work so much better now and with fewer mistakes. Maybe those dormant brain cells are awakening and reactivating!

Sunday, January 3

Notable notes from this morning's telecast:

The best of times and the worst of times is within me—all due to expectations.
You don't get what you want, need, hope, or wish for. You get what you EXPECT—and you don't have to know how!

Question: Why do messages like these hit me the hardest?
Answer: Because that is when I need them the most.
Are you listening, Marian?

Tuesday, January 5

The urologist prescribed a different medication for Mother. I hope it will be effective. Mother seems to think it is already! She desperately wants this condition to go away, poor soul. So do I! I may not have laundry to do tonight. Wouldn't that be wonderful?

LATER

I'm tired tonight. The least little thing irritates me. I just had twelve wonderful days at home, so why do I get so upset? Is it because I see Mother becoming more of a care and I don't know if I can handle it? I need to discover the reason. I'm resentful that I've given up so much to care for her. I feel unappreciated. If I wasn't here, though, she would be in a nursing home, just as her sisters were after the age of ninety. I couldn't bear that thought: the loss of dignity, the loss of self-esteem that she would experience—and the heartache I'd have.

Just finished rereading parts of this journal. The frustration I felt today was there a month ago, too. What does that tell me? I'm not sure.

Monday, January 11

I guess it all had to come out into the open. After dinner tonight, Mother and I sat at the table and talked for a while. I told her that a few years ago Jack tried to persuade me to agree to move her into a retirement home, but I told him I didn't think that was a good idea. Mother was so surprised, saying that my brother hadn't say anything to her. "And if he had," she added, "I would have said no."

I said I mentioned this because I wanted her to know how I've always supported her need for independence and living in her own home. I confessed, though, that I don't know if she appreciates that.

"Oh, but I do, Marian," Mother told me. "You've done so much for me. I don't know what I would ever do without you."

I said it would help if she told me that once in a while.

"That's not my nature," Mother responded.

I put my arm around her, looked into her face, and smiled. "Maybe you could change," I gently suggested.

LATER

There were many times today that I realized I would be glad when all this was behind me.

I'm so tired of being in my home only two or three days a week.

I'm tired of living out of a suitcase and sleeping on the living room floor in this small apartment.

I'm tired of not having any space of my own, not having anyone to talk with, and just plain not having any fun.

I'm tired…tired…so tired. There seems to be so little of me left any more.

Tuesday, January 12

Returning from the grocery store, I found the apartment empty. No sign of Mother. Then I remembered she had planned to visit a neighbor in an adjacent apartment.

Oh, it feels so wonderful to be alone! I discovered myself singing, "I love to be alone, alone, alone. Oh, how I love to be alone!" Is this childish on my part? I don't think so. I recall that story of the mother who, seeking to comfort her distraught little girl, said, "Honey, don't cry over the little things."

"But, Mama," the child asked. "What are the little things?"

Life is made up of little things, Marian. That is why you are celebrating these few, precious moments. Enjoy!

Saturday, January 16

How nice it is to have a couple of days back in Flint. I feel so energetic! Had a phone call this morning asking for my services as a tax preparer. Guess I've started my own tax business now. When one door closes, another opens!

Sunday, January 17

To get where I need to go requires courage. Meet experiences head on, move through them, and learn from them.

Those were journal notes I made while listening to this morning's telecast. Rereading them makes me feel better. The thoughts justify my frank talk with Mother last Monday.

LATER

We went to Mrs. Petrie's one hundredth birthday reception today. It was lovely. Yes, Mother wore the outfit I gave her for Christmas. She looked radiant! Mrs. Petrie proudly introduced Mother to the guests as "my oldest and best friend for seventy-five years!"

On the way home, Mother said she was pleased to be at the party, but confided that she doesn't want to live to be one hundred. That's a lot of birthdays to have celebrated!

Tuesday, January 26

"Do you enjoy being here?" Mother asked me tonight.

I thought for a second. "Why do you ask?"

She said that one of the neighbors wondered why she didn't move up to Flint and live with me. That sent my mind into convulsions. *It's none of their business.* Immediately, I went into a litany of all the advantages of staying here: her friends, her doctors, her church, a nice apartment which is her home. Mother smiled and nodded her head.

No, I don't enjoy being here, sleeping on the floor, having no privacy, running back and forth to Flint to take care of my home. However, since this is better than any alternative I can see right now, I make the best of it. I guess I didn't realize until now how much of life is a compromise.

Monday, February 1

Today I've been conscious of not saying or thinking, "I have to." It's surprising how that phrase can add pressure. Rather than saying, "I have to go to the store," I'm saying, "I'm going to the store." That simple change gives me an entirely different feeling. Could it be a throwback to childhood when I was told countless times that we had to do something? *You have to brush your teeth. You have to go to school.* That's another thought to ponder.

Tuesday, February 2

I had only twenty minutes of quiet time this morning before Mother got up. If she sees that I'm up, she gets up. I don't know what I'm going to do, except retreat to the basement. I need time alone the first thing in the morning to think, to journal, to meditate, to get focused. Without it, my day seems to fall apart.

LATER

I drove out to the parkway this afternoon and just sat in the car, hoping that being out with the trees and the ducks might soothe my rattled feelings. I needed time to be alone with my thoughts.

Evidently, only a small part of my need was satisfied.

Later, while preparing dinner, I mentioned to Mother that I'd lost a card I'd been saving for the grocery store's promotional. "Why, Marian! I'm surprised at you," she responded to my "confession."

That really blew me apart. "I'm not perfect," I yelled. "I wish people would stop thinking I was and that I can do everything—because I CAN'T"

Mother looked horrified at my outburst.

I went into the bathroom and cried for fifteen minutes. Afterwards, I apologized, assuring her that it wasn't her fault. I promised I'd always be there to take care of her. I hugged her and hoped she felt better.

I don't remember such an angry voice coming out of me, not for a long, long time. When the anger does come, I need to know the difference between what I can change and acceptance of what I cannot. I can only change myself. I cannot change the circumstances, but I can respond to them differently. This is what I'm learning. I have a long way to go.

Again, what did the little child say? "But Mama, what are the little things?" Is this what I must face every day?

Wednesday, February 10

It's a cloudy day and looks as if it might rain, but I don't mind. The outer appearances don't matter. It's what's inside that counts. I know that the sun is shining somewhere in this universe.

Just as the rain helps plants to grow, prosper, and mature, so do the "rain" and "clouds" in my life help me to grow spiritually. Yesterday's outburst was a thunderstorm!

Sunday, February 14

Mother watched the news telecast with me this morning, but she couldn't follow it. She said she was "all mixed up," not knowing where she was or what day it was. Her speech is slightly slurred, too. I wonder if she's had another mini-stroke.

Monday, February 15

Mother was busy this afternoon preparing old greeting cards to be mailed to St. Jude's Hospital for their occupational therapy program. While she was contentedly occupied, I stretched out on the sofa for a short nap. I was awakened by a THUD. There was Mother on the floor, her feet twisted in the rungs of the overturned chair, upended plants and dirt strewn all around.

After determining that she hadn't broken any bones, I laughed. It was, indeed, a comical sight! "Well," I said, still chuckling, "let's figure out how to get you out of there." I suggested that she roll over on her knees and then use the chair for support to raise herself. It took time, but she did it. Both of us were very proud of the accomplishment.

"Two good things came out of your fall," I announced after everything was back to normal. Mother looked at me questioningly. "Number one," I continued, "you know how to get yourself up if you fall on the floor. And, number two, the carpet got vacuumed!"

We laughed as we glanced at the plants safely back in their pots once again, looking none-the-worst from the experience.

I realized I had handled that "little thing" well.

LATER

Mother's arm developed a nasty looking bruise from the fall. I encouraged her to soak in a hot tub tonight before going to bed. She did, but had difficulty getting out of the tub. I didn't panic. We had learned from the previous experience. All turned out well.

Wednesday, February 17

I'm pleased with my tax business. I have only a few clients, which allows me to give each one the kind of service I would expect. And there's enough work to keep me challenged.

It's been a very good day! Mother sounded okay tonight. Her arm wasn't as sore today, but her back hurt. Yesterday's fall did have its effect.

Wednesday, March 10

During a quiet time this morning, childhood memories came to mind. I recalled how I hated to have Mother comb my hair—before I learned to do it myself—because she pulled it so much. Now, she complains that I pull her hair when I comb it, even though I try to be as gentle as possible. It's ironic to discover the many, often subtle, ways in which our roles have been reversed.

I thought about the dining room and kitchen in our family home, the swinging door between the two rooms, and how, as a first grader, I peeked around that door in the morning, looked sorrowfully at Mother sitting at the breakfast table sipping coffee, and pathetically said, "I don't feel well." Secretly, I didn't want to go to school because I was afraid of the teacher. Mrs. Race had bright red hair and never smiled. I was always afraid of doing something that would displease her. Mother never bought into my pitiful request, and I never told her the real reason for my feeling.

I'm sure there are many past experiences that are affecting my reactions and responses now. I need to get those out and release them. No doubt, there are many more memories like this one that will help me understand myself.

Sunday, March 14

It's difficult to carry on a conversation with Mother because of her hearing problem. It would be so easy for her to shut out the world around her. I don't want that to happen, so I keep trying to engage her in conversation.

It's not easy trying to meet her needs as well as my own. I need to take care of myself. There is no one else. I recall the airline safety message instructing passengers on the use of the oxygen masks: Put the mask on yourself first. Then take care of your baby or anyone else for whom you are responsible.

What does that mean in my situation? I know that if I don't take care of myself, I won't be able to care for Mother. But when I do put myself first, I feel guilty; when I don't, I feel resentful. Somehow, my life has fallen between the cracks.

Monday, March 15

I had two surprise phone calls from friends this evening. Both Virginia and Pat had good news that buoyed my spirits. How wonderful to have such kind, concerned friends! Their calls were just what I needed.

Wednesday, March 17

I may be at the point of accepting the fact that Mother won't be here much long. I see her strength slowly diminishing. She has always prided herself on being productive, having a goal for each day, and helping others. There are so few incentives for her now. It's extremely difficult to see my Mother, who was so vibrant and filled with endless energy, slowing down. The person who was always my anchor needs me now. I'm trying to accept that, as well as the fact that life will never return to what it once was.

Monday, March 22

I know the power of positive thought! It worked for Mother after her knee replacement. Those exercises hurt, but she did them with me by her side, encouraging and repeating the affirmation that the knee was getting better and better and better. That knee is just perfect today! Having the surgery was a wise decision. Without it she would have been in a wheelchair.

Sunday, March 28

I'm ambivalent when friends tell me that I've adjusted so well to my situation. When I hear that, I feel an inner resentment. *But you don't really know,* I say inwardly while smiling and nodding my head. I know they mean it as a compliment, but I feel misunderstood. I'm making the best of this experience, learning from it, and accepting it because the alternative of a nursing home is so absolutely repulsive. Maybe that's what others see as adjusting. Only God and I know the total situation.

Really, only God knows.

Monday, March 29

It's okay, it's okay, I tell myself as I see Mother steadily becoming more feeble. I am accepting the fact that she won't be here much longer in the body I now see. That's okay. This is a new level of acceptance for me, different from what I've experienced previously. I have a sense of inner peace now.

Mother is going up to Flint with me today for twelve days! I hope she'll be content. I think she recalls the many happy times when she helped me with yard work and major house cleaning tasks. Those days are no longer. I see her going downhill more each month. However, there are times she surprises me, like yesterday during her appointment with the foot doctor. She was able to put her socks and shoes on in record time with no help from me! Perhaps the anticipated trip to Flint gave impetus to that burst of energy.

Friday, April 2

It's feels so good to be in my own home. Mother had no difficulty in keeping busy while I did my monthly stint of volunteer work at the hospital this morning. She found some hangers in my closet to cover! Every time she comes up here, she goes through my closets looking for uncovered hangers. She finds only a stray one here and there. She has covered all of them.

Sunday, April 11

It's a beautiful morning. The sun is shining, making everything look bright and freshly renewed. This is Easter Sunday!

Notable notes from the telecast this morning:

The only barrier to experiencing a miracle is our unwillingness to accept it. We are so accustomed to engineering our lives, trying to produce our own miracles, that we miss the real ones.
Deep within us is a great magnificence. We must erase all doubt, all fear, and allow that greatness to emerge.

LATER

We enjoyed Easter dinner at Mother's favorite restaurant. All was well until we were returning to the apartment. Mother fell. I had walked a few steps ahead to open the door, too far away to catch her sudden fall. The shrubbery cushioned her, thank goodness. Later, she was indignant with me because I threw away her "doggie bag" which had landed in the dirt. "You could have washed it off," she informed me in no uncertain terms!

Monday, April 12

Changes are coming quickly. Mother had a weak spell at dinner. I noticed her leaning back and over to the side of her chair. She said she thought she was going to topple over. I helped her to the couch where she slept for over an hour. She was confused when she awoke, asking how we got home. We hadn't been out.

Tuesday, April 13

This morning, Mother told me her mouth felt numb and she couldn't see. I called the doctor and took her to his office immediately. Her blood pressure was 220/100. Medication brought it down significantly within ten minutes.

On the way home, Mother was disoriented. "Are we on the road?" she asked. She didn't recognize the apartment, but once inside, she said the furniture looked familiar. Her balance was affected, causing her to almost fall a couple of times walking from the car into the apartment, in spite of the secure hold I had on her. I was relieved to get her home safely.

Mother used her cane tonight, and seemed glad for the support it gave her. She was able to get herself ready for bed, requiring very little assistance from me. Her voice was stronger, too.

Another challenging day.

Wednesday, April 14

I didn't sleep well last night. I was listening, in case Mother called me, and planning what I'd do if I went home for a couple of hours today. I released yesterday and the future—any moment beyond this present single moment. I prayed for strength to do whatever it is I need to do.

LATER

I didn't go home. Mother slept most of the day. Her mouth was numb this morning, prior to taking her medication, but was okay by noon.

Cris called. She had arrived from California and was getting settled in at my Flint home which she'll use as a base while she visits in the area. I'll drive up tomorrow to see her and take care of the items on my "must do" list.

I'll make an appointment with Mother's ophthalmologist, too. Her vision is so impaired that she's unable to crochet now. That may be due to the blood pressure. If so, I need to know.

Thursday, April 15

I awakened early, my mind flooding with all sorts of dire thoughts and my stomach rebelling. I recognized it as fear. I'm afraid Mother is going to need my help full-time. I'm worried about my home. I can ask my neighbors to check on the house and call if there's any problem. I can go up to Flint once a week and take care of what's necessary. Yes, I can live down here and continue to to maintain my home.

I learned something last night while playing backgammon with Mother: I can help her cope with the loss of vision. She isn't blind, but I do need to be her companion and take the place of the satisfaction and joy she derived from her knitting and crocheting. Yes, there is much I can do, many lessons to learn. It was interesting how, not long ago, I was becoming complacent and almost bored with my life. How quickly that has changed!

LATER

I arrived in Flint around noon. Cris and I hugged, and I cried, unleashing the tears that had been welling up in my eyes during the drive the past hour. Cris assured me how important it was to release that emotion to keep it from building and building. Emotion, like steam, needs to be released before it erupts and causes damage. I'm so grateful for our friendship.

STILL LATER

I am exhausted tonight. I brought a desk lamp from home so Mother could have a direct light on whatever she was focusing on. It helped during our backgammon game this evening, but her vision seems to come and go. Sometimes she can see clearly. Then, in a second her vision is blurred. She can't recognize people, either. I showed her some pictures I'd had developed and enlarged, but she couldn't identify herself—the only person in the picture—even with the magnifying glass. I can only imagine the problem she's having.

Friday, April 16

As I sit here journaling early this morning, the tears are flowing. It helps to release the emotion. My tears are bringing me to that humble state of thought and realization that of myself, I am helpless, I am powerless. I can, however, depend upon a Power greater than myself to guide me.

Now, on to this day.

LATER

Good news! The ophthalmologist said there was no change in Mother's eyes. That relieved me immensely.

Later, after awakening from a nap, Mother told me that her mouth was numb, as well as her cheek, nose, and left hand. I called the doctor immediately and took her in, fearing an impending stroke. All was okay, but a CAT scan was ordered as a precautionary measure.

It was an exhausting, confusing, and somewhat frightening day for Mother. "Will you stay with me?" she asked as we drove to the hospital for the test. There was no question that I would! I almost stopped the car to put my arms around her and assure her I would be right there, that I wouldn't leave her.

The test frightened her. She didn't like the claustrophobic feeling of being in that tunnel. "I don't ever want another one of those," she told me on the way home. I hope the need never arises.

Mother was confused when we returned home. She walked out the front door of the apartment, thinking she was headed for the bathroom. During dinner, she asked, "Do my folks know where I am?" I wasn't sure who "her folks" were, but assured her they did. "When are we going home?" she asked, looking so bewildered. All I could do was put my arm around her and assure her that she was home, safe and sound.

At other moments, though, her mind was clear as a bell. She reminded me to be sure to pay the light bill and told me who had painted the watercolor hanging on the wall.

LATER

"Goodbye!" Mother said as I tucked her in bed with a good night hug and kiss.

I laughed. "Goodbye?"

"Well," she said, "in case I don't see you tomorrow."

Is that a premonition?

I'm tired. All the busyness, the frustration, and worry of this day has added up to plain, downright tiredness. I can't sleep too soundly tonight, though. I need to listen for Mother getting up to use the bathroom. I worry so much about her falling again.

Saturday, April 17

I placed my air mattress next to the hallway leading to the bedroom, so I could hear if Mother called or got up. She awakened as the sun came up, surprised that it was morning. "Is Dad home, yet?" she asked. (My dad died twenty-three years ago.) I sighed with relief when she dozed off to sleep again. I needed my quiet time.

I wonder what this day will bring.

Today's journal thought is perfect for me: **I know that my prayers are answered and everything I need will be supplied.**

LATER

The sense of feeling has returned to Mother's hand, although her mouth is still numb and her leg remains weak. The disorientation seems to have disappeared. She put her shoes on the wrong feet, however, and didn't know the difference! Since her balance is questionable, I reinstalled the shower chair.

After dinner tonight, a wave of exhaustion came over me. Looking in the mirror, I saw how very tired I looked. Now that Mother is improving, I need to take care of myself.

Sunday, April 18

Mother required assistance today with bathing, dressing, and fixing her breakfast. She said her hand was numb again and her mouth "felt big." She had had another dream about Dad, saying, "But he'll look different." Assuringly, I said, "Yes, but you'll know him."

Mother tries so hard to keep going. Even though it was a struggle for her, she washed the dinner dishes tonight. My prayer is that she be allowed to make her transition peacefully and quickly.

I am feeling good. I'm at peace. I know I'm not alone and that the help we need will come at the right time.

Monday, April 19

Last Friday, the doctor said that Mother's heartbeat was irregular. He asked if we had talked. I said we had and showed him the living will Mother had signed. "Good!" he told me. "Keep it with you." *Was he telling me something else?* I didn't ask.

As I massaged Mother's feet and legs yesterday, she said, "I wish I could do something for you."

"You have!" I responded. "You raised me and did many things for me when I couldn't. Now it's my turn."

Friends and acquaintances have said how beautiful the times were with their mothers before they died. I had no understanding of that feeling until now. My relationship with Mother is so peaceful. There is nothing more important in my life at this moment than taking care of her.

These past three years have been filled with learning. It's becoming clearer that my purpose in this life is to learn, to love, and to be of service. I have many more lessons to learn.

LATER

"Are the children still here?" Mother asked when she got up. It startles me to hear her ask "off the wall" questions like that. Not knowing where she was in time, I inquired who the children were. She seemed to be thinking of the grandchildren. "Oh, they had to leave to go home for school," I said matter-of-factly. That satisfied her. She didn't mention it again.

Wednesday, April 21

Mother was moving at a snail's pace this morning, more so than usual. She was so tired after eating breakfast that she needed my help in getting to the couch to rest. I had the feeling she was about to take her last breath.

I sat beside her, held her hand, put my arm around her shoulders, and silently prayed. *If it is your will, God, please take her now.*

It wasn't her time. She's sleeping peacefully and soundly, snorin' up a storm!

Later I had a crying spell. Why do I run the entire gamut of emotions? Earlier I felt so exuberant, and now I can't keep the floodgates closed. Cris told me to cry when I felt the need. I know tears are beneficial. It's just that I feel so vulnerable, so weak when I cry—especially in front of others.

Thursday, April 22

"I never thought it would come to this," Mother lamented as I helped her dress after a shower.

"What do you mean?" I asked, even though I knew.

"Needing someone to help me get dressed," she said sadly.

I paused, not knowing what to say. "Aren't you glad I am the one who's helping you?" I asked, putting my arm around her shoulder.

"Oh, yes!" Then she sighed. "I hope it's not much longer."

I hope not, either.

LATER

I'm tired tonight. I'm waiting for Mother to die. If others read that, they would think I was terrible. But I'm so tired. I want to get out of this cramped apartment. I want to be back in my own home and free from my responsibilities down here. I hope and pray it's not much longer. I know, however, that is not within my control.

Saturday, April 24

I didn't sleep well last night. The feelings of anger and resentment were too strong. *What am I angry at, or with whom?* I'm angry with Mother for causing me to live like this. *But why?* She can't help it. She didn't bring this on herself, and she certainly isn't one bit happy with being so dependent on someone. Then my anger must be *fear.*

But what am I afraid of?

LATER

During a phone conversation with a neighbor today, I mentioned how luxurious it felt to take a shower at home yesterday and not compete for space with the shower chair. My shower space down here is only the size of a postage stamp. The neighbor laughed. I told her it wasn't funny, but she continued to laugh. That upset me. *Doesn't anyone understand?*

LATER

I'm so angry, ANGRY, **ANGRY**. This journal is the safest place I have to vent my feelings. I thought Mother was going to fall tonight when I saw her climbing all over "my stuff" in the dining room. She was trying to reach the cord to close the draperies. In her futile attempt, the telephone was being pulled with every move, ready to fall on the floor, dragging the tablecloth and everything on the table with it. Fearful of a disastrous consequence, I yelled at Mother as I ran to grab her. At that very moment, her hearing aid fell out. She couldn't hear a word I said!

Maybe that was good. When we were settled once again, I told her how that upset me. "I wasn't going to fall," she said. Right! She's fallen so many times already, and she wasn't going to fall this time? What could I do?

I was so upset that I could feel my heart pounding—every beat louder and louder. Later, I felt a weakness in my arms and legs.

I'm still angry. I brought my air mattress into the living room, made it up, got ready for bed. Mother sat in her chair, passively watching me. I turned off the television. "Oh, is it time to go to bed?" she asked innocently.

"It's after ten o'clock," I told her.

"Oh, should I go to bed?"

"I don't care," I responded, turning out the light. After a few minutes, she toddled off to her room.

Now, I can't sleep. I'm out of patience with Mother because I've had to give up everything to care for her. I resent it. I am angry, angry—so angry I could scream. I need to write it all down.

1. Mother's frailty is not her fault. I need to recognize that so I can respond differently. (Easier said than done, Marian.)
2. Yes, I have made a sacrifice, but this is what I've chosen to do. The alternative is not even a choice for me.
3. I haven't really accepted the fact that soon Mother will no longer be in this life.
4. My thinking needs to be changed. It's erroneous. It's self-defeating. It will only continue to cause problems.

Slowly, I'm beginning to calm down. The tension is easing, and I can feel the warmth of circulation flow throughout my body. My need has been heard. Thank you!

Sunday, April 25

Mother and I had a long talk at dinner. She hoped she wasn't stopping me from doing anything. *Stopping me?* I've stopped everything to take care of her. I have chosen to do that.

We talked about the good, active life she's had and that her body is just plain tired now. She laughed at that! We talked about her five sisters, all of whom are deceased. I said she was the only one who has been able to stay in her own home past the age of ninety. Mother smiled. I went on to say that she wouldn't be able to stay here without my help. She told me how much she appreciated what I've done for her. How I needed to hear that!

LATER

Mother is too tired to do the dishes tonight. I see her going down fast, and I hope it isn't much longer. *How often have I said that?* In the past, she always had knitting or crocheting in her hands when she sat down. Now, she sits with her hands folded. It is so pathetically sad.

While at K-Mart today, I stood in the check-out line behind an elderly gentleman who was confused about the pen that the cashier handed him to sign his credit card receipt. He needed help and the cashier kindly obliged. As I waited, I could feel my impatience mount, and thought about going to another register. I just don't want to be around elderly people who need care like my mother. I don't want to see people who have had such active, independent lives be reduced to that state of helplessness. It's frightening. I don't allow myself to think that I could be like that someday, too.

Monday, April 26

I am much calmer today. I've shifted into low gear. Kathie, one of my calligraphy buddies, sent a box of suckers to Mother. She loves those suckers and was tickled that "the girls" had thought of her. Also, Alma called tonight. It's so necessary for me to talk with friends of my age.

Tuesday, April 27

Mother couldn't understand why the water for her cereal wasn't boiling. Thinking she'd turned on another burner, she "tested" it by touching the coils with her fingers. Oh, my! She couldn't see the one that was red hot. Another challenge.

Mother said she keeps thinking about Dad, wondering when he's going to come. I asked if he was coming here. "Yes, through this door," she said, nodding toward the front door of the apartment. "He's coming to get me. He's been gone a long time."

What do you say? Nothing.

Wednesday, April 28

"Is this Saturday?" Mother asked. Her days all run together. There's nothing to differentiate one from another. I wonder sometimes if I'm living in a nursing home. I need to change my thinking. Okay, Marian, what are the positives of this situation?

1. I have lots of time to do reflective thinking.

2. I don't have the guilt of having to place Mother in the care of someone else.
3. I have lots of time to write, journal writing and letter writing.
4. I have lots of time to read.
5. I could teach myself to crochet. That would certainly be an interesting challenge!

This afternoon, a neighbor dropped in for a visit. Mother told her that she wanted to die, that she was ready to go.

Thursday, April 29

I believe Mother is fighting her disability, not allowing herself to give up. She feels she must keep going, going, going. Jack was the same way, even exercising the night before he died. I'd be the same, too. There is so much pride in our family that it is very difficult to accept dependency. Yet, there is a lesson to be learned.

This has been a good day! I've been calm, understanding, and patient all day, although my body feels as if it has been wrung through a wringer backwards. I'm amazed at the 180 degree swing of emotions, from yesterday's anger and intense irritableness to today's calmness and peaceful serenity. With time, perhaps my emotions will level to a happy medium.

Saturday, May 1

The virtues of yesterday were too good to be true.

I'm in the basement. The anger is back. Mother was up early this morning, and I lost my quiet time, the main stabilizer in my life. She thought I was leaving early and that Marcia, my niece, was coming. I can't tell her anything until just before it happens if this is what she's going to do.

Thank goodness for this basement, even the hard chair I'm sitting on. It's not the most pleasant place to be, but at least it's quiet. Having time alone is so important to me that I'll put up with anything to get it, I guess. Without this time to recharge my battery, my day simply falls apart.

LATER

I had a neighborly chat with Carol, the tenant upstairs. She told me about Plymouth Inn, a nearby facility offering assisted living. She suggested that I check it out. At first, I recoiled at the idea but continued to listen. She said it was important for me to think of myself. That's true.

After dinner, I talked with Mother about looking into alternatives. It upset her. I tried to explain that I didn't know how much longer I could keep this up, now that she needed me full-time. It was hard for her to hear that and most difficult for me to say. It tore my heart out to admit this to her, but the pressure was building—seemingly beyond my control.

During the evening, Mother brought the subject up again—in financial terms this time. I assured her that she'd have enough to "pay her way" and that we'd check out places. Knowing there was no hurry seemed to make her feel better. We talked about the alternative of staying right here, in her own apartment, as long as I could have a couple of days off. She agreed that was important. We are thinking of solutions. Oh, how relieved I feel! I have no idea what will result, but I no longer feel like a prisoner with no hope of parole.

I think the emotional roller coaster I have been riding was due to the fact that I had braced myself for Mother's death, and it didn't happen. She's getting stronger, not weaker! I was denying that fact because I wanted this agony to end for both of us. It didn't happen. Now I'm learning the lesson of looking for solutions. The way will be made clear for both of us. This I truly believe.

Sunday, May 2

I awakened before dawn, my head aroar with what to do. Stay here? Plymouth Inn? Some other facility? I could keep this apartment so I'd have a place to stay as often as I wished if Mother were to move into Plymouth Inn. That relieved my mind somewhat.

I called Pat in New Mexico just to talk. She encouraged me to look for someone who could relieve me for a few hours twice a week. As I watched Mother this morning, I knew she needs to stay in her own home. There was no doubt in my mind. If she were in a nursing home, she wouldn't be able to sleep thirteen hours like she did last night, nor fix her own breakfast. I'll consider Pat's suggestion and look for someone to come in a few hours each week to relieve me.

What would it be like to be free for a few hours? The very thought is mind-boggling. It has been so long. Dare I even hope that the way will open, that the person I can trust and whom Mother would enjoy will be found?

Monday, May 3

"Should I tell Edith we're going to look for another place?" Mother asked so innocently today. I told her we wouldn't need to look if I could hire someone to take care of my yard, and if I could get away once in awhile. She seemed relieved. "You can go do anything you want to do," she told me.

I smiled. "You'd be more content to stay right here, wouldn't you?" She returned my smile and nodded her head.

The decision had been made.

LATER

I commented that today would have been Aunt Edith's one hundredth birthday, had she lived. Mother looked at me in astonishment. "Where is she living?"

I told her she'd died five years ago.

"You mean she's gone?"

"Yes, she's gone. You are the only one left in your family."

Mother was stunned. "They're all gone?" she asked incredulously.

I nodded my head.

"I should be gone, too," she said sadly, shaking her head.

I assured her that some day she, too, would be starting a brand new life. That pleased her! "Isn't that wonderful?" I mused aloud. "A new life!"

Feeling peaceful, I left to run a few errands. At the grocery store, I had a smile on my face and a desire to be friendly with everyone. As I was selecting bananas, I spoke to a gentleman nearby. "Aren't many green ones here today," I commented. He agreed, saying that one has to eat them fast when they're ripe. I noticed a young mother with her baby who was into everything. "She's giving you a hard time today," I remarked. "You bet," the mother said. "That's why I don't shop with her!" Speaking to total strangers was a relatively new behavior for me. Today I wanted to share the joy I felt!

Friends have said to me during this most recent crisis that I need to take care of myself. Yes, I understand that, but how do I do it?

My answer came later. I called Edith to thank her for the card she'd sent Mother and asked if she knew of anyone I could hire to stay with Mother. She said she would be glad to stay anytime! I accepted her kind offer, and we tentatively agreed on Saturday. Wonderful!

Thursday, May 6

This morning I asked Rick, the apartment complex manager, if he knew of anyone in the complex who'd be interested in earning some extra money by staying with my mother a few hours twice a week. He didn't know of anyone, but suggested that I write a notice to post on the bulletin board in each building. I will do that.

I took Mother to the doctor this afternoon. Her blood pressure was good, but her heart beat remains irregular. The last CAT scan report indicated three or four strokes within the past three years, mainly in the occipital lobe, which may account for the vision impairment. The strokes also account for the memory loss. The doctor prescribed a new blood thinner medication. I agreed with his decision to not treat the heart irregularity aggressively. I hope her heart takes her peacefully.

Again, the doctor asked me if Mother had a living will. I showed him the copy I carry with me at all times, and pointed out the "no heroics" clause. Nodding his head in agreement, he explained that the policy on not using life support systems varies in every locality and suggested I check that out with the Emergency Medical Service people, the medical examiner's office, or, as I mentioned, Hospice. I appreciated his concern and helpful suggestions. I'll make those calls tomorrow.

Friday, May 7

It was another sleepless night. I kept thinking about yesterday's conversation with the doctor. *How could I be assured there'd be no heroic measures?*

Things were on Mother's mind. too. She wondered if I wanted the door mirrors. She's preparing to make her transition, checking things off in her mind.

LATER

I talked with the receptionist at the Hospice office this morning. She was so kind. Yes, they do have an agreement with EMS for no life support, but suggested that I check with the fire department about their policy. She gave me a brochure describing Hospice services.

My next stop was the township ambulance service, right across the road from the apartment. I learned they do not honor living wills, but they do honor Hospice patients.

Returning to the apartment, I read the brochure and knew immediately that Hospice was the type of care I wanted for Mother. That's what she'd want, too. Since Hospice requires a doctor's statement that the patient's condition is terminal, I left a message for the doctor.

Meanwhile, I called the Hospice office to inquire about referral procedures, should the doctor agree. I talked with Cindy, the care consultant nurse. Her kindness touched my sensitive nerve, and my voice began breaking with emotion. Embarrassed, I took the receiver from my ear. In the distance, I could hear Cindy saying, "Hang on, Marian. Don't hang up. You need some help."

Tearfully, I told her that I was trying to find someone to relieve me. I spoke of my concern that Mother would be placed on life support, something neither one of us wanted, if I were to call Emergency Medical Services. How could I avoid it? She told me what the Hospice procedure was. That made me feel better, but my real need was finding a way to get some support. Cindy was right. I needed some help. I hoped and prayed that Hospice would be our answer.

I talked with Mother about Hospice, and she agreed that would be the service of her choice. The doctor returned my call later in the afternoon. He was sympathetic, understood all about Hospice, but I knew he wouldn't write any terminal statement. He said Mother could live for years and not have another stroke.

I hung up the phone and looked out the kitchen window. "Lord, what do I do now?"

I went into the privacy of the bathroom and cried my heart out.

Right now, I'm sitting in the car by the small lake which is down the road from the apartments. I keep asking over and over, "Lord, what do I do now?" My legs feel as if they can't support me. How can I go on? I'm emotionally and physically drained. Am I capable of releasing all worry about being with Mother full-time? Can I just take off, go up to Flint and do what I have to do? If she dies while I'm gone, how am I going to react? Right now, she is okay—but for how long? I have to let go…let go…just let go. I want this over. I've rehearsed it so many times, and it has been so real.

Yet, here we are.

LATER

I'm trying to sort out my feelings. If Mother is dying, I'll just let her go and wait for an hour before calling 911. If she dies while I'm away, so be it. At least, the body will be cold when I return. *How can I even think*

about it with such a harsh, uncaring attitude? Already I'm recoiling from it.
Can the death of my mother be reduced to such cold, unfailing words?

If what the doctor said is true, this could go on for a long time. I'm not sure I can hang on. I feel I'm losing it. Marian, let go…let go…let go…totally release…relinquish all. I am a vehicle, but God is the driver. Oh, I like that metaphor! I can picture that: my body molded like a car and Spirit in the driver's seat!

LATER

Next week, I will prepare meals and be company for Mother, but I'll get out of the apartment for longer periods of time. I'll walk down to the lake at the foot of the hill and sit there on nice days to read, to write, to meditate. I need to concentrate on just being. I've done everything I can and know how to do. Now, I need to let go of the control and practice letting God take charge. Can you do this, Marian? Can you?

Saturday, May 8

How I yearn for a relaxed, restful night of uninterrupted sleep. That probably won't happen, though, until this is all over. And I don't know when that'll be. I'm not in charge.

There are some positives, though. I'm learning why adult children put their parents in nursing homes. I will no longer be judgmental about that, nor will I harbor feelings of self-righteousness about my decision.

LATER

Edith came over this morning to stay with Mother while I went up to Flint for a couple of hours to cut the grass and take care of other necessities at my home. Just as I was ready to leave, the phone rang. It was Cris. I was so happy to hear from her! Then, while I was in Flint, Pat called. My two closest friends, my supports—both called today! I cried while talking with Pat, but told her to just keep talking. She understood. I responded between tears.

On the way back to Plymouth, I stopped to get take-out chicken dinners. Edith had brought a lemon pie which topped off a good dinner for the three of us. Mother enjoyed the meal, and I delighted in Edith's company—someone to talk with. I actually laughed, too! That felt good.

This has been an emotionally and physically exhausting day. I'm glad it's over.

Sunday, May 9

This is the first Mother's Day I haven't given Mother a card and present. I can't. It seems so false. Every day has been Mother's Day. When I see something in the store that she needs or might like, I buy it for her—not because of a special day, but because I love her so much. Not making a big deal out of today may be preparation for another year when she will not be here for me to honor.

My journal thought for today: **Just for today—for the next twelve hours—I can be happy.** Yes, I can do that!

Monday, May 10

Had a "surprise" greet me when I walked into the bathroom this morning. On the floor was one of Mother's soaked pads, as well as her wet underpants and pajama bottoms. And others think she could stay alone for a couple of days with Meals on Wheels? I'm going to try a different approach. If any "outsider" wants to know how things are, the answer is going to be "just fine!" I don't want to hear anyone say to me, "I know how it is" or offer suggestions unless they've had a similar experience or have lived this one with me.

I'm sitting at a picnic table on the edge of the lake a few blocks from the apartment. It is so quiet and peaceful, looking out over the still lake and watching the Canada geese—fifty or so this morning—search and scratch for food. I love this quiet retreat.

I need to straighten out my thinking, or I'm headed for trouble big-time. I thought Mother was going to die. I'd rehearsed all the details—

even to finding out what to do to avoid life support. Then, the reality that this may go on for years struck last Friday. I've been a wreck ever since.

LATER

I encouraged Mother to sit on the porch this afternoon. Two neighbors stopped by to visit. She enjoyed that!

I experimented with my new response when people inquired about my mother. "Oh, everything's just fine!" I said with feigned cheerfulness. Their reaction was amazing—a sigh of relief and a smile. No one wants to hear about problems. Why mention any?

I went for a walk tonight with Evelyn, one of our neighbors. We walked the same route Mother and I used to. I thought about the contrast. Just last year Mother could walk that distance of a mile. Now she can barely maneuver around the apartment using a cane.

I read the thought in my journal again: **Just for today—for the next twelve hours—I can be happy.** Then, try the next twelve hours, and on and on.

Can I do that? I'm trying.

Wednesday, May 12

Mother agreed to go for a ride in the car. I drove past Schoolcraft College where she'd worked as a volunteer for eighteen years, the highlight of her life. I hoped it would trigger a memory of the good experiences she'd had there. It didn't. In fact, nothing looked familiar to her. So sad.

That experience was a shocker. Mother is here in body, but her mind isn't what it used to be. God is a mystery and, so too, is life. I need to enjoy each moment and stop trying to look around that proverbial corner. I really don't want to know what's ahead.

Sunday, May 16

A new day, a new page in my journal. Today's guiding thought: **Life doesn't give me anything I'm not capable of handling.**

I sense there are changes taking place. I don't know what, nor do I want to know. I don't know what it is I need to learn. Maybe I'm not listening. Why is it so hard for me to listen? Am I afraid?

Wednesday, May 19

I am seeing how the effects of Mother's last strokes have caused more decline. On the way to the restaurant tonight, she told me what she wanted and asked me to order it for her. That was a first.

She loves the biscuits and honey served at that restaurant. Tonight she needed help pouring the honey out of the server. That, too, was a first. Also, I noticed how much heavier she leaned on me for support in walking. The bottom line, however, is that she enjoyed the outing. That's what's important.

I felt relaxed all day. This is the longest stretch of "feeling good" I've had since the first of April—nine whole days!

Thursday, May 20

Well, here I am in the basement. I told Mother it was only 7:30, too early for her to be up this morning. "That's okay," she said. "I'm up now."

I didn't agree that it was okay. I dressed quickly, packed up my books and journal, and headed for the basement. I have to, *must* have, and *will* have my morning quiet time—**undisturbed**.

Now I'm working at getting my joy back.

My life is arranged around Mother and her needs. It seems as if her death is constantly on my mind. I awaken frequently every night, or so it seems, wondering if she has died.

Saturday, May 22

I got up earlier this morning so I wouldn't have to go down to the basement for "my" time. Mother is taking her shower alone. I do have an ear toward the bathroom, though, just in case. I want her to do everything she can for herself. The day may come when she won't be able to shower herself, but until then….

What I'm experiencing is similar to what I envision a two-year Peace Corps assignment to be. I have left most of my possessions at home, living here with only the bare necessities. I am not defined by what I have, but what I am. This is an interesting time in my life. It's as if I've gone into the "desert for forty days and nights" and will emerge a different person.

Wednesday, May 26

Guess I have to get up before dawn to have my quiet time. Mother was up early again this morning, so here I am sitting on the hard chair in the basement writing and thinking. My thoughts have been so negative. I need to change that. I think I'll go to the movie tonight—do something for myself.

Monday, May 31

Mother was confused about what part of the day it was. She walked her usual route inside the apartment and then announced that was all she had to do until afternoon. It was 9:30 in the evening! An hour later, she thought it was 10:30 in the morning. Mentioning that it was dark outside clued her that it was night and time to go to bed.

I have the feeling that more challenges are coming.

Wednesday, June 2

I looked at Mother as she slept this morning. She had such a peaceful look on her face. I hadn't noticed that before. She has no concerns.

Today's journal entry: **What I give attention to is what I become.** Guess I'd better be careful what I focus on!

While showering this morning, I thought about last night's phone conversation with Pat. I talked about Mother's signs of dementia and said that unless you lived with it, you wouldn't recognize it as such. Pat was so supportive. I remember earlier, when I wasn't ready to accept the fact that Mother was getting older, friends were very gentle with me. They continue to support me at this stage of my life.

Monday, June 7

What a wonderful thing a day is! That's the thought I awakened with this morning. I know that when my mind is flowing positively, I'm relaxed and less tense.

I tried shoving the coffee container into the coffee maker this morning, but it wouldn't go in. I tried forcing it, one way and then another. *If I keep this up, it'll break, and then I'll have no coffee this morning.* Finally I stopped. Taking a deep breath, I realigned the container, putting it in the correct grooves. It slid right in, just the way it was designed to do.

I continued to think about that simple experience and how it relates to my life. When I'm out of alignment and trying to force things to happen, nothing goes the way I think it should. How effortless life is, in contrast, when I'm in complete alignment with God—just the way I was designed to be!

LATER

Last night, Mother said she dreamed she'd sold the cottage. "I just got disgusted one day," she told me. "I called the realtor and the cottage was sold in just a few days."

I laughed. "Yes! That's exactly what you did twenty years ago!"

Mother looked at me in total amazement. "You mean I don't have the cottage?"

Those are the moments only I am privileged to see. I consider it a gift. Being a constant part of Mother's life, I'm very aware of how much she has declined in the past two months. I'm so thankful for this time to be with her. I'm not as upset and angry now about her shortcomings. Instead, I'm beginning to feel almost a sense of awe at being here to experience this phase of life with her. Maybe I'm finally making peace with my true self.

Wednesday, June 9

I'm thinking about the conversations I overheard while waiting in the doctor's office yesterday: the aches, the pains, the sundry complaints of the physical body. As I listened to the litany of problems, I recalled my journal entry from the other day: **What I pay attention to is what I become.** I wanted to escape in the fastest way possible before I became any of those ailments!

Sunday, June 13

Notable notes from this morning's telecast message:

> **I can't allow circumstances to prevent me from enjoying life. People hold on to circumstances in order to feel like a victim, to enjoy feeling miserable, or to have others feel sorry for them.**

That really hit home! If I have to change my approach to my situation, how will I do it? If I feel like a victim, what do I do about that? Do I really feel miserable so that others will feel sorry for me?

Mirror, mirror, on the wall....

Tuesday, June 15

When I returned from the grocery store, Mother was sitting on the porch talking with her neighbor, Evelyn. Another neighbor had been over earlier. I'm so glad I made the decision to keep Mother here. Her familiar surroundings and neighbors mean so much, even more so now that her memory is affected.

I'm curious about my recent feeling of peacefulness. I am recalling times that had angered me only a few weeks ago—like not having any space and having to set up my bed every night and take it down every morning. Sometimes I would throw the air mattress on the floor and kick it to vent my angry feelings. Now, I have no feeling other than peacefulness. I like it. I won't bother to analyze it. Instead, I'll just enjoy and hope it lasts.

LATER

Rather than walking her usual route around the inside of the apartment tonight, Mother chose to walk outside. She decided to walk down past the office, a distance equal to half a city block. I reminded her that she had to walk back, too. "I'll show you what I can do!" she told me in no uncertain terms. And she did!

Talk about determination! Wow! But that's what keeps her going. She doesn't give up.

Friday, June 18

After a mental debate with myself, I decided to drive up to Flint this morning. I'm glad I did. In addition to picking up the mail and getting a few house tasks taken care of, I filled two buckets with roses from my garden. Mother was delighted! We have roses all over the apartment. Their fragrance and beauty are breathtaking!

Saturday, June 20

Something started Mother thinking about her death. She got out the memorial book from Dad's funeral. She used her magnifying glass to read the entries, but it didn't help. "I don't like to talk about this," she said, "but I won't be here much longer, and I want you to know I want the same funeral as Dad had. I want the same funeral home."

I told her I didn't think that funeral home was there now, and mentioned one in Plymouth to consider. She didn't know anything about that one, so I suggested that we check it out some day. She liked that idea. Our brief conversation was casual—just the way it should be. There was no sadness, no denial. It was natural and seemed so right.

Monday, June 21

I received an understanding letter from Pat today. I clipped a paragraph from it that I will want to reread many times:

> *"I've noticed such a change in your writing and thinking from a while back. You were so angry and bitter for a while. Now, I can feel the peace you've found. I knew you'd work it out. It was fascinating to see it happen through your written words. It was a natural process you had to go through. It's behind you now, and your mind is at peace and rest...."*

Tuesday, June 22

I'm still thinking about what Pat wrote. I needed that encouragement. Also, I have noticed people responding to me in a more positive, friendlier manner. That's the way it happens: first within, then without. Others reflect how I feel about myself.

The Michigan strawberries are in! I bought some from the market today and made a strawberry pie. It was delicious! Mother enjoyed it, as did the neighbors!

Thursday, June 24

My awakening thought was one I've read in several inspirational books: **An event is just an event.** It certainly applied to today's situation.

Mother didn't make it to the bathroom in time this morning, so I had a big clean-up job. My feeling, however, was not anger or disgust. In fact, I attached no feeling to the task. *So it happened. No big deal. An event is just an event. I will leave it in neutral.*

And I did!

LATER

I'm consciously telling Mother the time and connecting it with something significant. For instance, as I get ready to prepare dinner, I tell her,

"It's 5:00, so I'll turn on the evening news." I'm hoping that association will help her stay more oriented.

Saturday, June 26

Changed my routine this morning. Mother was up and almost dressed when I awakened. I took care of her needs before settling down for "my time." Why didn't I think of doing that before now? Yes, there were a few seconds of anger welling up inside me, but they quickly disappeared. I do prefer having my quiet time before doing anything else in the morning, but I can adjust. The important point is that I have it.

Wednesday, June 30

Mother put a blouse on last night instead of her pajama top. She didn't know the difference. During the night, she tried to flush her pad down the toilet, but it didn't go, thank goodness. She went back to bed with no protection. So—one more time

> the same drip, drip,
> > the same mopping,
> > > the same laundry.
> > > > Different day.
> > > An event is just an event.

Notes to myself:
1. Purchase plastic runners to protect the carpeting from Mother's bed to the bathroom.
2. Lay out extra pads and underpants for nighttime use.

Saturday, July 10

Mother rode up to Flint with me. On the way back to Plymouth, I stopped by the beauty salon to see Lena. She came out to the car to talk with Mother. As we hugged goodbye, Lena whispered, "This must be hard on you." Those understanding words usually elicit tears. Today there were none. "I've accepted it," I murmured.

And I believe I have!

Sunday, July 11

Notable notes from this morning's inspirational telecast:

No one can make you what you want to be. Only you can do that.
No event can make you happy. Only you can do that.
Don't depend on others to give you what you need.
You have all the power within you.

I must carry these thoughts with me today.

Tuesday, July 13

My sister-in-law, Theo, came over for an hour this afternoon. I enjoyed having someone with whom I could talk. I am so hungry for conversation that I latch on to anyone who can provide that for me. To tell the truth, I have become a little selfish about it.

I must stop trying to look around that elusive corner to see what's coming. It gains me nothing. In fact, I lose because I'm not taking advantage of the present moment which I'll never see again. What will be, will be. I know I'll be able to handle it.

The Fourth Year

Sunday, July 18, 1993

I noted this provoking thought as I listened to this morning's inspirational telecast: **We can be butterflies, but still have caterpillar thinking and acting.**

The fact that the moth needs to struggle out of the cocoon in order to gain life caused me to think that it's necessary for people to struggle sometimes, too. Challenges are a part of life. They prod us into growth. Recalling my own learning opportunities of the past three years, I know. I'm still struggling to break out of that cocoon and reach the butterfly's freedom.

In her beautiful children's book, *All I See,* Cynthia Rylant tells of a painter wearing an old overcoat and whistling Beethoven's Fifth while he sets up his easel in front of the lake every day to paint. When he's tired, he lies down in a canoe and drifts across the lake, staring up at the clouds.

Like that painter, I have the need to just drift at times. My favorite spot is the little lake down the road from the apartments. I love to go there in the morning, when very few people are around, to sit quietly at one of the picnic tables and gaze out over the quiet water. A half-hour enveloped in the quietness of nature, feeling the soothing effects of the warm sun and hearing the gentle, rhythmic sound of the water rippling against the shoreline, provides a serene peacefulness that allows me to return with a sense of renewal. God is and I am. I can continue, one day at a time.

I was happy to receive a letter from Zane today. Friends are truly one of God's most precious gifts.

> *"I was so pleased to hear the wonderful way you are working through the process....Seeking and stretching beyond our comfortable zone is never easy, and at our age it's particularly difficult because the tendency is to think we've seen it all, done it all, and know it all. Journal keeping has always been the salvation of my sanity. I know it is yours, also...."*

Friday, July 23

After a dental appointment in Flint this morning, I stopped by my house. It saddened me to see the yard choked with weeds and not be able to do anything about it. My poor roses. They need TLC in the worst way, but I can't take care of them right now. If they do survive, it'll be a miracle. For the present, everything in my life must be set aside for Mother's sake. I must not indulge in "caterpillar thinking." I can't afford it. The butterfly struggles only once to be free of its cocoon. Sometimes I do it daily.

I was so tired when I got back to Plymouth. I wanted to draw back into my cocoon and nap, but Mother decided to water the flowers. That required my help to get out the hose, turn on the water, turn off the water, put away the hose. She got her shoes muddy when she stepped into the wet flower bed, unable to see where she was going. That upset me. I had another clean-up task. My patience left a little to be desired. Poor Mother, she tries.

Thursday, July 29

It's the little things Mother needs help with. This morning she couldn't turn the bathroom faucet to regulate the water temperature. The other night she couldn't crawl into bed. Every so often, she leaves the stove on or turns on the wrong burner. She doesn't know when her hearing aid battery needs to be replaced and can't see well enough to do it. Those are a few of the little things that require someone being here full-time. I'm the best one to fulfill that responsibility—her daughter.

Tuesday, August 3

What a perfect day! I can't believe all that I've accomplished and so effortlessly. I not only cleaned the bathroom, but washed the windows and curtains, did two loads of laundry, did the ironing—plus grocery shopping and preparing dinner. I remained in the flow and it worked. Such a wonderful day! My caterpillar self wasn't even around.

Wednesday, August 11

I see Mother going downhill even more, and it's getting to me. She couldn't get up the single step to the porch today without help which means I have to be here *all* the time. That upset me. I cried and cried in the privacy of the bathroom. Then, as I looked out the kitchen window and watched her walk ever so slowly around the sidewalk circling the apartments, I cried again. I dread the winter coming on and being trapped in this small apartment.

I threw a book on the floor a couple of times today. I banged doors and felt like kicking things. I didn't know why I was feeling such strong emotion. I pulled out this journal and began writing:

1. I feel trapped. I feel smothered. Mother depends on me so much for everything, even for the time of day.
2. I'm worried about Mother getting worse. Then what am I going to do?
3. I feel alone—no support from anyone.

There! I think I have it all out. Now I'll look at it and see what I can do.

#1 Inform Mother that beginning tomorrow she is going to take her walk by the clock. We will plan in the morning what times she will go.

#2 Take it a day at a time. Today's problem is solved. Go from
there. Worry is nothing more than misplaced imagination.
It's wasted energy and I can't afford that.

#3 Forget the self pity. There is no person on this planet who can
be with me all the time.

Thursday, August 12

A much better day! Yesterday's self-counseling session with my journal
helped. Mother is watching the clock now, going out for her walks at the
times she said she would. That will help keep her oriented and me sane.
I'm trying to keep the "I have a choice" idea in my own mind. It helps.

Friday, August 13

My sister-in-law, Theo, came over tonight with her husband and
daughter, bringing cards and candy for Mother's birthday. I enjoyed having someone to talk to. It helped to relieve the monotony.

Mother received a lot of cards today which pleased her so much! I'll display them on the mirror in the living room so she can see how well she
was remembered by her many friends and family.

Sunday, August 15

Today was Mother's birthday—number ninety-five! We celebrated by
going to her favorite restaurant with Edith. Mother enjoyed her dinner
even more when I told her that it cost only twenty-two cents with her
birthday discount!

Later, she took a piece of birthday cake over to her neighbor, Evelyn,
walking ever so slowly across the parking lot by herself while I watched,
praying that she'd make it without a mishap. It was important for Mother
to carry on that tradition herself. She returned home smiling, proud of her
accomplishment and happy that Evelyn was so delighted with the cake. I

asked if she enjoyed her day. "Immensely!" she said, her blue eyes sparkling and her face glowing with a big smile. I was happy.

Saturday, August 21

A week later, and it's my birthday. I received several birthday cards today, a letter from my niece Carolyn, and a package from Cris with a two-piece travel cosmetic bag. I'll save that for the time when I'll be free to travel once again. Of course, I'll toss the one I'm using now. I won't want the memories.

I'm thinking about the decades of my life. This decade of my "fifties" has been the change time: retirement, redoing the house, Jack's death, new career in tax preparation, Mother's stroke, and now my confinement as I take care of her. I'm looking forward to the next decade as a time of new adventures.

Sunday, August 22

Today's inspirational telecast message was to stay out of the "spider web" of life by:

Paying close and loving attention to myself.
Keeping a sense of humor.

Interesting! Now, I have to watch for spider webs *and* caterpillars!

I've been thinking about the negative emotions of fear, anger, and depression as being signals for help. They are normal emotions, unless they are allowed to "hang around" forever. I can't allow myself to get caught in any spider web with them!

LATER

Called Edith tonight. She told me her nephews had moved her sister into a nursing home. It upset her. It's not easy to care for one's parent. The decision of how to do so is a personal choice. What Mother and I are doing is right for us, but would not be for everyone. You do what you need to and in the way that is best for all concerned.

Monday, August 23

HAPPY BIRTHDAY to me! This is my fifty-eighth birthday. It will be a very ordinary day: the usual routine of showering Mother, shampooing and setting her hair, cleaning the bathroom, grocery shopping.

LATER

I prepared an excellent dinner with all my favorites, including a special angel food birthday cake "spiked" with raspberry gelatin and served with a dollop of whipped topping and fresh raspberries. Mother enjoyed the dinner, but didn't realize it was my birthday.

I received five phone calls, including one from my cousin, Evelyn who lives in British Columbia. What luxury! Being remembered with calls and cards tells me I'm not alone.

Tuesday, August 24

Mother decided to water her plants today, a laborious task for her. She filled a small pail with water, carried it in one hand while her other hand managed the cane, and slowly made her way to each plant. Methodically she dipped out a cup of water for each one—not differentiating the artificial from the living. I didn't say anything. I wish I could have laughed and made a joke about it. When will I accept the reality that she is no longer the capable and self-sufficient woman I always knew?

I'm losing my mother.

Wednesday, August 25

Every morning when I get up, I glance into Mother's bedroom and pause to watch her sleeping—to make sure she is still breathing. I have to do that before I can do anything else.

LATER

We had ice cream for dessert. Mother tried to scoop up her serving all at once, having forgotten how to use her spoon to break it into bite size portions. It irritated me because the behavior is so childlike. Tonight, however, I recognized my irritation as a signal and changed my thinking. I patiently showed her how to use the tip of the spoon. It worked! How sad, though. How pathetically sad.

Thursday, August 26

I received the call tonight that Mrs. Petrie had died. I can only feel happiness for her. Mother's concern was that she didn't suffer.

Mother asked about my birthday. She was surprised it had passed, and she hadn't wished me "Happy Birthday." I kissed her, assuring her that the wish was just as good today. She didn't remember the special dinner, cake, cards, and phone calls just three days ago.

Sunday, August 29

Mother slept until I awakened her at noon. She had been dreaming about writing her obituary, saying she'd talked with a newspaper reporter and showed him all her bowling trophies and the honorary diploma from Schoolcraft College. I asked if she'd said everything she wanted. She nodded. "I've had a busy life," she said reflectively. I agreed.

Tuesday, August 31

I attended Mrs. Petrie's memorial service this evening. Paul related some memorable anecdotes, illustrating the strength of his mother's character. I'm sure that Don and Paul feel grief, but they must also feel relief. It was difficult for them to see their mother slowly diminish. I'm experiencing it, too. It's heartbreaking, especially knowing there is absolutely nothing you can do to stop it—and it may become worse.

Mother has failed since her birthday. I see it in many subtle ways: sleeping more, that far-away look in her eyes, the fatigue on her face, the slower pace. I hope it's not much longer.

Wednesday, September 1

Mother mentioned she was thinking about Mrs. Petrie, but was hesitant to elaborate. I encouraged her to tell me anything she wanted. She said that wasn't something to talk about. I assured her that dying is a part of living, that it's similar to trees losing their leaves in the fall and their rebirth in the spring. That thought seemed to ease her mind, but she didn't say anything nor ask any questions.

Thursday, September 2

I'm thinking about Jack and Bob dying two months after their birthdays. Dad died a month after his birthday, too. I wonder if Mother will do the same. Strange how the mind puts that together.

Tuesday, September 7

I read that every conscious choice a person makes can influence aging. *I wonder how old I really am.* After all the conscious choices I've made during the past four years, am I older or younger than my years? That's a challenging thought!

I had two clean-up jobs today. Mother's eyesight and coordination are so poor now that she needs assistance with personal hygiene, but she doesn't realize it. She did accept my help, though. I just hope the incontinence problems don't become worse.

Wednesday, September 8

While I shopped at the mall this afternoon, Mother wrote letters to her granddaughters, Carolyn and Elaine. She asked me to read them. I looked at the letters, and my heart almost broke. *They were totally illegible.*

I "decoded" as best I could and mailed both copies to my nieces. I hope they sense the love that inspired their grandma's effort.

LATER

While rereading some notes I had clipped in my journal, I came across the idea of tithing ten per cent of my day to God. That figures out to two hours and forty minutes. But I can't take out all that time. The idea hung around, though, continuing to intrigue me. I wondered how I could do it.

Later, it occurred to me that I could designate one hour in the morning (my usual quiet time), one hour before going to bed, and ten minutes a couple of times during the day. Taking that time out will make the rest of the day better. I will be able to accomplish more in less time and with less effort because of aligning with God. Also, it should take away the resentment I feel about not having time for myself. I'm beginning today!

Saturday, September 11

I enjoyed shampooing Mother's hair and helping her shower today. I believe the positive response was due to the meditation time I had this morning. All the time I was helping Mother shower I thought: I'm so fortunate to be able to do this!

The other day, a friend told me that caring for her mother during the last year of her life was the greatest gift her mother could have given her. I thought it was the other way around for me—until this morning. Now I'm beginning to see that it *is* Mother giving me the gift.

Thursday, September 16

Mother suggested that I look into senior housing for her. I told her she was beyond that, that she needed more care than what would be available in a retirement home—and that *right here* was the best place for her. "But it's too hard on you," she argued. I appreciated that understanding. She agreed that if we make any move, it will be to a two-bedroom apartment so I could have a room of my own.

Tuesday, September 21

While sitting in the basement waiting for the laundry to finish, the thought occurred that I should check with the funeral home about arrangements. It would certainly be easier if I made those decisions now. I won't mention this to anyone because it might sound cold and unfeeling. I recall how fragile I was in just helping to make the arrangement for Bob's, Dad's, and Jack's funerals. I will be solely responsible for Mother's. It will be easier to make the arrangements now when my head is clear and my emotions under control.

Thursday, September 23

I am so relieved to have it all behind me. I actually selected a casket, vault, notice cards, and gave all the necessary identification and background information on Mother. I can't believe I did that!

Making those decisions wasn't difficult, but getting myself inside the funeral home was. As I drove into the parking lot, I thought about turning around and driving away. That would have been very easy to do. Instead, I pulled into a parking space, turned off the ignition, took a deep breath, and told myself: You've come this far, Marian. You're going through with it.

Mother doesn't know I made her arrangements, but I know she'd approve. I remembered her wish to have a casket "like Dad's." I did my best to comply.

LATER

I felt so sorry for Mother tonight, sitting with nothing to do. I gave her a foot massage and that brightened the evening for her. The physical touch, generating the love that flowed between us, had a mutual healing effect.

Tuesday, September 28

Mother "bugged" me all day about some banking business which I can't take care of until Friday. I've explained it so many times. Either she doesn't understand or she forgets. I just ran out of patience today. I'll be glad when Friday comes so I can take care of it. No one knows, unless one has lived with it, the irritation of having to repeat and repeat, explain and explain, over and over—to think you finally "got through" only to have the same question asked a few minutes later. Mother used to have such a good business head. Now the simplest task confuses her. It's so sad.

Thursday, September 30

Mother slept most of the day. She did go out for a walk four times, though. She seems depressed, but smiles so sweetly at any little attention I give her, such as gently awakening her for meals, tucking her in bed, helping her dress—just all those little things. I'm glad I'm here for her.

Sunday, October 3

Mother seemed "out of it" today, although she walked double her route three times. That's her only activity. She's so persistent, thinking she must get six walks in a day.

This afternoon I suggested she might enjoy going to the grocery store with me. Just as we were getting into the car, I noticed that her slacks were wet. When I said they would have to be changed, she objected but did come back into the apartment with me. She had her pajama bottoms on, too!

Monday, October 4

I took Mother to the doctor this afternoon for a routine check-up and flu shot. I'm always relieved when the report is good. Her next appointment is January.

Tuesday, October 5

I'm relaxed, more patient and compassionate. When I think back to three years ago, I know I've come a long way. It hasn't been easy, and I certainly don't want to return to the beginning of this journey. I know that when Mother is gone, I will feel sadness—but there will be no regrets. I've done my best to make these final years good ones for her. My prayer is that she be allowed to die in her own home, preferably sleeping away peacefully—and that I'm with her.

Theo and her husband dropped by for a short visit this evening, bringing tomatoes from their garden and a piece of cheesecake. As we hugged goodbye, Theo said encouragingly, "Keep your chin up."

Some days I need to do more than that. Much more.

Wednesday, October 6

Mother got up earlier this morning. She was taking an extraordinarily long time getting dressed, so I went in to check on her. She'd put on a skirt and was trying to find the jacket to go with it. "Why are you dressing up today?" I asked.

She looked at me in surprise. "Why, we're going downtown!"

"Oh?" I said in astonishment. "What for?"

"We're going to explore four stores. Don't you remember?"

Mother was never a shopper, and the thought of "exploring" four stores was not even imaginable. "Which four stores are we going to?" I asked, curious to find out where her thinking had taken her this time.

"Oh I don't know," she responded, "but you do!"

I suggested that we do our "exploring" in the afternoon. She was agreeable, thank goodness!

Mother's mind is going. Is this another stroke? What am I going to do?

LATER

Mother didn't forget about the shopping expedition, but decided she didn't feel up to it today. I made no attempt to persuade her otherwise, either!

She said she felt a little tipsy, confirming my fear of another mini-stroke. I stayed home, afraid to leave her alone.

Thursday, October 7

I'm thinking about the design and message I'll use for the Christmas cards I'll make this year. I'll browse through some poetry books in the library to find something appropriate. John Greenleaf Whittier comes to mind as a good beginning source. I want to have the cards finished so I can begin the enclosure letters by Thanksgiving. That project will satisfy my need to do something creative.

LATER

Mother looks so pretty with her hair newly permed! She wore a skirt and her dress shoes to the beauty shop. I was shocked, though, when she came out of her bedroom with her half-slip on the outside of the skirt. She didn't know the difference.

What's going to happen next?

Monday, October 11

I'm learning the importance of showing compassion, understanding, and support—of just being there when one's presence is not specifically solicited. A letter or a card in the mail means so much to me. Many days I've braced myself going to the mailbox, hoping there'd be a letter—but not really hoping because I didn't want to feel the emotional letdown of seeing an empty box. I know others have their own lives. How significant it is, though, to take time to visit, to call, or to write a note to someone who needs support. It's that giving of one's self to another that really counts. I hope I never forget that.

Tuesday, October 12

Mother said that she'd like to go over to the cemetery in Canada to see if Dad's name had been engraved on the stone. I assured her it had been, adding that it wouldn't be very pretty there now because all the flowers would be gone. Her own death is on her mind.

I changed the subject by asking if she'd like to drive over to the bowling alley Thursday morning and watch her friends bowl. Her eyes brightened with that thought! Mother was a very good bowler with ten trophies to prove it. "But you won't be able to sleep all morning that day," I laughingly warned her. She won't because there'll be a reason to get up.

Thursday, October 14

Everyone at the bowling alley greeted Mother with warm hugs and kind words. "I didn't know who all those people were," she confided to me later. She enjoyed the attention, though.

I pre-funded the funeral arrangement today. The two hardest tasks are done: selection and payment. Now I can deal with all the other details. I have peace of mind.

Saturday, October 16

It's a cool, rainy morning, but I love it! In reviewing some of my notes this morning, I found this gem: **Think of thoughts as in a parade. Let the ones you don't want pass you by; snatch, grab the ones you want!** I like that idea!

LATER

Mother put on a dress this morning. I asked what the occasion was. "I'm going to church!" she answered brightly. I told her that was fine, except today was Saturday. "Oh, I thought it was Sunday."

She asked if I liked the blue dotted dress she had on. I said I did and then asked why. "Oh, I thought this might be a good one to give to the undertaker." She is preparing for the transition yet to come.

Sunday, October 17

Talked with a friend today who said my life wasn't so hard because Mother wasn't sick or in physical pain. I'm sure this person was trying to help me think positively, but I'm ultra-sensitive these days. The comment caused me to realize once again that each person's pain is personal. It isn't appropriate to tell anyone that what he or she is going through is *nothing*. I need to remember that in talking with anyone in the throes of stress. It's their private world, just as this is mine.

Saturday, October 23

Another gorgeous day ahead! I'm enjoying my undisturbed mornings this week, now that Mother sleeps until noon. I look forward to this time for letter writing, planning, just doing whatever I choose. It's absolutely vital for me to have time for myself.

I'm reading *Believing In Myself*,[6] a meditation book written by Earnie Larsen and his sister, Carol Hegarty. Today's thought, a quote by Dr. Francis Braceland, was especially meaningful: **The sorrow that has no vent in tears may weep in other organs.**

We admire strength and toughness, but when emotions are suppressed, something is going to give. That's why I prick the potatoes before baking, to give them vents so they don't explode in the oven. Allowing myself to "vent a little along the way" will definitely prevent a blow-up down the road. I honestly think I've been doing that. That's why I'm feeling less distress in my back, shoulder, and arm.

Wednesday, October 27

It's a gray, gloomy morning. Rain is predicted. I've enjoyed watching the tree across the street turn from all green, to green and yellow, to all yellow, to a luminous yellow. Now, half of its leaves cover the ground

6   Larsen, Earnie, and Carol Hegarty. *Believing in Myself*. New York: Simon & Schuster,Inc., 1991.

beneath. Soon it will be just bare branches, resting until they sprout forth with new leaves six months from now.

The cycle of life continues.

Monday, November 1

Mother wants to crochet a bedspread for Marcia's wedding gift, just like the one she crocheted for herself. Oh, my! I reminded her that it took over six months to make hers—and that was twenty years ago. As an alternative, I suggested that she leave hers to Marcia. No response. Mother had it in her mind that she was going to crochet a bedspread for her grand-daughter—and that was that.

I suggested practicing, but Mother firmly informed me that she didn't need any practice in crocheting. "You're not very encouraging," she told me.

Quietly, I thought back on the past three years and how I've been her strongest support and greatest "encourager." I said nothing.

After dinner, Mother found her needlework broomstick and struggled with the crocheting for over an hour. She did manage to get a few stitches on the broomstick before giving up. "It's too hard to see at night," she said, putting the yarn back in the bag. I agreed, but knew it was more than the light.

She was confused tonight, too. "I miss saying good night to you when you're not here," she told me as I tucked her in bed. I assured her I'm always here at night, but my words couldn't break into her thought. "It's nice to have someone to say good night to," she said sadly.

Tuesday, November 2

Mother didn't work on the bedspread today, choosing to cover hangers instead. She has lowered her sights, but she can't do the hangers, either. I'm at a loss as to what she can do.

I massaged Mother's feet and legs tonight and manicured her finger-nails. She enjoyed the TLC. Maybe I should fuss over her more.

Called Cris and had a wonderful telephone conversation. She has decided to move back to Michigan and will look for a place to live when she's here at Thanksgiving. It'll be great to have her closer!

Sunday, November 7

In order to have what you want, you have to be willing to give it up. To have security, I have to give it up. We have to move through some experiences, unpleasant as they may be, in order to achieve what we want or desire.

That was the message on this morning's telecast. I'm not sure what it means or what it looks like in life. To have security, I have to give it up? I must move through these experiences to have what I want? Am I tied to security on one hand and avoiding experiences on the other? Marian, you'd better put this one away for a while and ponder it some other time.

LATER

Mother hasn't given up the bedspread idea. She was after me to get the yarn for her today. I asked how much yarn she would need. "Oh, six skeins should do it," she said. I knew it would take far more than that—like sixty—but was relieved to hear her say only six.

STILL LATER

Mother was so pleased when she saw the bag of yarn I brought home! She started to work immediately. After a few minutes, though, she put it aside, saying her eyes bothered her. I predicted that, but said nothing. A few minutes later, she picked it up and began the initial chain of stitches.

"How much is sixty-five times five?" she asked.

I told her three hundred twenty-five and asked why she wanted to know.

"Well, that's how many stitches I need," she said in a tone that seemed to indicate I should know that.

"How did you come up with those numbers?" I asked.

She said she'd counted sixty-five scallops on her bedspread and multi-plied that by the five stitches in each scallop. I was really impressed with her thinking! Secretly, though, I doubt the bedspread will ever be finished.

Making that chain was more difficult than Mother anticipated. She asked me to do it for her, saying she couldn't see very well. I saw the writing on the wall; she would be asking for help constantly. Her eyesight is so poor, her memory is so erratic and failing, and that bedspread is a major project. I don't need this in my life right now.

I'm upset about this whole thing. What was this morning's message about surrendering in order to have what you want? Would it hurt me to work with Mother on this project that she seems to have her heart and mind set upon? How much time am I wasting by being resentful over a project that seems to give her so much pleasure?

Saturday, November 13

I just reviewed my journal entries for the past week and cannot believe it. One day was a carbon copy of the next.

Subject: the bedspread.

It reads like a bad melodrama.

What began as simple requests from Mother to help now and then, somehow multiplied with each passing day. While she slept, I ripped out and redid her muddled attempts in an effort to help. That didn't work. I knew the futility, but she didn't.

"Why don't you give it up?" I asked in desperation.

"Once I start something I must finish it," she calmly told me while continuing to put the crochet hook in the loop and missing.

I decided to devote one hour a day to helping with that project. That didn't work, either, because she continued to struggle and plaintively call for my help.

Why is she holding on so tenaciously to this impossible project? Three years ago, she had given up so easily on knitting and crocheting and I fought to encourage her. Now it is the opposite. She is the one who is fighting, and I have given up.

The tears flowed and flowed this morning. I don't know why. They were not tears of frustration, but of sadness. I know my mother is dying. This bedspread project might be her last grasp on life. She knows she is slipping away, but she will fight to the very end—and I'm not able to do anything to change it. I can't. What I can change, however, is my thinking.

Part of my reason for discouraging the bedspread project was that it didn't fit my picture of Mother going downhill and my wish for all this to end. Maybe God is telling me one more time: You are not in charge, Marian. You need to accept, surrender, and learn.

What do I need to learn? Perhaps my perfectionist nature has prevented me from asking that question before.

LATER

I found this note tucked away in my journal: **Feel your feelings! The roller coaster effect is normal, but stay focused on your purpose.** What a relief to know that this dizzying roller coaster effect I'm feeling is normal! I've had some strong feelings these past days, and who knows what's ahead. I need to ride out the roller coaster, but keep focused on my purpose of caring for Mother and providing an environment where she can have the highest quality of life possible. Everything must be kept in perspective.

STILL LATER

As I changed my thinking today, good things happened:

1. Mother was more talkative—and I listened.
2. Mother crocheted the chain for the bedspread—all three hundred and sixty-five stitches! She couldn't do it the other day.
3. I *offered* to put the stitches on the broomstick. This time it pleased her.
4. I feel good!

Thank you, God! I'm learning. Oh, how I'm learning!

Tuesday, November 16

In my reading this morning I learned that my negative thoughts and feelings have no power of their own. They receive power from the attention I give them. Therefore, if I release negative thoughts and feelings from my mind, thus giving them no attention, they will very quickly become powerless and fade away. Whatever I give my attention to will become my intention. If I can only remember that.

I'm discovering that my greatest assets are within me. I'm living a very simple life, but I've received an indescribable richness I didn't know I had. This experience is teaching me a great deal. I'm learning as I could not have learned in any other way.

LATER

I was overwhelmed with tears many times today. I know Mother is losing ground and won't be here much longer. I hurt when I see her so feeble, unable to do for herself as she always did, unable to take a bath herself, unable to crochet or knit, unable to walk without difficulty. I'm so thankful, though, that she's able to do as much as she does.

Sunday, November 21

Cris flies in from California today. I'll be so happy to see her!

I bought a cacklebird for Thanksgiving—something different from the traditional turkey. The anticipation of a new taste piqued Mother's interest. When I told her that I would be visiting Cris tomorrow afternoon, her concern was if I'd be back in time to fix the cacklebird! Her memory and concept of time continue to diminish. Thanksgiving is four days away.

Monday, November 22

Mother awakened at noon, as usual. After she'd had her breakfast and was set for the afternoon, I left to meet Cris at her aunt's home.

Cris and Aunt Angie were so supportive, listening with compassion and understanding to my caregiving experiences, concerns, and especially what it was teaching me. I needed that. There were no tears, not even a little one. I was so proud of myself!

"You look wonderful!" Cris commented to me several times. That made me feel good.

Then, as we hugged goodbye after a delightful three hours, she told me I was at peace. "It's here," she said pointing to my heart, "but it shows outside."

Wednesday, November 24

Mother and Dad would have celebrated their seventy-first wedding anniversary today. What a wonderful remembrance!

Another often-recalled memory occurred twenty-nine years ago. Following tradition, we had gathered around the dining room table in our family home in Detroit to celebrate Thanksgiving. It was a happy occasion. I remember how excited Bob was to tell us about the bicycle he and Theo had just purchased for their five year old daughter, Kathy, for Christmas. Little did we know that would be the last Thanksgiving we would celebrate with Bob—and the last time he would help select Christmas gifts for his two young daughters. Little did we know what was ahead: Bob's cancer diagnosis, three surgeries and long hospitalizations, fifty-nine cobalt treatments, and death six months later. The fond memories of my brother will always remain with me.

LATER

Mother got up earlier this morning, saying she couldn't sleep because she kept thinking about crocheting. Right after breakfast, she was in her bedroom with the yardstick, trying to figure out the pattern in her bedspread! The futility of her efforts no longer bothers me, as long as she's content.

While Mother slept this afternoon, I worked on the calligraphy for my Christmas card. It's ready for printing now. Later, I found relaxation in the kitchen, baking muffins—the yummy maple syrup/bran recipe—and a pumpkin pie for tomorrow.

Thanksgiving Day

It's a gray, sunless day, but quiet and peaceful. That's how I feel, too. I saw a young, serene face looking back at me in the mirror this morning and privately marveled at how beautiful I looked. Yes, I said it—although it was with great hesitancy that I wrote the word beautiful. It has been said that it takes humility to see beauty in one's self. Am I? I'm not sure.

LATER

Mother got up mid-morning, earlier than usual. Eating breakfast exhausted her, so she slept on the sofa for the next three hours. Georgia, one of our neighbors, came over for a short visit while I prepared the cackle bird for roasting. I enjoyed our conversation, especially the good laughs!

STILL LATER

Dinner was on the table, but Mother was detained in the bathroom. I checked on her and discovered everything was wet. The dinner waited while I got everything, including Mother, cleaned up. Thank goodness, we didn't have guests!

Saturday, November 27

An absolutely miserable day—so miserable I couldn't write in my journal until late tonight.

Mother got up at 8:00 this morning, "robbing" me of my quiet time. That was the last straw. I've enjoyed that time alone for the past five weeks and thought the routine was set. Maybe I was too comfortable.

I was upset all day. I couldn't even speak to Mother this morning. I busied myself with household tasks, hoping that the physical activity would help me to gain control of my emotions—and change my attitude. It didn't help. I cried in the privacy of the bathroom. That didn't do it, either. I drove out to the parkway where I cried until I thought I'd never shed another tear.

Tonight I played the role of a willing martyr, telling Mother how much I'd given up and how unappreciated it appears to be. For five weeks now, she has slept until noon. I enjoyed that time alone in the morning. Today it was taken away from me and I want it back.

Dear God, what is happening to me? What kind of person am I becoming? This is my mother. What am I doing to her?

There's a hard lesson here for me, but I don't know what it is. Mother's behavior is so like that of a child, and I'm treating her more and more like one.

Later, I jokingly told her that I'd lock her in her room if she got up too early. "There's no lock on the door," she informed me.

We both laughed! Yes, there is some humor in this. Deep down, though, I'm afraid I am being pushed almost to my limit.

Monday, November 29

Awakened to a delicate blanket of snow. It gives an aura of lovely quietness, but I wasn't feeling it this morning. I was overwhelmed with a sense of sadness, and many tears have flowed. Am I still in the tomb of yesterday? Is it because of the approaching holiday season, the winter coming on? The freedom of the outdoors will be gone for the next four to five months. I think that's it: the loss of freedom, both outside and inside of me.

I've shed so many tears lately. It just destroys me. I was startled awake by a dream this morning. I was putting Mother in a nursing home and I couldn't decide where. I'm glad it was only a dream. I pray she'll be able to live out her life right here in her own home.

Well, on to this day, whatever it may bring. I'll print the Christmas cards, making that my project for the day.

Tuesday, November 30

"We need to get the clothes ready for the undertaker," Mother said as I helped her dress after her shower.

"Oh, there's plenty of time to do that," I responded matter-of-factly.

She said "it" wouldn't be long, adding, "You never know, I may go very quickly."

I assured her I'd take care of everything, but I did expect her to tell me what I should do from wherever she is! We both laughed!

LATER

Mother was very feeble tonight. She readily accepted my help in getting up from her chair, and leaned heavily on my arm for support as I led her into the bathroom. By 9:00 she was exhausted and wanted to go to bed. I helped her get ready, tucking her in with a good night hug and kiss.

Friday, December 3

It's a dark, foggy morning—certainly not an "attitude brightener" beginning of the day. I had a restless night because of a sinus infection.

I've been thinking about what I'd do for a friend in my position. What would I like someone to do? Write letters or call, that's what! Just to know that friends are still there means a great deal to me. Hearing about their activities takes me away for a few minutes and helps keep me in contact, especially since I'm away from my home. It's interesting because their lives continue while I feel mine has stopped.

LATER

I took Mother to the church volunteer work group this morning to visit her friends. There were only four in the group whom she knew.

Several told me what a good daughter I was. Hearing that sends such angry vibes throughout my body. I'm not taking care of my mother because I want to be thought of as a *good daughter*. I'm doing it because I couldn't bear to see her in a nursing home. I'm doing it so she can stay in her own home and live with dignity. I'm doing it because I want to avoid the pain I'd experience if she were somewhere else. I'm doing it because I love her. The ladies meant well, though, and I need to accept that.

I don't like returning to places I've left and I think Mother feels that way, too. She said she enjoyed herself this morning, but the group had changed. That's true. Nothing remains the same. She is better off with her happy memories.

Saturday, December 4

Mother thinks she can stay alone. Then, in the next breath, she says she has only a few days to live. I told her I've heard that for three years and asked why she says it. "Because I'm ninety-five," she told me.

I laughed, telling her that with her good health she'll live to be over a hundred! She shook her head and said she should go into a nursing home.

"I couldn't bear the thought of that," I said, putting my arms around her and telling her how very much I loved her.

Tucking Mother into bed tonight, I hugged her, saying I loved her so much. I apologized for anything I'd said that may have hurt her.

"I love you," she told me so tenderly. "I couldn't do without you."

Monday, December 6

I give up. Just as I got up this morning, Mother did, too. I thought she'd go back to bed when I told her it was too early to get up, but she refused, saying she had "something" to do. *My quiet time had been taken away again.* I asked what she thought she had to do. She said she had to go some place, but couldn't think where.

I've shed so many tears, but Mother doesn't shed one. I wonder if she has no feeling. In one way, I want to see at least a tear or two, but I know it would tear me apart. Her stubbornness and strong will may not allow her to show any emotion.

I can't control when Mother will get up, but I can control myself. That's it! I've been trying to control her. I can't, nor do I have any right to try. The only person I can control is me. I will change my routine by getting up earlier. I may even like it!

What was that advice I couldn't understand a month ago? **In order to have what you want, you have to be willing to give it up.** I am beginning to understand.

Tuesday, December 7

This early hour before dawn is completely undisturbed, totally quiet, and ever so peaceful. My time alone this morning was wonderful, giving me strength and purpose for the day.

I've been thinking about this idea: **Love is what we are born with; fear is what we learn here.** There's some unlearning I need to do.

Friday, December 10

I felt sorry for Mother tonight, sitting in her rocking chair with folded hands and looking so pathetic. She couldn't crochet, saying she'd lost her place. My attempts to help were of no avail. I tried to think of something she could do. The idea of a simple knitted dishcloth, like those she enjoyed making a couple of years ago, sprang to mind. I found the directions and two balls of yarn left over from the previous project. After casting on the required number of stitches, I sat beside Mother and watched as she slowly knit her way through the first rows. Her mood brightened immediately! She was delighted to be doing something she enjoyed. Even though I had to fix her mistakes frequently, at least she's experiencing some sense of accomplishment.

Saturday, December 11

I don't know how to begin describing what I just experienced. I need to, however, in order to know it really happened.

As I sat on the sofa this morning with my eyes closed, it took only a few moments to get into my meditative "inner space." I began pushing back my thoughts on both sides, as if digging a sand tunnel, until I was nestled in what appeared to be a soft, quilted air mattress. I was suspended in space, feeling very safe and secure. Looking around, I saw an opening that began to gradually widen as I floated nearer, revealing a vast expanse beyond. I could see forever! Slowly, and like a perfectly orchestrated symphony, this immense space began filling with beautiful, exotic flowers of every variety imaginable. The rugged mountain peaks in the background stood like majestic sentinels. Everything was so breathtakingly beautiful that my eyes began to flood with tears. I wanted to explore this seemingly boundless expanse of exquisite beauty, but I was afraid to venture out. I remained safely nestled in the floating air mattress, hovering at the entrance which was guarded by great boulders on either side. Did they represent my thoughts which I had to push away before I could go further?

The rest of the experience was such pure feeling that I can find no words adequate enough to describe it. I don't know how long I remained there in its cool ecstasy—just looking. I didn't venture out to touch, to feel, to understand. What was there to fear?

What happened in those moments? I don't know. Was I given this time of incredible beauty when my anguished emotions could take no more of what has become a squirrel cage existence?

Will it occur again? I don't know. If it was a trick of the mind, I'll accept it. If it was daydreaming, it served its purpose of giving me the tranquility my spirit longs for.

But it was far more. I believe it was the brief touch of God's hand on mine.

Monday, December 13

Things may happen to me and around me. What is important, though, is what's happening in me.

I'm thinking about how much I've grown in so many ways during the past three and a half years. I used to count the time until I could get away to go back home for a few days. That certainly has changed! Last fall I sensed a change and began spending more time here and less at home. Then, whammy! By April 1st, I was here full-time. What a tailspin! The emotional yo-yo was dizzying, and the feeling of being trapped was suffocating. Nine months and many stormy times later, I've finally calmed my body and mind.

LATER

I'll call today to check about having the touch tone service added to Mother's phone line. That will allow me to connect with my home answering machine and be available to continue my tax business. My way through this change is becoming clearer.

Tuesday, December 14

I helped Mother with her knitting of the dishcloth tonight. It's heartbreaking to see her knit like a child who is just learning. I think back to all the knitting she did for the Red Cross during the war, as well as all the baby blankets, booties, hats she had knit over the years for her grandchildren and friends. I recall the numerous ski hats and mittens she made for the church to give to needy children, and the countless number of lap robes she made for folks in nursing homes. Her needles used to click rapidly and rhythmically, row after row. Now, every stitch is a task in itself.

Saturday, December 18

Today is Marcia's wedding! I called this morning to wish her happiness on this very significant day. I won't be at the wedding, but I wanted her to know how much she was in my thoughts. She told me she looked at her dad's picture last night and cried. I'm so glad she remembers Bob.

LATER

Mother tried to walk too much today. She is so determined to take one or two outside walks every day. Sometimes I walk with her, but she prefers to walk by herself, using her cane. Watching her slowly make her way around the sidewalk behind the apartment today, I saw that her gait was unsteady and her body was sagging. She was ready to fall. I ran out to rescue her, and she fell into my arms. She was so tired.

STILL LATER

The dishcloth is finally finished! Mother is so pleased. It will be interesting to see if she mentions making another one. I'll help, of course. How could I not when she is trying so hard?

Tuesday, December 21

I decided our apartment needed to look more festive. Placing the Christmas tablecloth and a holiday centerpiece on the dining room table helped. That small touch added a little holiday cheer to my own mood, too.

Sam, from Schoolcraft College, came over in the afternoon and surprised Mother with a gorgeous poinsettia plant! Mother was pleased to know her friends there hadn't forgotten her.

Thursday, December 23

While I was in the basement doing the laundry this afternoon, Norm, our neighbor across the hall, came down. He asked about Mother and mentioned that he had cared for his mother, too. "I don't know what you're doing to take care of yourself," he remarked, "but you seem okay." I was pleased because his observation told me that the inner peace I felt was showing on the outside.

Friday, December 24

This has been such a pleasant holiday. The idea of the "alternative Christmas gift" was embraced by the family and worked great! In lieu of family gifts, we gave to charities this year. I enjoyed making my cards and writing the enclosure letters. That's the most meaningful part of the holiday season for me. The letters I've received are treasured gifts.

Shirley, Mother's friend from the church, came over this afternoon. Both of us enjoyed her visit. When she was leaving, the tears welled up in my eyes. That happens so frequently now. Shirley hugged me and said I would really miss Mother, having lived with her like this. I shook my head. "Yes, but it will also be relief," I told her, my voice cracking with emotion.

That's the first time I've said that to anyone other than Cris and Pat. Shirley nodded her head and seemed to understand.

This is Christmas Eve—a very quiet one. I don't mind. Mother said it wasn't any different than any other evening to her.

Christmas Day

Today was very quiet. One of the neighbors and her family stopped in to wish us "Merry Christmas" on their way to dinner. They were our only visitors. No phone calls, either. I fixed a turkey dinner, complete with Mother's favorite pumpkin pie. She told me she enjoyed the meal.

While I entertained myself by watching a couple of basketball games on television, Mother worked on the bedspread. Yes, that is still a project. She kept asking me for help, but every suggestion I made was not acceptable.

As I watched families coming and going from the apartments today, I reflected on the Christmas holidays of years gone by when I'd make the trip from Flint to Detroit, Utica, or Plymouth—wherever Mother and Dad were living—sometimes driving on snowy, unplowed roads. We celebrated the day by making calls to Bob's home and Jack's, delivering gifts and having the fun of watching the grandchildren open them. I was always exhausted at the end of the day, but happy to have enjoyed it with my family. It was the right thing for me to be doing at that time in my life. Now I'm in a different part of my life. This may be the last Christmas I have with Mother.

Sunday, December 26

Brrrr! What a frigid, cold night! My bed-on-the-floor isn't too warm when the temperature drops to zero.

One of Mother's friends came over this afternoon, and we had a "show 'n tell" time! I brought out the tablecloth Mother had crocheted years ago, as well as the quilts she had made. Included was the "Sunbonnet Sue" quilt that she'd made for me soon after I was born and had adorned my bed during my growing-up years. It brought back warm memories as I looked at its tattered edges, recalling the matching games I played with the pieces of material used in Sue's sunbonnets and dresses. Each piece, left over from the many dresses Mother had sewn, had its own history. Mother had made a twin quilt for my doll's bed, too! The "show 'n tell" was the highlight of the day. Mother was pleased to see all of her work again and to have her friend admire it.

Monday, December 27

Another month almost gone—and another year. My thoughts this morning are on smiling. All sorts of good things happen when I smile. A smile lifts my cheeks and gives me a natural face-lift. It makes others feel more comfortable and at ease. It gives me a brighter, more positive outlook and perspective. A smile keeps me thinking of all I have to be thankful for, and makes me feel warm and cozy all over. I'll choose to dedicate this day as SMILE DAY!

Some day I may write an article on caregiving. It is a lonely, solitary responsibility. I'm afraid to express my feelings to others because they may be misinterpreted as whining or complaining. I learned that early on. The caregiver is expected to be the bulwark—ever-loving, ever-kind, ever-patient. The only person to be concerned about is the one needing the care. Wrong! The caregiver has needs and feelings, too. The focus of my message would not be on what I've done in a physical sense, but rather what my emotional needs have been. There have been so many times I've cried out in despair and frustration that no one understands. Perhaps my writing would reach out and let another caregiver know that there is someone who understands. But does anyone really understand?

Thursday, December 30

All was well until this evening when Mother experienced trouble knitting a dishcloth. She was making this one for the neighbor across the street. I ended up ripping and restarting it *nine* times tonight. I was so frustrated because Mother didn't do what I asked, thus making numerous and unnecessary mistakes. My patience was tested to the limit.

Finally I sat beside her, calmly watching every stitch while she knit four rows. She did well under my watchful eye. Needing a break, I asked her to stop and rest for a while. She stopped for all of one minute, then picked up the needles and resumed knitting, oblivious to the mistakes she was making. "Why did you do that?" I asked in desperation, shaking my head as I looked at the muddled mess.

"I just wanted to do it," she told me.

I give up.

As I tucked Mother into bed tonight, she told me to forget about what happened. I kissed her good night and said I would.

Saturday, January 1, 1994

I'm recalling Mother's comment to me last night as I placed an afghan under her feet to support them more comfortably. "Oh, that feels better! You are always there when I need you," she said, breathing a sigh of contentment. I pray she will always feel that way until she draws her final breath.

LATER

Georgia, one of our neighbors, knocked at the door this morning and offered to get a newspaper for me while she was running errands. How wonderful it is to have someone so thoughtful nearby.

Jo, a friend from Flint, called this afternoon. It's comforting to know that I haven't been forgotten.

Theo came over this evening and showed us Marcia's wedding pictures. Mother's poor eyesight didn't allow her to see them, but she enjoyed the company.

This has been a good day.

Monday, January 2

Mother insisted on knitting by herself today. When I asked why, she responded, "Because I'm used to doing things independently."

"But," I argued, "you can't see well enough."

"My eyes will improve if I keep at it," she informed me as she continued to work the knitting needles.

I can only imagine how difficult it must be to accept that she can no longer function as she once did. She believes that if she perseveres long enough, she'll overcome any obstacle. That attitude worked for her in the past. Why not now? I fear it's different this time.

Wednesday, January 5

As I was brushing my teeth this morning, I envisioned the morticians rolling Mother's body out of the apartment. The experience was so real that a gush of tears engulfed me, and I sobbed for a few seconds. I tried to erase the thoughts from my mind as I continued on my morning routine, but the tears kept coming intermittently.

I'm sitting on the sofa now, the emotional impact of those earlier moments still affecting me. This is the second consecutive morning I've had this waking dream of Mother's death. When this is all over, I'll be able to smile, to laugh, and be joyful about the beautiful life Mother had—and treasure these past years. At the moment, however, the emotion of what is ahead is tearing me up.

Thursday, January 6

The first snowfall of the year has blanketed the ground—white, quiet, beautiful. Eight inches of it! I walked around the complex this afternoon, so enjoying the glistening beauty and muffled quietness that I discovered myself singing!

Mother seems so childlike now, stuffing food into her mouth and spilling food on the floor. A dog would have a feast under our table! I clip a paper towel on her, like a bib, to keep her blouse clean. Her muscle coordination is poor, due to the strokes. Saliva drools from her mouth, as well. Poor soul, she can't help it.

It's difficult to be a parent to your own parent, especially when she does things that you, as a child, were admonished for—like eating before meals. When we finished dinner tonight, Mother commented, "See? That little piece of candy didn't affect my appetite."

What do you do? I swallow and say nothing.

Monday, January 10

We played solitaire tonight. Mother dealt the cards and I played them. That's all she's able to do since her vision is so impaired that even the jumbo size cards fail to help. This unique version of solitaire is something different to do, and we can enjoy it together.

"I love you!" Mother said, as I tucked her into bed tonight. I don't recall hearing her say those words with such deep affection, although I always knew she loved me. She said she prays for me every night. That brought tears to my eyes.

This has been a special day. It's difficult to describe the feeling I have and the peace there seems to be between us. I want to remember this moment. I want to remember Mother telling me, "I love you."

Tuesday, January 11

I've been going non-stop for the past twelve hours. We went up to Flint for our routine dental appointments. Thank goodness, I had learned from the last experience to bring a full change of clothes for Mother.

Sometimes it's difficult to explain things to Mother, such as why she has to take antibiotics before dental work due to the knee replacement. She asks the same question again and again. It would be easier to just say, "Take these pills." But I try to treat her as an adult. After all, she is my mother.

I need to allow more time when I take Mother any place. It's easy to estimate how long it will take me, but I need to add more time for her. She walks so slowly. Everything she does now is one speed: slow. I must accept it and make the necessary time adjustments. When I don't try to fit in other activities and allow Mother the time she needs, it's better for her and easier on me. Normally, I would have stopped by my house while in Flint today, but that's an activity for another day. Yes, I'm learning.

Friday, January 14

Mother's back bothered her again tonight. She wants to help by washing the dinner dishes, but standing puts too much strain on her back. I need to talk with her about using that kitchen chair I have at home. She is reluctant to use aids, but maybe she'll accept that. I'll approach it from a "let's see if it helps" suggestion.

I helped Mother brush her teeth tonight and was surprised she accepted my help. I said the dentist told me to help her—which he did! "He didn't tell me that." Mother said indignantly.

He did, but she probably couldn't hear him—or forgot.

Saturday, January 15

Received a cute card from Pat in today's mail with the printed message, **"Friendship multiplies our joys and divides our sorrows"** and Pat's postscript, *"How true! Just thinking about you."* Those are the kindnesses a caregiver needs—this caregiver, anyway!

Cris called this morning to tell me that she leased a townhouse and will be here in March. She'll be within an hour's drive. Happy day!

Mother ripped out all of the bedspread—that infamous bedspread she'd been working on. She said she found a mistake near the beginning. I didn't say anything, but that was only one of many! She spent the whole evening ripping. It didn't upset me, and it kept her occupied. I have no idea what she plans to do—if anything. I'm not concerned.

You've come a long way, Marian!

Sunday, January 16

I believe Mother had another mini-stroke tonight. She had no recall of the pie I had made this afternoon, even though she had watched me make it. She was so surprised when I served it for dessert.

She was dizzy all evening and said her head "felt funny." She rested on the couch all evening. As I helped her get ready for bed, she said she wouldn't be able to finish the bedspread for Marcia. "Would you please tell her?" she asked. I assured her I would. She smiled.

Perhaps, that's the end of the bedspread project after two and a half months. I certainly hope so. I sensed that Mother was putting things in order.

Wednesday, January 19

One of my tax clients called this morning. She was confused about the two phone numbers I had on the answering machine greeting. Briefly I explained the situation. "When I burn the toast tomorrow morning," she said, "I'll remember that others have greater problems."

She commented how wonderful it is, what we do to care for each other. "This is my mother," I said in response. "I know I won't be caring for her forever, but I have to live with myself forever."

Monday, January 24

Mother had another accident this morning. She tried to clean it up, but it was far more than what she could handle. Her efforts resulted in a bigger mess. I didn't get upset. As I cleaned, I kept repeating in mantra fashion: *An event is just an event. An event is just an event.*

Poor Mother, she doesn't know what's happening and wishes she would die. She slept most of the afternoon. I looked at her pale, wrinkled face and was so saddened. Then I looked beyond that outer appearance, and all I could feel was love.

My constant prayer is that she doesn't suffer.

Wednesday, January 26

I awakened from a nap this afternoon with a start when I heard my name being called—very softly and gently from a distance. I saw Dad! He spoke no words, but I sensed he was telling me that my job of caring for Mother was coming to an end and that he would take over soon. That was so comforting.

Sunday, January 30

Mother was looking for the bedspread tonight. Yes, that infamous one. I told her she had ripped it back, and it was there in a ball on the table. She insisted that wasn't all of it, was very certain there was more. I couldn't help her, but was thankful she didn't accuse me of throwing it away.

Tuesday, February 1

When Mother got up at noon, she said she was going to take a bath. The next sound I heard was the water running! A shower wasn't in my plan today, but that was okay. We had plenty of time. Mother was so proud of herself for suggesting a bath without my reminder.

While I was showering her, she asked if I enjoyed myself last week when she was away.

"Away?" I asked. "Where were you?"

"Oh, I don't know, but I was away for a few days."

I chuckled to myself!

Mother gave me another reason to chuckle tonight. As I tucked her in bed, she told me that Jack had asked Bob for a loan. For a moment, my deceased brothers were evidently living in her mind. "Oh, what was that about?" I asked to find out more details.

"I can't remember," she said, "but I told him not to do it!"

I'm so glad I can laugh!

Thursday, February 10

"I guess it's time for me to go," Mother said while she ate her breakfast oatmeal. She'd dreamed that her mother was calling her. Maybe her time is nearing. Only God knows.

LATER

Mother said she can't finish knitting the dishcloth. I guess she's given up. She can't see to knit or crochet now and is accepting that fact. It must be very difficult for her.

Sunday, February 13

I thought about yesterday's phone conversation with Cris. I had told her about the other night when I felt so sorry, then guilty, about Mother having nothing to do. Cris' comment was that I had the patience of Job. I didn't think of it as patience, but rather as concern for someone I loved who was now so limited. It was compassion for another human being—who happens to be my mother.

During Mother's shower and shampoo today, I wasn't as patient as I have been. She is so slow. Waiting for her to do something can seem like an eternity. Needing to get some of my patience back, I thought about what I had done on better days. I recalled that while she washed her face, I would change the sheets on her bed. Then, to speed things up a little more, I would help her get dressed. Also, I would put out her breakfast things, and then do something else while she cooked her breakfast oatmeal at her own pace and in her own way. Because I didn't stand around waiting, I had patience.

I did that today. What an amazing difference it made!

Wednesday, February 16

Mother is still looking for the bedspread, claiming she had it half-finished. I can't believe how adamant she is about it. I just keep still, listen, and nod my head. I'm so thankful she hasn't accused me of throwing it away.

Sunday, February 27

I'm filled with self-pity this morning. I thought about all the fifty or more letters I've written during the past two months and the meager response I've had. I look forward to the mail delivery each day. I am so excited when there is a letter that I make it a special occasion by waiting for a time when I can savor its contents, relaxing with a cup of coffee. I love letters! I read them over several times, whenever I need to know that someone cares.

LATER

It's amazing how water can help resolve what's on my mind! My morning shower absolved my self-pity. I realize now that I've been putting conditions on the letters I've sent. If they are truly written from love, then I can forget about any response or return. Love will return—maybe not in the same way it was given, but it will return, often multiplied.

The other night a friend told me that I would return to my old routine when I came back to Flint. My immediate response was an emphatic "No!" I am different now. My thinking has changed and so have I. I want to throw open the windows of my mind. I want new experiences. I want to be free, free to be me because I'm beginning to discover what a truly wonderful, beautiful person I am! I want to put the past behind me, but take its learnings and move on.

Thursday, March 3

When Mother walked out of her bedroom this morning and saw me sitting at the dining room table writing letters, she was so surprised. "Why Marian! Where did you come from?" she asked. "I thought you were away all night."

She does get confused, especially when I tell her plans in advance. Last night she asked when I was going up to Flint, and I told her. Now I realize I will need to be more vague in my responses. That's difficult because I could never lie to my mother.

Friday, March 4

Mother was awake for only a total of six hours today. I see her going down even more. She was unable to keep her dinner down tonight and had an accident as well. Cleaning up didn't bother me, though. I just kept repeating to myself: *An event is just an event, neither good nor bad. Only thinking makes it so. An event is just an event....*

Received the kindest note from my friend, Zane, today. She had awakened last Monday morning at four o'clock thinking of me. Her note concluded: *"Just know that in quiet moments, I think of you."*

I was very touched.

I'm thinking about everything Mother has done for me. She was the one who nourished me, who protected me, who taught me to care for myself, who taught me about life from her experience. She encouraged me when I had no hope, she loved me unconditionally, and she was always so proud of my accomplishments. I was inspired by her example of independence and service to others. Her strong faith in God led me to know a Power greater than myself. She asked so little and gave me so much. Now, as I see her life coming to an end, it's difficult to watch her body slowly weaken. Her unwavering spirit, however, still remains resolute and strong.

Tuesday, March 8

Unintentionally, I didn't kiss Mother good night. I was preoccupied, unaware that she was going to bed until I saw the light go out. Just as I heard her crawling into bed, I remembered and went in to kiss her. "Oh, I'd miss that!"she said smiling.

That good night kiss sends an important message. Mother seldom returns it, but I know her love is shown in many other ways. Often, she tells me, "I pray for you every night."

Saturday, March 12

I had a restless night, punctuated by several dreams about Mother and her death. I awakened with an overwhelming sense of grief, stomach all in knots, tears streaming down my face. It was so real. I saw friends offering to help with the physical details and I gladly allowed them because I had no strength. My thoughts were centered on how devastating the grief was.

And I thought I was prepared?

Oh, how much I have to learn.

Monday, March 14

The "funeral feelings" from yesterday were still with me when I awakened this morning. Tears came as I thought how it would feel to get up and know that Mother was gone.

LATER

When I reminded Mother that this was shower and shampoo day, her response equaled a five on the Richter scale! "Who said so?" she demanded to know, looking me straight in the eye.

"I said so!" I laughed. And I've been chuckling ever since. When I mentioned it later, Mother didn't recall ever saying such a thing!

As I helped her get ready for bed tonight, she held both of my arms, looked deeply into my eyes, and said so lovingly, "I don't know what I'd do without you." Tearfully, I hugged and kissed her.

That was a love moment I want to always remember.

Thursday, March 18

I believe that some day I will write a book about these past four years. We, who are or have been, caregivers for a parent are in a group with a special bond. We don't talk about our responsibilities. We just continue doing whatever we have to do. We entered the caregiving situation from different stages in our lives. For many of us, the caregiving responsibilities have been an intrusion, often followed with resentment and anger. My experience has presented many lessons which have been hard and difficult at times, yet necessary. I'm learning, but I have a long way to go—a long way, indeed.

Sunday, March 20

On the way to the post office this morning, I was attracted by a balloon display proudly announcing: "Daniel: 6 pounds, 4 ounces." I smiled, thinking about the happy parents. Then, turning the corner, I saw people gathering at the funeral home. Within a single block, there was the beginning of life and the end, happiness and sadness.

And that's the cycle of life.

Saturday, March 26

Mother burned her oatmeal this morning. I wasn't watching closely enough, and she left the burner on high. Scrubbing that pot was hard work. It didn't help my attitude to hear Mother laugh about the incident.

I'm so tired of cleaning. I don't know how much more of this I can take. I feel that I give and give and give—and nothing comes back to me, not even "I'm sorry" from Mother when she burns the oatmeal.

Something is happening. I don't know what, nor do I understand why. I keep thinking there is a reason, a purpose for all this. But what? Why am I so accepting one moment and then so visibly upset another? Have I been accepting? Do I want something in return?

I feel so alone.

Sunday, March 27

I cried myself to sleep last night. I'm still hurting this morning and will have to make a choice: Do I want to stay miserable, or be happy and content? It's up to me. It's my choice. Right now, though, I feel abandoned, and so terribly alone.

Wednesday, March 30

Again, my awakening thoughts were on Mother's funeral. And, of all things, I was busy arranging transportation for everyone! That's ludicrous.

Last night must have been the night for dreams. Mother told me about another dream she'd had. She was in a coffin! "Make sure I have a smile on my face!" she told me.

I will.

Thursday, March 31

When I kissed Mother good night, she asked what we had to do tomorrow. She has always had a reason for getting up each morning. I didn't think about that before answering, "Nothing,"

"Oh," she said sadly. "Nothing to get up for."

Then I reminded her she needed to take a bath when she got up.

"Oh, I do, do I?" she said, smiling impishly.

She has a purpose for tomorrow, such as it is.

Sunday, April 3

What a good Easter Sunday this has been! I felt peaceful all day.

The strawberry/rhubarb pie I'd made was a winner, well worth the effort of going to four stores to find the rhubarb.

Quietly observing all the families coming to visit their parents or relatives, I thought about all the holidays that I had done the same. It wasn't a sad memory. That part of my life has passed. Now I'm into new experiences.

Mother wasn't feeling well and slept most of the day. She did go out for a walk, though, and washed the dishes later in the evening. I'd left them for her to do so that she could continue to feel useful.

Friday, April 8

Mother looked so peaceful sleeping this morning. There was even a smile on her face. I know she's content, at peace, and worry-free.

Yes, Mother knows she is being well cared for. During dinner last night, she recalled that I had interrupted her afternoon walk, suggesting that she'd walked long enough. "You evidently watch where I go when I walk," she told me.

I laughed. "Yes! I have to keep tabs on you!"

Mother smiled and nodded her head.

Saturday, April 9

These past four years have not been easy, by any stretch of the imagination, but in many ways they have been good. I will be able to go on with my life in a different way because of what I've learned.

I have such a caring, loving feeling toward Mother. She is like a precious flower that must be handled with tender, loving care. Her love for me is demonstrated in so many ways: the warm touch of her hand on mine, her sweet, demure smile, her words to others that I take such good care of her. Yes, I'll miss her greatly, but I will be at peace knowing that I had done my very best to make her last years comfortable and fulfilling.

Wednesday, April 20

Sam and the President of Schoolcraft College visited this afternoon. Mother was delighted to see them. She was honored to know they'd taken time from their busy schedules to see her. They brought some delicious peanut butter cookies, freshly baked in the college's culinary arts kitchen. Did Mother love those! The visit was the highlight of our day.

Sunday, April 24

I watched the telecast this morning and wrote these notes:

> **A cocoon is a safe, protected place. It's fine for a retreat,**
> **but in order to grow, we have to break out of that comfort zone.**
> **Nothing that goes into a cocoon emerges the same.**
> **A butterfly, not a caterpillar, comes out of a cocoon.**
> **The cocoon stage is a time to prepare, to gather all the**
> **resources, to get ready for the good that is about to happen.**

I know I'll want to refer back to those thoughts.

Thursday, April 28

Watching former President Nixon's funeral last night brought an awareness of grief's exhausting emotion. I empathized with his brother, the sole surviving member of the immediate family. That's what I'll be, too. He was all alone, just as I will be.

Friday, April 29

"Where is Bella?" Mother asked me this morning.

Stunned at first, and not knowing where she was coming from, I asked if she meant Aunt Bella, one of her six deceased sisters.

"Yes," she said. "She was here for a visit last night, and I wondered where you put her to sleep."

I thought for a second before opting for the truth. "Aunt Bella wasn't here. She died ten years ago."

"Oh, no," Mother denied. "She was here last night and must have just left."

What could I say?

Mother looked around the apartment, shaking her head. "She's gone now. When is she coming back?"

I told her I didn't know. Piqued by curiosity, I pursued the subject, asking how Aunt Bella got here—car? train? bus? Mother didn't know, except that she came alone.

What's strange about this is that Aunt Bella never visited us in Detroit, only at the cottage. And never would she stay overnight because she couldn't sleep in any bed but her own! The mind does play some strange tricks.

Later this afternoon, while I was in the basement doing the laundry, Mother locked me out! I had to go outside and come in through the patio sliding door which was unlocked, thank goodness.

"Why did you lock the door on me? I asked.

"I forgot where you were," she answered.

What a dichotomy! She inquired about a sister long gone whom she believed to be in the apartment today. Yet, she locked the door on her daughter who has been her constant companion for over four years.

Tuesday, May 3

Mother was sleeping so peacefully that I hesitated to awaken her at noon. She was reluctant to get up, even after fourteen hours of sleep. Part of the excessive sleeping is due to the natural slowing down of her body, as well as boredom and, perhaps, depression. There is so little she can do now. It's a humbling, sad experience to watch the slow demise of your mother.

I received a letter from a friend whom I hadn't heard from in a year. She offered to help me if I'd tell her what I needed. I could think of nothing. I should have told her that the best help I can receive is through letters and phone calls. I crave for conversation, the welcome sound of a friend's voice giving me a new and a fresh outlook. I look forward to Pat's letter each week. We have written faithfully to each other every week for the past four years. What a wonderful friend!

I think I'll treat myself to a movie this week. "Grumpy Old Men" is on at the local theater. I need some good laughs.

Sunday, May 8

Today is MOTHER'S DAY. Rather than going out for dinner, I'll prepare a special meal in honor of the occasion. That will be easier for both of us. We'll have baked chicken and lemon chiffon pie—two of Mother's favorites. Later, we'll go out for a drive through the parkway.

Georgia was so happy when I delivered her newspaper this morning. Her son was coming over later to take her out for breakfast. I imagine I'll see several families coming by to take their mothers out for dinner and spending the day with them. I write that with a little sadness.

Tuesday, May 10

This was the day of the solar eclipse. I saw it occur on my drive to Flint. The sky took on a grayish cast as the moon passed in front of the sun. The next solar eclipse will be May 20, 2012. My, that sounds like light years away!

Wednesday, May 11

Mother got up at noon, as usual. I showered her, shampooed/set her hair, and while she was eating breakfast, I changed her bed linens and cleaned the bathroom. Then it happened.

I don't even need to fill in the blanks. This journal is already peppered with the details: the mess everywhere, another shower, the cleaning, the laundry. I was tearful the rest of the afternoon, and I don't know why. Was it fear? Fear of what may be ahead for me? Fear of not being able to handle it? Fear of realizing what was happening to my mother? Oh, how I wanted someone—anyone—to put their arms around me and tell me that everything was going to be okay. There is no one.

Wasn't it interesting that this upsetting experience occurred just after I had finished listening to a tape in which the speaker talked about life "banging on our hoods" when we get too comfortable? Well, my hood just got banged on—royally! What do I do about it? How long will it take me to settle down? What do I need to learn?

Thursday, May 12

I was reluctant to open my eyes this morning. Yesterday's experience still had not been entirely released from my mind. In the morning's silence, though, I heard a small, still voice within me say ever so gently, *I am always with you. My love is always there.* I sensed a rush of warmth, of comfort, of love enveloping all of me—and saw yesterday fading…fading…fading away.

Okay, Marian, retrieve the learning, but let the event go.

What is the lesson here for me?

1. I allowed fear to take charge yesterday. I need to stop and let God take charge.
2. Recognize that fear has many faces; anger is one.
3. Know that fear and faith cannot occupy the same space. It's up to me to consciously choose.

LATER

Four individuals told me today how much Mother has "gone down." I know she has failed considerably these past four months. I live with it. I know this can't go on forever. A change is coming, but I don't know what or when. That's where faith has to occupy the empty space—or fear will.

Saturday, May 14

My creativeness has expanded into note cards! One of the neighbors gave me a calendar with lovely art work by handicapped artists. I used the pictures to make note cards for the neighbor. She was thrilled! Creative projects like that keep me level-headed and allow me to deal with this situation I have chosen. They provide a welcome release, permitting me to be in a world of my own, if only for a short while.

Sunday, May 15

My sister-in-law, Theo, called tonight with a dinner invitation. A while ago, I had mentioned how I would enjoy a prime rib dinner. She remembered! Her kind and thoughtful concern touched me.

Monday, May 16

The doctor thought Mother's dizzy spells and strange feelings were due to blood pressure fluctuations. She could be having small strokes, too. He asked about her memory, agreeing that the dementia had increased.

Taped to the door of the doctor's examining room was a copy of the "Wisdoms of Life" which I liked so much I've made it a part of my journal.

1. I was given a body.
2. There are lessons to learn.
3. The lessons I don't learn have to be repeated.
4. Others are a mirror of me, reflecting what I love/hate about myself.
5. There are no mistakes, only lessons.
6. How I live is up to me.
7. All the answers are within me.

Number three is an eye-opener! I better pay attention the first time!

(Just recently, I learned that Cherie Carter-Scott is the author of these "wisdoms," plus three more, which have been published in her book, *If Life is a Game, These are the Rules.* [7] Thank you, Cherie!)

7   Carter-Scott, Chérie. *If Life Is a Game, These Are the Rules* . New York: Bantam-Doubleday Dell Publishing Group, Inc., 1998.

Friday, May 20

Mother suffered a frightening weak spell tonight after dinner, similar to the other night. It seems that these spells are lasting longer and occurring more frequently. I'm not afraid, although it bothers me to see her so uncomfortable. I feel so helpless not being to alleviate her discomfort.

Sunday, May 29

Cris and her aunt invited me over for a Memorial Day celebration. What a wonderful afternoon the three of us had! I wanted those two hours to last forever.

Mother slept most of the time I was gone. I picked up one of her favorite chicken dinners on the way home. She enjoyed that treat! We had a gelatin dessert which I served in her beautiful, antique sherbet glasses. I thought it was elegant! Sadly, Mother didn't recognize the crystal as her own and asked where I got them. I like to use as many of her pretty things as I can. We use her good china every day. Why not?

Monday, May 30

Memorial Day! Still in the afterglow of yesterday afternoon, I prepared a picnic dinner to celebrate the day. Mother really enjoyed it!

Norm, our neighbor across the hall, remarked how much Mother was slowing down. He had noticed as he observed her walking today. I thought back to three years ago when we walked around the entire complex. Now, Mother can hardly walk around the back of the apartment. She is failing, but she looks absolutely beautiful! Her skin is such a healthy, rosy color, so smooth and soft.

Mother mentioned selling the two remaining cemetery plots. Also, she was concerned about fixing up her sewing machine to sell. I guess she's getting ready to move on. And I'm ready, too.

Wednesday, June 1

I received a surprise package and letter from Kathie, a calligraphy buddy, today. The box was full of little surprises, individually wrapped. There were gourmet coffee packs, candy, a rubber stamp, bubble bath, lotion, note pad, book mark, and a coffee mug with a little bear saying: *Please bear with me!* That was a great morale booster! Kathie's letter was upbeat, too. I could sense the bittersweet relief she was feeling now that the responsibility of caring for her mother is over.

As I kissed Mother good night, she said, "I love you!" with such depth of sincerity that I could not keep my tears in check. Kissing her again, I whispered, "I love you, too, so very much."

Thursday, June 2

At 8:30 this morning I heard a THUD. I shot into the bathroom and found Mother sitting on the floor against the wall, looking befuddled. She had lost her balance while reaching for a towel. I tried to get her up, but it was impossible. I checked to see if Norm's truck was there. It wasn't. I tried a few more maneuvers to get Mother on her feet. Nothing worked. I didn't panic, but calmly assured her that we'd figure out some way. Thinking about my next step, I went back to the kitchen window. There was Norm's red truck! He came over immediately, and we were able to gently lift Mother into bed where she slept soundly for the next two hours. She seemed none the worse for the experience.

The neighbors have been wonderful! Norm gave me his work number and said to call him there any time. I could get help from the apartment complex manager or the maintenance men, too. I feel secure.

Saturday, June 4

I placed my mattress close to the hallway last night so I could hear Mother call. Flexibility is one advantage of the air mattress. I can place it wherever I choose.

Mother needed help getting out of bed this morning, an effect from yesterday's fall. Her sore arm muscles made it painful to feed herself, so I held her cereal bowl up to make it a little easier. Later, she seemed afraid to have me leave, even to make a short trip to the grocery store. We'll use moist heat and aspirin today and see if that helps to ease the discomfort.

Sunday, June 5

I thought about why I became so upset last night turning the heating pad on and off for Mother every two minutes. (Whenever she felt a little heat, she claimed it was too hot.) The reason might have been in my own words when I said to her, "You're acting just like a little kid." It is so difficult to accept the fact that Mother is no longer the parent I knew. Just when I think I've accepted the role reversal, something like this occurs and I discover I haven't achieved it at all. I wonder if I ever will.

Monday, June 6

I pulled my mattress into Mother's bedroom last night to be closer to help her during the night. It's very painful for her to walk. Aspirin and the moist heating pad give her the most comfort. I'm relieved that the doctor will see her this afternoon.

LATER

It took two hours to help Mother dress, prepare her breakfast, and assist her to the car to go to the doctor's office. The hip x-ray was insignificant except for osteoporosis and arthritis. A bone scan was recommended.

Tuesday, June 7

I'm not sure how much longer my body can take sleeping in two hour intervals. I'll make it somehow. I must. I can't take the chance of Mother getting up alone and falling, so I awaken every two hours to check on her.

She required a lot of assistance today. Reluctantly, she used her walker. Grabbing on to furniture and the walls is all the support she needs—so she thinks!

I feel so confined. The thought of this being a permanent situation, and maybe getting worse, is one I don't want to even entertain. Right now, it would create a suffocating "spider web" around me.

Thursday, June 9

Not much rest last night. I was up with Mother four times and just cat-napped in between.

What an afternoon! It took four hours for the bone scan. I groaned inwardly when the technician said Mother would have to drink three large glasses of water. That's a mighty tall order for someone who is incontinent and unable to walk without assistance. Needless to say, it was a very tiring afternoon for both of us. Mother welcomed the wheelchair ride to the car.

I know Mother appreciates what I'm doing for her, but I wish she'd tell me. When I'm tired, as I am right now, I begin to feel put upon, unloved, and unappreciated. Then resentment moves in. A "thank you" every so often would help soothe the weariness.

Friday, June 10

I received my words of appreciation tonight! As I kissed Mother good night, she said, "I love you!"

I looked at her in mock surprise. "That's three times you've told me that tonight!" We both laughed.

Then, Mother looked at me seriously. "And I mean it!"

That deserved another kiss!

Sunday, June 12

Poor Mother was up for only four hours today. The pain is pulling her down. We'll try the new pain medication. I'll put my mattress near the hallway tonight, closer to her room. I must figure out some way she can awaken me. Perhaps an extension cord with a light switch that I can hook up to a lamp in the living room would work.

My niece, Marcia, sister-in-law, Theo, and her husband came over to visit. Theo suggested raising Mother's chair with wooden blocks to make it easier for her to get up. I agreed to let her do it.

Monday, June 13

A hot, muggy week is predicted. I'm not looking forward to that.

I was up twice with Mother last night, and catnapped in between. Watching her gradual decline is so difficult. I look at the leaves on the trees, noticing how some wither and fall off immediately, while others may begin to wither, yet linger on and on. We are like that, too. Mother is just gradually declining. God is in charge. This I must remember and totally accept.

LATER

This was another sleeping day for Mother. The stronger pain medication takes the edge off the pain but makes her drowsy. She didn't make it to the toilet in time this afternoon, so I had a mess to clean up. It wasn't as bad as the other day, though. I was grateful. Poor Mother, she tried to help. I appreciated her effort, but....

My journal thought for today was a good one: **I'll do something to brighten someone else's day.** And I did, for two neighbors! It's Michigan strawberry time so I shared the luscious berries I'd bought with a neighbor. Also, I replanted Georgia's sick petunias, actually squeezing the water from their water-logged roots! Both neighbors were delighted, and my attitude brightened, as well.

Tuesday, June 14

The bone scan report was negative. The doctor's diagnosis is "pulled ligaments" which will take four to six weeks to heal. There's nothing that can be done, except medication to relieve the pain and moist heat.

Theo and her husband dropped by with the chair blocks, but they were too high. Drilling the holes for the legs a little deeper will solve that.

Thursday, June 16

I'm recalling last night when I was eating dinner alone and thinking about death. It is no longer the feared experience it was when Bob, Dad, and Jack died. My first experience with death came when I was twelve years old. Grandma had died. While we were driving to Canada for the funeral, Dad explained death to me. "It's just a body," he said. "If you touch it, you'll feel that it's cold and hard. The life that was there has gone on."

I have felt Dad's spirit during this past year. I saw him one night—different form, but I knew him. I believe he was waiting to take Mother home.

Friday, June 17

"I had a dream last night," Mother told me as she ate breakfast. This time she was bowling! She didn't learn to bowl until she was seventy years old, and the game has been her favorite ever since.

Mother enjoys telling me about her dreams. Earlier this week she dreamed she'd been typing at the church. Two nights ago, she'd been working at Schoolcraft College in her dream. She is active in her dreams, doing exactly what she had done in life. The mind is so mysterious. Mother recalls the past clearly, even in her dreams, but has difficulty remembering yesterday.

LATER

Mother continues to fail. She lacks interest, wants to die, and sleeps all but four to six hours a day. Now her appetite is waning. She is incontinent in bladder and bowels. Almost every day there is an accident, but she can't help it. I'm becoming very experienced in the clean up department. However, I don't care to add that skill to my resume!

Theo brought the blocks for the chair tonight and put them in place. Mother liked the height, saying it was much easier to get up now. Score one for Theo!

Tuesday, June 21

Tears flowed as I was washing dishes tonight. I'm losing my mother. I'm ready to let her go, realizing this is no life for her now and that it can't go on much longer. At the same time, my heart grieves the tremendous loss it will be. When the time does come, it will be an emotional challenge like I've never experienced.

Friday, June 24

Mother is still planning a birthday party for me! She started yesterday, suggesting that we invite a couple of the neighbors. Today she added another name to the list. That list keeps growing!

I laughed when she asked me how old I'll be. "Do you remember when you were fifty-nine?" I asked. She shook her head. She was fifty-nine when I graduated from college, thirty-seven years ago.

LATER

"You are so good to me," Mother said as I tucked her in bed tonight.

I'll treasure that! I was so emotionally choked up, all I could do was kiss her again.

Saturday, June 25

During our phone conversation last night, Cris asked if I ever felt like running away. Good question! I thought for a moment. "No, not really, " I finally responded. I'm never relaxed when I'm away from Mother, even though I do need a break every so often. That's one of the advantages of the Flint trips. But I can't recall wanting to run away. Who would take care of Mother?

I called Pat this morning. When I heard her voice, my smiles dissolved to tears. I explained my reaction in a letter I wrote to her today.

> *"I'm very vulnerable right now. The sudden, overwhelming, surges of emotion happen so fast. I know it's grief, that it's normal, but it is hard on me and very difficult for others. It seems to come when there is kindness shown to me. It's as if everything that has happened during the past four years is roaring down on me like an avalanche. Very few know and understand what it's been like. Because you do, I can share my feelings with you more easily. With others, I maintain a controlled facade because that's what people want to see. I cannot expose my vulnerable self. I know it is grief, but it's still frightening when it happens so suddenly."*

Sunday, June 26

Mother is feeling better. She was awake for five hours today, ate well, washed the dishes, and even walked several times around the inside of the apartment—using the walker!

She continues to plan my birthday party. She added Cris' name to the list today. "Five from here, and Cris makes six." she told me. Laughing, I said we'd have to rent a hall if the list got any longer!

"Oh, they can put a table down the middle." she countered.

"Where?" I asked.

She thought for a moment. "Oh, you know. That place where we always go."

Later, she asked, "Do you think we should go over there and make arrangements?"

I assured her there was plenty of time. My birthday is two months away.

Tuesday, June 28

The party was still on Mother's mind today. She even had the seating arranged! She was a little confused about the food, though. She thought everyone would have the same chicken dinner she always orders.

I wonder if she is arranging this party for me after she is gone. I continue to play along.

Wednesday, June 29

I'm still looking for something Mother could use for a signal to awaken me during the night. Georgia suggested talking with Norm.

Great idea! Norm knew exactly how to do it and will have something together by tomorrow. I wanted something so that Mother could turn on the living room light from her bed. Norm is fixing it so the light will not only turn on, but flash, as well! Jokingly, he said he could rig up a siren and bells, too, if I wanted that! I think the flashing will do just fine. With the simple push of a button, Mother will be able to let me know she needs me.

LATER

This morning Mother told me what she wanted to wear on Thursday. I asked her what was important about Thursday. "Why," she said, "that's the day of the party!" She's two months early.

I'm feeling so relaxed right now. When I forgot to put out Mother's pills at dinner, I joked about not doing my job. "I'll have to fire you!" Mother said in mocked seriousness. I laughed and said she'd never find anyone as good. She agreed.

As I tucked Mother in bed tonight, she said, "If I don't live until tomorrow, I want you to know how I've appreciated everything you've done for me." Oh, my! Amidst an avalanche of tears, I kissed and kissed her, telling her that I loved her so much.

I'm still crying. Mother is slipping away. I'm already experiencing the sadness I will feel from losing someone I love so very much—my mother.

Saturday, July 2

Norm finished the signal light today. It's a piece to behold, elegantly mounted on black walnut wood and polished to perfection. He even glued green felt on the bottom to protect the furniture. I am so pleased! Mother has no difficulty in pushing the large, industrial size button which causes a lamp in the living room to flash continuously. Now I'm only a flash away! I feel more secure, and I'm sure she does, too.

Sunday, July 3

This party jag that Mother is on is now driving me crazy. My birthday keeps getting closer. I don't know what I'm going to do. Her thought is sweet, but I don't like parties given for me. I'd rather just go out to dinner on my birthday and have a quiet celebration. The thought of having to make arrangements for a party that I don't want irritates me. I hope she forgets it as she has other things.

Monday, July 4

I had a strange sensation last night. I was stirred into consciousness by a brilliant light which was alternately invaded by swirls of darkness, giving a marbled effect. The constant motion was dizzying.

Mother has died.

I started to get up to check on her.

No, she is safe. If she is gone, there's nothing I can do right now.

The night's trauma carried into morning. An upset stomach caused me to lose my breakfast. I can't get sick. Who would care for Mother?

LATER

It was mid-afternoon before Mother got up. She didn't eat much today and was so restless this evening. She walked...she sat...she got up...she walked...she sat...she tried doing the dishes. Nothing satisfied her.

Georgia came over to visit and saw Mother's restless behavior. She was concerned and made me promise to call her any time. Usually, she turns her phone off at night, but said she would leave it on tonight. We have a "tap signal" for the window, too, just in case.

Thursday, July 7

It was a miserable night, so warm and humid. I was awake every hour—and Mother was up to the bathroom every hour or so.

Georgia called me before dawn, thinking she'd heard me knock. I mentioned that Mother was going down fast. "Yes," she agreed. "I see it every day." I'm grateful to have someone right next door who can help.

Friday, July 8

Mother got up earlier this morning. For some reason or other, I was upset, suddenly becoming so tired of the routine. There was laundry to do, and I really dreaded going down into that hot, musty basement.

Mother started in on the party again, saying she wanted to make arrangements for it at the restaurant. I could no longer play along with the game. "I don't want a party," I told her. It was a cruel thing to say because I really deflated her. I felt so guilty.

We discussed "the party" at dinner. Once Mother gets an idea in her head, it takes the equivalent of an air hammer to change it. I asked her how she came up with this idea, considering that she doesn't like to be around a lot of people. She thought I'd like it, and it made her so happy.

"Why is this so important to you?" I asked.

"Because you are so important to me," she responded.

That did it! I hugged her and cried, telling her that those words meant more to me than any party ever could. That's what I'll treasure. Thank you, dear Mother, for telling me.

Saturday, July 9

I received this note in today's mail from my friend, Jo, in Flint.

> *"Dear Marian,*
> *Standing before my mailbox with your letter in my*
> *hands is like standing before a feast. And that's exactly*
> *how I feel when I receive one of your dear notes.*
> *Your everyday gentle care of your mother is truly*
> *wonderful. You model what life is all about—love.*
> *Thank you for giving us, your friends, a glimpse of*
> *what should be! "*

Her words touched me deeply.

Tuesday, July 12

Enjoyed baking muffins today. Mother's eyes sparkled when she awakened to the aroma of her favorite bran muffins. She loves them, and so do the neighbors!

The signal flasher is working just great! Mother has used it only three times, but the sense of security it gives me is invaluable.

Wednesday, July 13

Theo called to ask if it would be okay to come out for a visit. Absolutely! Just before she arrived, Mother had another accident. I was able to quickly get her shoes and slacks off and newspaper on the floor, so the clean up was minimal. I'm getting to be an expert at that.

I enjoyed talking with Theo. We tried our best to include Mother in the conversation, but it was difficult. Later, when I mentioned how enjoyable the visit was, Mother commented that Theo didn't talk very much. The truth is that Mother isn't able to hear well enough to follow a conversation. How sad it must be to be shut inside your own world.

Friday, July 15

Mother's short-term memory continues to diminish. She sat in the living room for a few minutes tonight after washing the dishes. Then, she returned to the kitchen.

"Who did the dishes?" she asked, surprised to see the clean, empty sink.

I told her she had.

"I did?" she asked in total astonishment.

Saturday, July 16

It's been four years now since Mother's first stroke, four years of gradual decline. So far, we've been able to meet the challenges. I wonder, though, what's ahead and how much longer.

I wonder, but I really don't want to know.

I'm recalling a note I'd made in my journal during last Sunday's inspirational telecast: **Looking outside for answers is futile. They are all inside me!**

I will remember that in the days to come.

The Fifth Year

Wednesday, July 20, 1994

Is Mother gone?

That was my awakening thought this morning. She is constantly on my mind, even when I sleep. Whenever I'm up during the night, I peek in to see if she's okay, if she's still breathing. It was hard to tell this morning. Then her toes moved.

As has become the norm, Mother slept most of the day.

She was anxious to get her hair cut this afternoon. The trip to the beauty salon, though, exhausted her. She couldn't keep her dinner down tonight and went to bed early.

I am alone most of the time, but not free to do much, except go to the grocery store and drive up to Flint. I don't like to be gone very long. I'm grateful that I'm able to entertain myself.

I have come a long way, but....

Robert Frost's poetic words continue to have increased significance these days—"and miles to go before I sleep."

Sunday, July 24

Mother decided to take her "long" walk today. I stopped what I was doing to sit on the patio and watch. I had told her that I didn't think she was ready for the long walk. If she couldn't make it home on her own, there might be a problem. My fears, however, were unwarranted today.

"I'd been thinking about taking that walk for two days," Mother told me later. It was a challenge for her. When I asked what she'd have done if she had not been able to walk back or had fallen, she replied simply and matter-of-factly, "I'd just stay there."

Monday, July 25

I'm still concerned about Mother walking farther than I thought she should yesterday. It is more than concern. It is anger. I was preparing for her death. Now, she's beginning to rally—and I don't like it. That's a terrible thought, but I'm so tired of being confined like this.

I guess I'm not handling this situation as well as I thought I was. Things were going along too smoothly. Somehow, I'll work through these feelings. I just flipped the pages of my journal back to July 16th and read again: **Looking outside for answers is futile. They are all inside me!**

LATER

I made my weekly trek up to Flint this morning. All was well until I returned to the apartment. Mother didn't keep her promise of sleeping, or staying in bed, until I returned. She was sitting at the table eating her cereal, dressed in an ill-matched outfit that looked absolutely awful. I was so angry. Mother ended up crying, probably because I'd frightened her. I've been crying for four years, and she hasn't shed a tear. I told her that from now on, since she thinks she's so capable, she can dress herself and fix her own breakfast.

Do I need to allow Mother to do more for herself? This sudden show of alertness and independence is a shock to me. Is that wrong? She's not dying—not at the moment. It's this yo-yo effect that's so difficult.

Tuesday, July 26

I may have figured out the cause of my intense anger. I was mentally prepared for Mother's death. I had been packing up things to make it easier for the closing of this apartment. I had the funeral mentally planned. I had rehearsed my emotions. I'd even begun to think what I would do when everything had been taken care of, and I was back home. I felt at peace, secure, and happy in the comfortable routine I'd established.

I had put Mother into that routine, too. I thought she was dying. Out of my love and concern, I was doing everything for her, including making final plans. That was false. And when anything is false, it doesn't last. It all came to a screeching halt yesterday when Mother showed me that she was very much alive and kickin', asserting her independent rights which I had been trying to take away.

Now, what will I do? What have I learned from this experience? Listen, Marian: *Stop* trying to look around the corner and planning for what you think might be there. Live now, because that's all you have.

LATER

I apologized to Mother for yesterday's outburst. I said I was sorry I hadn't allowed her to do more for herself and asked what chores she wanted to do. As she named them, I wrote: fix my breakfast, do the breakfast dishes, empty the pad pail, make my bed, do the dinner dishes, dress and undress myself. I posted the list on the cupboard as a reminder to myself not to do those tasks. Mother smiled, pleased with the solution. So was I!

"You might have to remind me to do those things," she warned me. "I don't always remember." Kissing her, I assured her I would.

It won't matter if her bed isn't made until 9:00 at night, if the dinner dishes aren't done until 9:30, or if either is done. She will do the tasks at her own time, when she feels up to it. I will allow that to happen. It's very important that she feels useful, that she's doing what she considers to be her fair share.

All is well once again. As I kissed Mother good night, I mentioned what a good day she'd had. "I love you!" she told me so tenderly. "We can forgive." I agreed and kissed her again. At the age of ninety-five, she is still teaching me life's lessons.

Wednesday, July 27

Mother turned on the wrong stove burner to cook her cereal this morning. I discovered it when I saw her ready to put her hand on the red hot burner "to see if it was hot." We had a little discussion about that. Testing the burner with her hand was what she always did, she told me. We agreed that I would turn the stove on for her from now on, but she could still cook her own cereal. Meanwhile, all the stove knobs have been removed and put away in the cupboard out of her reach. Maybe I need to invest in a set of child-proof knobs.

Saturday, August 6

The signal light is worth its weight in gold! Mother flicked it on at 4:30 this morning. She was wandering around in her bedroom, wondering where I was—afraid she was alone. She was so relieved to see me that she grabbed my hands and hugged me tightly.

Thursday, August 11

Mother had a surprise pre-birthday party today! Shirley, her husband, and the pastor came over with a cake, complete with candles. We sang "Happy Birthday" while Mother made a wish and blew out all the candles—with a little help. It was good to see her so happy.

Birthday cards are filling the mailbox! As I taped another card to the expanding display on the living room mirror, Mother smiled and nodded her head. It pleases her to be so well remembered.

A beautiful plant arrived from Carolyn, her granddaughter in California. It's name is especially significant—Peace Lily.

Sunday, August 15

Today is Mother's ninety-sixth birthday! I can't believe she has lived this long. She is healthy, looks beautiful, and seems content. Most days she can dress herself, fix her own breakfast with assistance, make her bed, and wash the dishes. Her eyesight is good enough to allow her to get around, but not to read, crochet, or watch television. The hearing aid helps her to hear one person speak directly to her. She sleeps well—and long, like eighteen hours a day. We do have much for which to be grateful. Ninety-six years is a long time to live and still be in your own home.

LATER

Marcia and Kathy joined us for dinner at Mother's favorite restaurant. This was the third party to honor this year's birthday. I think Mother enjoyed the outing with two of her granddaughters, but not like she has in previous years. She seemed to be in a world of her own. That saddened me.

Saturday, August 20

Mother was up earlier than usual this morning. It irritated me, but I said nothing. I took my coffee out on the patio and leisurely sipped it while thinking about what I could do to make this a good day. Driving up to Flint to cut the grass was an option, but that didn't thrill me. Then, I thought about Cris. I called. Yes, she was home and was excited about getting together today!

I told Mother my plans, assuring her I'd be back in time to prepare dinner. She seemed pleased to know she would have the afternoon alone. I said she'd have a good day, free from my nagging. She laughed, happy that the sofa was all hers for the day!

Cris prepared a light lunch, and then surprised me with a chocolate cake she'd baked in honor of my birthday! I was touched. We talked all afternoon, sharing so much. She supported me for "escaping," saying that both Mother and I needed it. If I had any feeling of guilt about leaving Mother for the afternoon, she removed it. In fact, she urged me to escape more often.

When I returned to Plymouth, I felt like a different person. As I tucked Mother into bed tonight, she said she loved me, even though she didn't always show it. We've made progress! We are never too old to learn—even at the age of ninety-six, bless her heart!

Yes, it was a very good day.

Sunday, August 21

I walked around the complex twice this evening. It gave me time to sort out the intense emotions of the past few days and to think how they could be avoided in the future. I know Mother can stay alone for a few hours. Why don't I feel free to leave, as I did yesterday? If there are prison bars to my days, it's because I agreed to put them there.

Mother got ready for bed herself tonight and has now turned out the light. She didn't say good night.

TEN MINUTES LATER

The signal light began flashing. When I walked into Mother's room, she was holding out her arms to me. She hugged and hugged me, caressing my face so tenderly with her hands, and saying, "I love you so! I love you so!" with such deep affection. I held her close, my face moist with tears. It was a very touching moment.

Monday, August 22

I awakened before dawn—crying. I'm having a difficult time letting all this go. I'm hurting. I can't hide it—nor can I deny it.

Mother was up early this morning. I considered going up to Flint, but drove to the mall, instead. I shopped around for an hour. I didn't enjoy that like I used to. I'm not the same person I used to be, either.

LATER

I walked around the apartment complex for thirty minutes tonight. That felt good! Georgia was waiting on the patio when I returned. We talked all evening. She makes me laugh, and how I need that!

Received a few birthday cards and letters. Cris sent a package with three gifts which I'll enjoy opening early tomorrow morning. Georgia and I plan to go out for lunch tomorrow. I'm looking forward to that.

Tuesday, August 23, 1994

HAPPY BIRTHDAY to me!

I postponed the lunch date with Georgia because Mother didn't get up until I awakened her early this afternoon. She slept almost the rest of the day, too. She's back in her old sleep pattern.

Having to give up today's plan didn't bother me. I sat at the computer and wrote letters. Mother didn't know it was my birthday. She gets so mixed up on days. It doesn't matter. I didn't prepare a special meal, nor did I bake a cake as I did last year. It wasn't important.

Two friends from Flint called. I enjoyed those phone conversations, as well as all the cards and letters I received. I've reread the letters several times. Cris sent a beautiful floral arrangement. I do have wonderful friends!

Wednesday, August 24

I wonder what this day will bring. I can't plan ahead. I must remain in the present moment, concentrate on it, and use it to the max.

LATER

Had another birthday surprise! Carolyn and Jerry sent a floral bouquet, uniquely arranged in an ice cream soda glass filled with candy. When I called to thank them, Carolyn said she'll know tomorrow if she can make a stop-over in Detroit during a business trip next month. It would be so great to see her!

Thursday, August 25

What appears to be an obstacle is really an opportunity for me to grow! That's a good one for me to think about, especially after this past, emotionally-charged week.

Received a long letter from Cris. Since Mother may live a long time, she suggested I consider moving her to my home in Flint and making the family room into her bedroom to avoid the stairs. She offered to help. I'll give it some serious thought.

LATER

No, we'll just stay here. I'll try to get out more, and that should help. I need to keep everything simple. The emotion of closing this apartment and disposing of furniture will be hard enough, but doing it while Mother is here would be more than I could handle now.

No matter where I am, there I am.

This is a problem of attitude adjustment. My thirty minute walk this evening seemed to be one step in that direction. What I'm really longing for is the freedom to come and go as I please, to do things and go places with friends, to be responsible only for myself. All of those will have to remain on hold as long as I'm in this situation.

Friday, August 26

Mother asked about the flowers she'd ordered for my birthday, hoping they had arrived today. They didn't. She said she had reminded the neighbor to order them. Evidently, the neighbor didn't think Mother knew what she was talking about. I felt so sorry for Mother. She looked so dejected.

I told her about a pair of walking shoes I saw at the mall the other day and liked. "Would you like to buy those for my birthday?" I asked, hoping that the suggestion would ease her disappointment.

She smiled. "I'd like that. I wanted to do something for you."

We hugged each other. I told her I'd get the shoes tomorrow.

Saturday, August 27

What an experience we had at dinner tonight! Mother upchucked her meal—including her upper denture. In my haste to get everything cleaned up, I inadvertently flushed her teeth down the toilet! Poor Mother. I hope the dentist still has the impression.

"That was an expensive flush!" Mother commented.

We laughed! I love her sense of humor.

I'll call the dentist on Monday. In the meantime, I'll fix soft food meals. Always another challenge.

Tuesday, August 30

The decision to plan not to plan is working well for me. Mother's unpredictable schedule continues to be just that: unpredictable. One morning last week she was up and dressed by 8:15. Then, she slept on the couch the rest of the morning and most of the afternoon. The next day she didn't awaken until 2:00 in the afternoon. I have decided that my best plan is no plan; just do whatever, whenever, and however. Remaining flexible seems to be working so far.

Friday, September 2

Edith called tonight and tried to be helpful, bless her heart. She suggested that Mother could stay in a nursing home for two weeks to give me a break. I couldn't do that to Mother. Besides, the process of bringing it about—not to mention the shock to Mother—made me cringe. I thanked her for being concerned.

Even though I don't want a two-week vacation, I'm beginning to think about daytime help. If it is what I need to do, I will be guided to the right person.

Monday, September 5

Labor Day! I recall the sadness of this day years ago as we packed up to leave the cottage. Putting the shutters on the windows, saying goodbye to our summer friends, taking the last swim in the cool waters of Lake Huron, and bidding farewell to the carefree days of fun and laughter were all part of the traditional weekend.

I am facing a different goodbye now. Will it be the last Labor Day with Mother? Questions, questions. No answers—yet. I need to simply enjoy each moment. That's all I have.

When Mother and I kissed each other good night, I added the child's rhyme she often said to me years ago: "Good night, sleep tight. Don't let the bed bugs bite!" She smiled. "I'll see you in the morning," she said. And then added, "if I'm still here."

I thought about that later and wondered.

Tuesday, September 6

I enjoyed walking this evening with Fran, a neighbor across the street. She asked about Mother, and I told her about the birthday celebration. "You're a good daughter," she said so sincerely.

I looked at her and smiled. "I've made a commitment," I said calmly, yet definitely. I was surprised at my response.

Later, as I continued on my walk alone, I thought about it. It's true! I'm not being *good*. I've made a commitment to care for Mother in her own home, and being a *good* daughter has nothing to do with it. I haven't made many commitments in my life, but when I do, there is absolutely no turning back.

I'm committed to caring for Mother, not out of obligation as her daughter, but because of a promise I have made of my own free will and choice. I have chosen to care for Mother in her own home for as long as I'm able. I have accepted that commitment, and when it is fulfilled, I will be at peace.

LATER

I'm rereading the wonderful letter I received from Zane today. She's a great friend. We are just beginning to know each other.

> *"Dear Marian,*
>
> *'As the marsh hen secretly builds on the watery sod, Behold, I will build me a nest on the greatness of God.'(Sidney Lanier) The word nest seems to be the key word. I am forever building my nest…the secret, safe and wonderful place in my mind that is just for me to go to find comfort.… When someone or something seems to invade my nest, I flail around in a muddle of discontent, disbelief and disconnectedness. My questions to God are wild, many and, of course, full of self pity.*
>
> *The good thing about all of it, as you have discovered, is that God always provides an answer and that answer is always: Why do you balk about the challenges I'm allowing you to experience? There are no accidents. I want you to consider this as another opportunity to grow.*
>
> *I stomp and storm and argue that I've done enough growing for one person in one lifetime. I like my nest just the way it is. Eventually, I play all this out in my mind and realize the 'opportunity' was for a purpose and I have grown because of it.*
>
> *You have just experienced it with your mom. Out of the blue, from a corner you never expected, another opportunity is poking around in your nest, disturbing the comfort zone once again.…"*

Saturday, September 17

What an absolutely wonderful day we had with Carolyn! I met her at the airport at 9:00 this morning, the beginning of the best day I've had in a long, long time. While Mother slept, we talked and talked. My hunger for conversation was abundantly satisfied. I felt so good! Later in the day, we went out to the cemetery to put flowers on Jack's grave. That was a very tender and emotional time for both of us.

Carolyn gave Mother a lot of attention. This may be the last time she sees her grandma. Poor Carolyn experienced my responsibilities, too. Mother "messed" and "barfed," but that's life around here. Carolyn is the only one who has actually seen all that. I was sorry she had to experience it, but she wasn't. "I'm glad," she told me, "because now I really know."

My cry has been that no one understands.

One person does now.

Monday, September 19

Mother went down another notch today. Her speech was noticeably more slurred. I wonder if she's had another mini-stroke.

Tuesday, September 20

My application to volunteer in the AARP Tax Aide Program has been accepted. The state coordinator called today to ask if I wanted to work in Flint or Plymouth. Not knowing where I'll be at tax time, I chose Plymouth. The training begins in January. That seems like a long time away.

During dinner, Mother asked what I was going to do with her wedding ring. "What would you like me to do?" I asked.

"I want you to have it," she said.

One more sign of what occupies her thoughts these days.

Wednesday, September 21

Today was NEW TEETH day for Mother! She needed only three appointments for her new partial denture. The new teeth not only look better than the old ones, but fit better, too. Mother is pleased, especially because there are no more dental appointments.

Tuesday, September 27

I'm thinking about approval and how I interpret *good daughter* as being synonymous with approval. Maybe that's why I recoil so when anyone tells me I'm a good daughter. I don't need anyone's approval for doing what I'm doing. In fact, I really don't care what others think. I'm caring for Mother because I've made a commitment to do so. It's more than just a commitment, though. It's a covenant that was made with love, a very deep love for my mother. I pray for the strength to fulfill it.

Thursday, September 29

Mother wet all over the bathroom floor this morning and then proceeded to go back to bed wearing wet underpants. All she could say was, "I didn't know."

The day went from bad to worse. I sobbed for an hour. Mother tried to comfort me, not knowing she was the cause of my pain. Later, when I apologized, she couldn't remember that I cried.

I called a local home health agency this afternoon for information about hiring someone to stay here one day a week to give me some respite time. I don't know what Mother's reaction would be to having a stranger stay with her. I don't think she'd like it. I'll have to think about that.

I needed some time alone this afternoon. I drove out to the parkway and sat in the car for about an hour. I yearned to stay longer, but there was dinner to prepare.

Friday, September 30

The idea of moving Mother to a two-bedroom apartment has resurfaced. I had rejected it previously because the mere thought of moving exhausted me. Now I see it from a different perspective.

While Mother was eating her breakfast, I discussed the advantages of a two-bedroom apartment. She realizes I need a room of my own. She was happy that we would stay in the complex.

I talked with Rick, the apartment manager, this afternoon about our need. He said he'd let me know as soon as an apartment that we'd like becomes available. We are number one on the list! Meanwhile, I can begin to prepare. Now I have a focus, a direction. No longer do I feel like I'm at the end of my rope—one that was ready to break.

Saturday, October 1

I bought plastic runners to protect the carpeting from Mother's bed to the bathroom. The incontinence problem is increasing. The next step will be a bedside commode.

I began cleaning out a couple of kitchen cupboards today. Even if we don't move, the cupboards will be clean.

Sunday, October 2

I wrote letters to a couple of friends this morning and tried to keep the tone upbeat. My life is on such an emotional roller coaster that I don't want my written words to express any of the "low" times. There's no point in putting those feelings in letters to friends. They would only feel helpless. This journal is the place for those feelings.

Monday, October 3

After I'd helped Mother get squared around and settled for the afternoon, I decided to treat myself to a movie. It was one I wanted to see and turned out to be an excellent choice. I extended my respite time with a trip to a restaurant for an indulgence of onion rings and a Coke! Just being away for three hours was helpful. No one knows the daily isolation I feel.

The enjoyment was soon taken away, however, when I returned to the apartment and had a call from the neighbor. While I was gone, Mother decided to go to the mailbox—without her walker. The wind blew the front door closed and it locked. She did have her keys, but couldn't see which one to use. She knew the sliding glass door on the patio was open and tried to get to it—but went in the opposite direction, totally confused. She was walking beside the bushes in the front of the building, hanging on to them for support, when the neighbor came to her rescue.

I was almost hysterical. What frightened me most was the fact that no one knew where I was. Mother said she almost fell twice, but it was probably more than that. She is now under strict orders to not even think about going out the door if I'm not here.

And I have another problem. I'm afraid to leave. Before going to sleep tonight, my brainstorm was to get a pager. I simply can't continue to be imprisoned in this apartment.

Thursday, October 6

All I have is <u>now</u>. Concentrate on the moment, Marian, and stop trying to focus on what's ahead.

I don't know what the future holds, nor do I want to know. After yesterday, I know this moment is all I can handle.

Friday, October 7

The highlights of the day were receiving three letters and taking Mother to the dairy for a sundae. She really enjoyed that!

Cris' letter was so supportive.

> *"Hi Marian!*
> *I continue to admire and envy your refusal to accept frustration and defeat, and your determination to maintain control over your life.*
> *The periods of self pity (which are justified and permitted) are never very long. And when you redirect your energy, you come back stronger than before!"*

Cris is like a sturdy life raft in my life. She is always there for me.

Saturday, October 8

Mother was so weak today that she didn't have the strength to dress herself. She accepted my help, shaking her head and lamenting, "I never thought it would come to this."

What could I say?

Wednesday, October 12

Theo and her husband came over this afternoon. They mentioned the quilt display which will be part of their annual church bazaar next month. I brought out the quilts Mother had made years ago and spread them out for an admiring party. Mother agreed to loan three of them for the display. I don't know how my mother had time to do quilting while raising three children. Two of the quilts were made before I was born. Those are true heirlooms!

Mother asked Theo to come out for a day to give me a break. I was so surprised. She's more sensitive to my needs than I realized! Theo agreed and asked me to give her the menu. I thanked Mother for her thoughtful suggestion.

Tuesday, October 18

I'm witnessing the most gorgeous sunrise! All is well. The sun did rise again! It also brought exciting news.

Rick called to say he had an apartment for us. The one I'd thought would be perfect had just become available! I had put thoughts about that apartment out of my mind, believing if it was to be, it will be. Two-bedroom, ground floor, see-through apartments do not vacate often in this complex, so I wasn't thinking seriously about moving. Rick's phone call changed my thinking immediately!

Later, Mother and I walked over to see the apartment and she gave her "stamp of approval!" We talked with the neighbors, whom Mother knew well. They are so tickled that we are moving in! Eleanor dearly loves Mother and is so pleased she'll be closer.

I'm on cloud nine! More S P A C E! A room of my own! Larger rooms and closets! A bathroom twice the size of this one!

Moving day is October 31. I'll be very busy for the next two weeks.

Saturday, October 29

I've been reading my journal entries from the past week and am amazed that so much was accomplished—and I'm not exhausted. I've cleaned all the vertical blinds, the windows, the louvered doors (all ten!) and polished the hardwood floors in the closets of the new apartment. The kitchen cupboards are organized, as well as the bathroom. Our clothes are neatly hanging in the closets.

Mother helped pack her china and has said she'll wash all the pieces after the move. That'll give her something to do, making her feel that she has helped. And I don't care how long it takes her!

The layout of the new apartment is identical to this one. The only major change will be the location of the master bedroom, which will be Mother's. That may confuse her temporarily.

Carolyn called to find out about the new apartment. Teasingly, she told me I was old enough now to have a room of my own! We laughed.

Mother and I walked over to the new apartment after dinner. She was so pleased to see the closet filled with all her clothes, including twenty pairs of slacks. I guess she was afraid I was going to throw out her clothes. Little does she know what I did discard. I'll never tell, either!

Eleanor came down to chat for a few minutes. Bless her heart, she offered to stay with Mother any time I needed to be away longer than usual. Doors do open when least expected.

Monday, October 31

Moving Day!

It's a rainy morning, but nothing could dampen my spirits today, as I continued to carry things into the new apartment. I thought I was Mary Poppins when my air bed, which I tried to carry over my head because I didn't want to deflate it, almost took off with me! Wouldn't that have been a scream!

When the movers arrived, Theo and her husband took Mother to their home for lunch and the afternoon so she wouldn't have to be in the confusion. When they returned later in the day, I had Mother's bed made and everything in place. The new apartment looked like home.

Mother seems content tonight. So am I! So am I!

Wednesday, November 2

In the middle of the night, the light began flashing. I shot out of bed like a rocket, not knowing what to expect. Mother was trying to get out of bed on the opposite side to which she was accustomed. She was totally confused. "I'm losing my mind. I'm losing my mind," she kept saying over and over.

A couple of aspirin and lots of TLC soon put her back to sleep, but I stayed awake for over an hour. During her next trip to the bathroom, I rearranged the furniture so she could get in and out of bed on the side she was accustomed to using. All is well once again.

Friday, November 4

Mother was confused again last night. This time she wandered into my room, trying to find the bathroom. It certainly was a foreboding experience to awaken from a deep sleep and see someone moving around on a walker, giving a ghost-like aura. Halloween was last week!

Saturday, November 12

Mother was pleased to see the lace cloth she'd crocheted fifty years ago adorning the dining area table. It is a beautiful piece of work! I remember watching her crochet each of those medallions and then, what seemed like magic to my ten-year old eyes, fasten them together to make this exquisite table covering. What a treasure!

LATER

My mother has wheels! We checked out front wheels for her walker at an orthopedic services center this afternoon. Mother really liked them. She adapted to the new feel immediately, surprised at how much easier it was to maneuver around. In fact, she moved around so much faster that I teasingly told her she'd need a driver's license!

Thanksgiving Day

This will be a quiet day. We had a family celebration last week when I invited Theo and her husband over for a "house warming" dinner in our new apartment.

Instead of the traditional turkey, I prepared "cranberry chicken" for our dinner today. That's a very simple recipe: mix a can of cranberries with eight ounces of Catalina dressing and a package of dry onion soup mix. "Slather" it over boneless, skinless chicken breasts and bake for an hour. It's delicious!

LATER

Mother rode up to Flint with me this afternoon. I had a long list of things I wanted to bring back to the apartment, as well as the usual "must do" list. Mother seemed to enjoy the outing, although she slept most of the time. Nevertheless, it was a change for her. That's important for both of us every once in a while.

Wednesday, November 30

Mother is looking for a job! She told me about it at breakfast.

"Where are you looking?" I asked, curious to know where her thinking had taken her this time.

"Hudson's," she said without missing a beat.

"What will you be doing?"

"Oh, I don't know," she said. "They'll have something for me."

I told her the stores had already hired their extra Christmas help by now, but that didn't deter her. "Why do you want a job?"

"To put in my time," she answered.

"How would you get there?"

She paused, and then giving me that why-are-you-asking-me-such-a-silly-question look, said, "Why, I'd just take the streetcar."

She was thinking of years gone by when Hudson's Department Store was in downtown Detroit, and we did take the streetcar to get there.

Work is so important to Mother. In her mind she believes she is capable of doing everything she ever did. We play the game.

Sunday, December 4

I finished matting and framing the family composite picture today. The 30x36 piece is impressive hanging over the sofa in the living room. When I look at the five of us in that picture, I have a true sense of belonging. Mother feels that, too. She told me tonight, "When I'm resting on the couch and look up and see that picture, I feel my family is watching over me."

I put up a few Christmas decorations today. Mother seemed pleased with the festive appearance. The prettiest time is in the evening when only the Christmas tree lights illumine the room.

Wednesday, December 7

We were greeted with six inches of snow this morning. It truly looks like a winter wonderland! This is a perfect day for writing Christmas cards, and that's exactly what I'll do.

LATER

While we were playing cards tonight, Mother asked what day it was. That is not an unusual question, but then she asked what month it was.

"What month do you think it might be?" I asked in an effort to find out what she was thinking. She guessed March, then May. I suggested she look around at the decorations.

"What month do we put up Christmas decorations?" I asked, turning on the tree lights.

"November?" she guessed in a soft, hesitant voice.

"You're close," I answered, as if we were playing Twenty Questions. "What month is Christmas?"

"Oh, December!" she said with a sense of glee.

That is so sad.

There's no way of describing the heartbreak one feels in watching your parent—the person who was once so strong and capable, the person you depended upon—slowly become so fragile, helpless, and confused.

Saturday, December 10

Eleanor came downstairs to visit and have a cup of coffee with us this evening. Mother asked her if she'd ever worked for Rose, the lady in charge of the bowling alley. Eleanor said she hadn't, but was interested in why Mother asked. "I'm thinking about getting a job there!" Mother told her.

Eleanor about fell off her chair in surprise, but played along by asking Mother what she'd like to do there. "Oh, I'd keep the scores!" Mother answered with enthusiasm. She was the scorekeeper during her last years of bowling and a good one, too. Those were happy years for her.

Tuesday, December 13

Each day is like a good book. I never know exactly how things will work out. Today was a perfect example.

I was as happy as a "kid let loose in a toy store" this afternoon while doing a homebound friend's Christmas shopping for her two granddaughters. It was such fun filling the shopping cart with all the things three and five year old girls would love: books, crayons, a Teddy Bear, a

Barbie doll, a puzzle, a couple of games, an artist's easel. I was so pleased I was able to get everything on the list.

My happiness, however, didn't stop there. When I showed all the treasures to Mother this evening, little did I know the extended pleasure we would have looking over each of the gifts and imagining the excitement the girls would have Christmas morning when they opened them. Mother loved the little bear, especially its sweater and hat. I think it reminded her of the sweaters and hats she used to knit. I enjoyed reading aloud the books I had selected, pleased with the choices. It was a delightful evening.

Thursday, December 22

"Where did you come from?" Mother asked this morning, dumbfounded to see me.

When I told her I'd been here all the time she was surprised. "Why, I thought you'd gone away. When did you come home?"

She finally concluded that she was "all mixed up" and readily accepted my suggestion of returning to bed and sleep. I tucked her in and then took my shower—with many tears.

LATER

Several people have asked me what I do all day? They can't imagine how I occupy my time. I'm thankful to have many and varied interests. I've enjoyed finding new recipes in the newspaper and trying them. Writing an average of five letters a week to friends and family is an activity I look forward to, especially when it's in response to a letter received. Journal writing, reading, and walking are ways I keep myself mentally, intellectually, and physically alert. Rubber stamping cards, calligraphy projects, matting and framing pictures have all given me creative pleasure. And, now, the tax season will soon begin. That will occupy some of my time and thinking, definitely! I never lack for something to do, and for that I'm grateful.

Saturday, December 24

We have lived in our new home for only two months, but it seems like we've always been here. I feel settled, content, and able to handle whatever challenges may be ahead. It's amazing what a difference an additional two hundred square feet of space can make!

Eleanor just brought us a plate of freshly baked cookies! It's wonderful to have such a good neighbor and friend.

LATER

What a privileged experience I had this afternoon! The student who received Mother's scholarship at Schoolcraft College came by to meet her benefactor. I had tears to think that this young, twenty year old wanted to visit my ninety-six year old mother to say, "Thank you!" She wanted Mother to know how much the scholarship meant to her and what she was able to do because of it. It was so touching to see the two of them sitting beside each other on the sofa, and to feel the respect and honor being given by someone just beginning her life to someone who was ending hers.

LATER

My niece, Marcia and her husband Dave, came over this evening. Mother likes Dave, especially all the undivided attention he gives her. Dave is a nurse and has some understanding of the extent of care I give. Marcia was surprised that I bathed Mother. Perhaps she wants to believe that Grandma is the same self-sufficient person she has always been.

Monday, December 26

We drove up to Flint this afternoon. My mailbox was overflowing with holiday cards! Mother seemed to enjoy the outing. She feels more secure when she's with me.

Mother astounded me tonight when she said that my brother Jack's two daughters, Carolyn and Elaine, weren't sisters. It appears that the confusion is increasing. Her stamina has decreased noticeably, as well as her appetite. Also, I'm hearing what may be described as a heart cough—that very dry, unproductive cough.

The signs are there.

Wednesday, December 28

I bought a new car! Mother is happy about the color. "It'll be a Red Wing car!" she said, remembering I'm an avid, loyal fan of the Detroit Red Wings ice hockey team. We enjoyed a good laugh about that. Her clever thinking amazed me.

Friday, December 30

This morning I thought about limitations and how they are a matter of perception. While living in the old apartment, my space was limited because of my thinking. Once I opened my mind to moving into a larger place and let that need be known, the result was the perfect apartment, the perfect location, the perfect neighbors, and the perfect amount of space.

Another lesson learned, Marian!

Saturday, December 31

The last day of the year, and what an interesting twelve months it has been. I've experienced some of my highest and some of my lowest moments, hours, days this past year. I have taken giant steps in my growth and look forward to the new year with three hundred sixty-five more days of opportunity—each with twenty-four hours! What a gift!

Sunday, January 1, 1995

This is the year I'll be sixty! It doesn't depress me, though, not like the beginning of the last decade did. I don't feel sixty, but having never been there, how do I know? I feel no age.

LATER

"What for?" Mother asked when I awakened her this afternoon and told her it was time to get up. She'd been sleeping for the past fourteen hours! She got up an hour later, but slept most of the afternoon and evening on the couch. She no longer has a purpose.

Tuesday, January 3

Mother was up earlier than usual this morning, and then sat in her rocking chair before getting dressed, which was more unusual. "I'm so tired," she sighed, "from putting all those books together." This time she was working at Wayne State University and "all those people coming in asking her to do this and that" just tired her right out! "I'll never do that again," she declared, shaking her head with another sigh of fatigue. Her dream was so real.

My cold has really hit today. I'm very concerned about staying healthy. Mother needs me.

Thursday, January 5

I've had some thoughts this morning about what others may think regarding how I'm caring for Mother. Do I really care? Because of the deep psychological dynamics involved in *mother*, no one can really say anything. What do I want others to say? More than anything, I want understanding. What I'm doing is not easy, but I don't want pity. I want my needs for conversation, for friendship to be fulfilled. I want to know that I'm not alone, that I haven't been forgotten, and that friends will be there when my life takes on still another change.

My whole life during these past five years has been devoted to Mother. I've watched her change from being very independent and self-sufficient to finally accepting that she can no longer do everything for herself. She's con-tent now. She's still able to walk to the bathroom...still able to laun-der her stockings each night...still able to make up her bed...still able to dress and undress herself with some assistance…still able to eat…and still able to wash the dishes each evening. Thank goodness for all that!

Friday, January 6

My cold is running the full course. Mother has been up and down all day, worried about me. It is so much harder taking care of myself when I have to take care of her, too.

The ambulance took someone from our building to the hospital tonight. That always saddens me, reminding me that that day may come for Mother.

Both of us slept most of the day. When I thought of things I needed to or should do, I couldn't muster the energy to do them. My body needed rest.

Saturday, January 7

Received Pat's weekly letter today. I have reread parts of it several times, appreciating the supportive message.

> *"Marian—it makes me feel so good to know that you have made a meaningful and productive life out of a situation that could have served to make others bitter and resentful. Your resilience is truly astounding! I wonder what it is that makes some people so resilient and others fall apart and resign from life…."*

Sunday, January 8

It was "sleepless in Plymouth" last night. Poor Mother coughed *all* night. I didn't know what to do to help her. I couldn't give her the medication that helped me because of her high blood pressure. All I could do was elevate her head with pillows and offer cough drops. Finally, just before dawn, I crawled in bed beside her and held her hand to let her know she was loved and not alone.

I called the doctor early this morning. He recommended an over-the-counter medication which gave immediate relief. Mother is getting some sorely needed rest now. I am so relieved.

Guess this "bug" is making the rounds. The neighbors have it, too. The medicine is controlling Mother's cough, but she can't keep food down. Her face shows a weight loss and, definitely, the fatigue from last night's coughing marathon. The doctor will see her tomorrow.

Monday, January 9

Today's journal thought: **Explore something that excites you.**
That'd be great if I felt better and Mother was okay.

Then I stopped and changed my thinking. *Why not?* I haven't been able to do anything for three days now except the necessities of living and playing nurse. It's about time I added something exciting to my life. I have no idea what it will be, but just the anticipation is exciting!

LATER

I figured out how to use a new application on my computer. That was exciting! In the process of doing that, I wrote a long-overdue letter to a friend; that made me feel even better. And later, I had fun creating a birthday card for Theo, using one of the rubber stamps I'd just purchased.

Today's thought did have power!

Plus, the doctor had good news for us! Mother is in no danger. It's just going to take time for her body to fight the virus.

Saturday, January 14

Mother's cold seems to be giving up the fight, but she is very weak. The effort of getting dressed, even with my help, exhausted her this morning. I keep encouraging her to drink liquids. A half a cup of water is like a gallon to her!

Tuesday, January 17

Mother didn't have the strength to eat today. I sat beside her, my arm around her shoulders, and fed her. She didn't object to that in the least. It was a very close, loving time for both of us.

As I helped her get ready for bed tonight, Mother said I was treating her like a baby. I smiled and asked if that bothered her. "No," she said. "I kind of like it."

Thursday, January 19

Mother continues to lose ground. Gradually, she has given up one area of control to me and then another. Now she is allowing me to feed her and seems to enjoy it. If I reread my journals, I could chart the decline, especially since last June when she fell. Instead, I choose to think back over the years and realize that her long life has been productive and happy. I'm grateful that she has been allowed to spend her last days lovingly cared for in the comfort and familiarity of her own home. I cherish this sacred privilege I have been given to be her caregiver.

Mother decided to fix her own cereal this morning, but I had to feed her. She had no energy to lift the spoon herself. I asked if she'd like Eleanor to check on her while I went up to Flint this afternoon. She smiled. "Yes, if it would make Eleanor feel better," she said. That's my mother, always thinking of the other person!

LATER

Mother enjoyed Eleanor's visit and gave her the highest compliment. "She's just like you!" she told me.

"In what way?" I asked.

"She helped me on and off the couch, just like you do, and offered to do other things, like get me something to drink."

Eleanor was very pleased when I shared that compliment with her. Their friendship is a win-win. I am deeply grateful.

Friday, January 20

I put the commode beside Mother's bed tonight to make it easier for her, as well as to conserve her strength by not having to make four or five trips to the bathroom during the night with her walker. This is a much better arrangement for both of us. I can shower leisurely now that Mother has her private bathroom!

Sunday, January 22

Mother ate just half of her cereal today before becoming exhausted. I fed her the rest. It was the same at dinner. She is so weak. The signs are there now. She is slipping away.

Monday, January 23

Rose Fitzgerald Kennedy died yesterday at the age of one hundred four. Hers was a life of tragedy, ecstasy, and triumph. "The birds sing after a storm, so why shouldn't we be happy, too." is one of her quotes I want to remember.

Mother took off her wedding ring tonight. She wants me to wear it, as well as her engagement ring. I'll take both rings in for resizing tomorrow.

Tuesday, January 24

Flint had ten inches of snow, thus it took me a little longer to shovel the driveway. My house was a welcome sight. I know I need to return to my home for at least a year after Mother makes her transition. I will need time to readjust to a different way of living.

Riding up to Flint and back with me this afternoon seemed to revive Mother. She was able to eat dinner by herself tonight. My hopes were diminished a short time later, however, when she began moaning, groaning, and shaking, saying her head hurt. I gave her an aspirin, put a cold cloth on her forehead, sat beside her, holding and stroking her hands. That seemed to ease the discomfort.

Thursday, January 26

I'm wearing Mother's rings, and they are beautiful! Mother is so happy to see them on my finger. I have the warmest feeling when I look at them, realizing they are symbolic of my parent's marriage and love into which I was born.

I'm tired tonight. I'm weary of caregiving. All I want to do is rest and not be responsible for anyone or anything.

Sunday, January 29

Mother wasn't feeling well tonight. As I helped her to the couch to rest after dinner, she said that she looks forward to me "putting her down." I cradle her head and shoulders, similar to putting down a baby. It's all I know to do. I have no book or anyone to guide me.

Tuesday, January 31

Wow! January sure did fly by. It's been only a week since Mother has been feeling better. She's still pathetically weak. I continue to feed her, although it is only the last half of her dinner now. I don't mind in the least. It is a very loving time for us. Few words are spoken. None are needed.

Wednesday, February 1

This was a Flint day and my annual doctor's appointment. He declared I was perfect and had "the health and body of a thirty year old!" He added I was remarkable for my age group, whatever that means. I felt on top of the world as I bounced out of the office.

Tuesday, February 7

This was my first day of volunteering with the AARP Tax Aide program. Mother is happy I'm doing this. She's a great advocate of volunteerism. The tax returns I prepared today were simple, and the people were grateful for the service. I enjoyed the short respite from my caregiving responsibilities.

Mother was anxious for my return. I saw her watching at the window when I turned into the driveway. She was hungry at dinner, but upchucked most of it. Maybe her anxiety had something to do with that.

Friday, February 10

Mother had a dream about the clothes in which she wants to be buried. "I want my blue suit, like in my picture," she said referring to a recent church directory picture.

I said I would abide by her wishes. "Are you planning to leave soon?" I asked.

"Yes, any day now," she responded.

Monday, February 13

After a good night's rest, I feel much better this morning. Today's thought is to **stay in the flow**. Just cruise along, doing what I need to do, but allow the current to carry me. Don't push any faster, and don't resist. Stay in the flow.

My reading from the current issue of the *Science of Mind*[8] magazine was thought provoking. When I *choose* to do things, rather than thinking I *have* to do them, the effect is totally different. Everything is a choice. I clean the house, take showers, do the laundry because I choose to be clean. I prepare balanced meals because I choose to be healthy. I'm living down here because I choose to care for Mother. When I choose to do something, I enter the task more relaxed and with a sense of joy, rather than with tension and resentment. I've always known how important it is to have a choice. Now I'm beginning to understand why.

8   Jennings, Rev. Jesse. "Doing More and Better," *Science of Mind* , February 1995, p. 65.

Tuesday, February 14

What a pleasant surprise I had today! Pat sent a beautiful arrangement of cut flowers. I was truly touched, not only by the beauty of the flowers but by Pat's loving thought. She is such a supportive friend!

Wednesday, February 15

While I kept Mother company at breakfast, she told me about a dream she had last night. She was raking the lawn and sowing grass seed at the cottage. I laughed, commenting that she must really be hungry after working so hard in her dream. She looked at me in a no-nonsense way and said very emphatically, "That was *not* a dream."

Oh, okay! Who am I to gauge the distance between a dream and reality? Perhaps it is closer than I think.

Thursday, February 23

I drove up to Flint this morning to meet a new tax client. When I returned, Mother was dressed, had fixed her own breakfast, but had left everything, including the milk, on the kitchen counter. She was so relieved to see me walk in the door. She thought I'd been out all night! *Wonder what she thought I was doing.* From now on, I'll be sure she sees me in the morning before I leave. There's never an end to this learning.

I'm so tired tonight. This has been an energy-sapping kind of day.

Friday, February 24

Visited with Eleanor and her husband for a few minutes this morning. We enjoyed some good laughs. I need to do that more often.

As I was helping Mother get dressed today, she told me I was spoiling her. I asked if she liked that. "No," she answered, "but I'll take all I can get at my age!"

That's exactly the way I feel, too. She may be one spoiled mother, but she deserves every bit of it.

Sunday, February 26

A note from this morning's telecast: **Strength is the energy of God.** I certainly could use a refill!

I'm so tired of having to plan everything I do around Mother's unpredictable schedule. I resented rushing around today to complete all the necessary errands—seventy-five per cent of which were for her—and make sure I returned before she awakened. I am so tired of this giving, giving, giving. If strength is the energy of God, where was it today?

Monday, February 27

Mother looked weary this morning when she awakened. She told me she didn't want any more work to do.

"What have you been doing?" I asked, curious to hear about this recent dream.

"I washed the kitchen curtains and the bathroom, too, " she told me proudly. "You should see how nice the kitchen curtains look now. Do you think I should wash the shower curtain, too?"

I suggested putting it in the next load of laundry.

Tuesday, February 28

I've chosen to write in bed tonight. I want to be absolutely quiet. The only sound I want to hear is the scratch of my pen across the page of this journal. I'm reviewing the events of this day, although it would be far easier to just "close the book" and forget it all.

I was uptight all day. Very resentful. Easily irritated. Mother decided to get up at ten o'clock this morning, which wouldn't have bothered me except that I wanted to finish the laundry I had started. At the time, the last load was in with just ten minutes left. Mother, of course, couldn't wait, so I had to take care of her "getting up" needs between running back and forth to the basement. I had too much "piling in" on me and couldn't handle it.

I don't understand this feeling of resentment. Is the accumulation of the past five years getting to me? I think I'm handling everything well, but then these feelings creep up and I begin to wonder and question. I'll just take it a day at a time and know that this, too, will pass.

Friday, March 3

Do something you love doing today and enjoy it!
Yes, I did! The day was filled with good happenings.

First, the upholsterer came and I selected new fabric for two chairs. Mother was pleased, and so am I.

Later, Mother agreed to my suggestion to have a hearing evaluation. She needs a new aid, one that will stay in place. Perhaps an "in the ear" model would work.

Then, while at the store this afternoon, I saw one of my tax clients. She expressed how pleased she was with my work and said that she referred her sister to me. That compliment brightened my day.

The good happenings didn't stop. When I paid the rent for this month, the office receptionist told me how much she liked the hangers Mother covered for her a couple of years ago. I relayed the compliment to Mother. "Should I make some more for her?" she asked, pleased with the recognition of her work. I wish she could.

Then, to cap a great day, we won both variations of solitaire tonight. Mother was delighted! She loves to win. Her competitive spirit is still very strong.

Wednesday, March 9

Today's journal thought hit home! **Accept and experience all your feelings. They have much to teach you.** With all the feelings I've been having lately, I have loads to learn!

LATER

I can't believe this day. Four times I had to rinse out panties Mother had wet—one an hour. Then, she dropped a pad into her commode, and I had to fish that out. "Did I do that?" she asked when I showed it to her.

I'm expected to take care of everything, to clean up the messes, and still keep on giving. I seldom hear words of appreciation, although Mother has said several times, "I don't know what I'd do without you." But hearing the simple words of "thank you" or "I'm sorry, I couldn't help it," once in a while would be a comforting help.

There was a bright spot to the day, however. Marcia and Dave came for dinner. Since tomorrow is Marcia's birthday, I made it a birthday dinner, complete with cake and ice cream. Everyone thoroughly enjoyed the meal, and I relished the opportunity for conversation. Fresh voices! Fresh thoughts! Believe me, I took full advantage of it!

Tuesday, March 14

Another gorgeous morning. I raked the small patio garden and was thrilled to see spring flowers beginning to emerge. I don't know what they are—hyacinths? crocuses? maybe tulips? It's exciting to see the new growth and anticipate the hidden beauty. Each time I look out at that tiny garden, I have a new idea for planting it this spring.

LATER

Mother is having incontinence accidents more frequently. I wonder if the lack of control is due to one of the several mini-strokes she's had. I learned something today, though, which saved me a lot of work and Mother much embarrassment. She struggled to get off the sofa from a nap and needed to get to the bathroom immediately. I knew she'd never make it, so I brought the commode to her. That was easier for both of us. I continue to learn!

Sunday, March 19

I unearthed the rubber stamping materials today and played! I'm thrilled with the Easter card I created. I had so much fun making that card, whistling and humming while I worked. It's been a long time since I've felt that much joy.

Tuesday, March 21

My bedtime reading last night was from a book I've loved, *In the Flow of Life* [9] by Eric Butterworth. As I often do when rereading favorite books, I allowed the pages to turn randomly and began reading where they stopped. Last night, I read the pages on death.

I liked what I read. The author suggested that rather than waiting until a time of bereavement, keep the thought in mind now that life keeps flowing continuously without any time frame, without a beginning or end.

I like that. Life just keeps flowing on. It's a peaceful thought.

Wednesday, March 22

This was definitely not a good day for Mother. It was mid-afternoon before she got up. Eating breakfast exhausted her, and it didn't stay down, either. Just as I finished that clean up, she had an accident. A short time later, I had still another change of clothes to rinse and launder. Within less than two hours, I was the exhausted one.

Mother did tell me that she was sorry, and I thanked her for that with a hug. I can only imagine how humiliating it must be for her.

Friday, March 24

Mother's mind is playing tricks on her. Tonight she asked me about "the girls who take money from my account, give it to charity, and give the interest to me." I didn't have a clue.

9   Butterworth, *Eric. In the Flow of Life*. Unity Village, MO: Unity Books, 1991.

Mother is slowly ebbing away. She doesn't eat much now—only a spoonful of everything. It's important for me to serve a variety of foods in order for her to get a balanced diet, limited as it is.

Sunday, March 26

I wonder what I would have missed had I not chosen to care for Mother during these last years of her life. I wouldn't have known the tremendous love we've shared, the tender feel of her soft, frail hand in mine, nor would I have shared in her dreams which have given me a glimpse of what is to come. As the speaker said during this morning's telecast: **Every situation I find myself in has been planned as an opportunity for my growth.**

Saturday, April 1

A peaceful night's rest and a beautiful morning. Snow is predicted—a typical April Fool's gift!

Cris arrived with a bouquet of miniature carnations in delicate shades of pink and white. Quickly, she transformed them into artistic arrangements so their beauty could be enjoyed in every room. Then, while I prepared dinner, she talked with Mother and helped her recall our long friendship and all the things Mother had made for her: covered hangers, slippers, and the necklace/bracelet set she was wearing. (That delighted Mother so much that she offered to make another set for her!) Mother seemed to enjoy the conversation, especially having Cris' undivided attention.

Mother never ceases to surprise me with her memory recall and lapses. Yesterday, when we talked about Cris' anticipated visit, she remembered where Cris sat the last time she was here for dinner a few months ago. And she was right! Sometimes her memory is so sharp and clear, other times so confused.

Friday, April 14

Watching Mother's decline and living with it full-time may be getting to me. It depresses me to see her so feeble, knowing it will only get worse. In spite of two crying sessions today, an afternoon nap, and a two mile walk this evening, I'm very, very tired emotionally. When this is over for me, I will want a long reprieve from having to physically care for anyone. I will want to run and be free.

Saturday, April 15

This afternoon a floral arrangement arrived from Alma, a friend from Flint. The card said she was thinking of us at Easter! It was a delicate and beautiful arrangement: a white basket, decorated with lavender ribbon to match the blooming African violet plant, nestled with English ivy. I called to tell Alma how her loving gift miraculously turned my morning slump into a beautiful day.

Sunday, April 16

This is Easter Sunday.

Last night Mother asked if I was going to work today. When I told her it was Easter, she thought for a moment. "Where are your new clothes?" she asked.

"In the store!" I said with a laugh.

She caught the humor and laughed, too.

LATER

Mother could hardly finish her dinner. Gently, I helped her to the couch, thinking she'd rest for a while. Wrong! She was up within two minutes to wash the dishes, of all things.

I'm back to feeling like a yo-yo—up and down, up and down. One minute Mother acts as if she's at death's door, and the next minute she's up and at 'em. I can't change it. I'm just going to have to accept and flow with it.

Saturday, April 22

Why is my body so tired this morning? What have I been doing that I can sleep as deeply as I did yesterday afternoon for forty minutes, sleep soundly all night for eight hours, and still feel tired?

Sunday, April 23

Real learning comes <u>after</u> I think I know everything. I heard that thought on this morning's telecast and have been rolling it around in my mind ever since. Where am I at this moment? I know I'm far, far from knowing everything. But, if I ever do come to that point, is there still another level of learning?...miles to go before I sleep?

LATER

Mother asked what she should do if I died, wondering how I wanted her to settle my estate. I told her to stop thinking like that unless she expects to live fifty more years! She laughed. Sometimes, Mother acts as if she's ready to "check out" any minute; other times, she talks about out-living me. She must think that because Jack, Bob, and Dad are gone, she has to look after me. She's still a mother, and a mother's love for her child is deep and unwavering. That is a comforting thought.

Monday, April 24

I was able to participate in a matting/framing workshop at a local art store this afternoon. I enjoyed the two hours and came away with a variety of mat cutting ideas I'm anxious to try. I didn't worry about Mother, but neither did I waste any time returning. All was okay.

Sunday, April 30

Thoughts from this morning's telecast:

Be honest with your feelings.

**Repressed anger is dangerous because it can be expressed unex-
pectedly in "not so pretty" ways. Recognize your
feelings and express them at the time, while you're in control.
Constructive use of anger becomes love!** (That's interesting!)

LATER

I applied what I learned. Mother started to get up early. I wasn't ready
to compromise my quiet time to take care of her needs, which included a
shower and shampoo today, in addition to the usual routine. I could feel
the anger beginning to well up inside my body. Calmly, I explained to her
that the inconsistency of her sleeping habits didn't allow me to establish a
routine for myself, something that was very important and necessary for
me. She accepted that, returned to bed, and slept until noon!

I'm so glad I was able to get those feelings out. I was able to identify
the anger immediately and then express my feelings in a calm and reason-
able way. The anger was dissipated almost instantaneously. And the miracle of it was Mother's understanding!

Monday, May 8

I'm sensing that a change is imminent. I recall a similar feeling around
this time of year eight years ago. That resulted in retirement four months
later. Then, two months before Mother's first stroke five years ago, that
ominous feeling of change emerged again.

I'm beginning to wonder if....

LATER

Just as I turned out the lights to go to bed, Mother put on her signal
flasher. She wanted me to stay with her. Assuring her that I was right
there, and always would be, she lovingly touched my arms, stroking them
and holding my hands. I stayed with her for a few minutes before tuck-

ing her in with good night kisses and words of love. She said she loved me, too.

Fifteen minutes later, I heard her get up and went in to check. "I didn't call you," she said, surprised to see me. It comforted her, though, to know I was there.

Tuesday, May 9

Getting back into the groove! Enjoyed baking muffins today and sharing them with the neighbors.

Mother slept all day. In fact, she has slept for twenty-two out of the past twenty-four hours. During her awake time this evening we played cards. She seemed more focused than she has been lately. That was her only activity today.

Wednesday, May 10

Just before I left to run a couple of errands, I checked on Mother. My instinct was correct. She'd had an accident and wasn't aware of it. As usual, she watched me clean up the mess without saying a word—until I asked. She told me she would have thanked me, but was waiting for me to finish cleaning up everything. Oh, my.

She believes that all this is temporary and that things are going to get better. I had to be frank. "I hope for both of us that things won't get worse," I told her, "but we had better accept that they might and work with it."

I know that was a hard pill to swallow, not only for Mother, but for me. We can't kid ourselves.

I am alone. I have no one with whom to share this responsibility. In my low moments, I toy with the idea of hiring someone to stay with Mother a day or two. That wouldn't resolve anything, though, because I'd still worry. Mother tells me she wouldn't know what to do without me. Her time is short, and I want to be with her.

Thursday, May 11

After another accident today, I told Mother she might need to wear a diaper, that the pads were not enough protection. "Those pills I take are the problem," she told me. She said nothing as I cleaned up the mess. Neither did I.

Later, in the privacy of my room, I cried. Mother cannot accept that she's in the condition she's in, and I cannot force that acceptance. She continues to fail. Her appetite is diminishing; the number of hours she sleeps are increasing. She is becoming more feeble, unable to control her bodily functions. Now I'm thinking about diapers? Where is the quality of life?

Friday, May 12

Pat's weekly letter arrived today. It was so supportive and encouraging that I was compelled to write this immediate response:

> *Already I've read your welcomed letter twice! My greatest need is conversation. There is almost none with Mother. She doesn't hear well enough. I interact with the television, with books, and with journal and letter writing.*
>
> *There aren't many visitors or phone calls these days. As time goes on those have diminished. We are an "instant" society. We are great about rushing in when there's an emergency, but, when the "cure" isn't instant, folks tend to get on with their own lives and give only a fleeting thought to those with long-term needs. No one likes to be around sadness or anything that would remind us of our own mortality. I understand that and have tried to be upbeat when talking and writing.*
>
> *You and Cris have heard my tears, my anger, my resentment, my bitterness, my struggles. Others have no idea. I am a strong person, but I have my moments of weakness and times when I need someone to help me see what I cannot see for myself.*

Mother continues to sleep almost twenty hours a day. She has no desire to step outside, unless it's to the car to go some place.
I have no idea what's ahead but know I'll meet the challenge.

Saturday, May 20

Mother emerged from her bedroom this morning wearing only her pajama top. When I asked where she was going, she told me she was going to get up.

"You don't have any clothes on," I told her.

I helped her dress. Then she went back to bed and slept for another four hours!

While Mother slept, I did what I loved best. I baked muffins to share with the neighbors and an angel food cake to go with the rhubarb/strawberry compote I'd made. That was delicious! Eleanor had a sample taste and heartily approved.

Mother got up at noon and emphatically told me that she was tired of "those scissors."

"What scissors?" I asked.

"You know, what I had to use for that work," she told me.

"What were you doing?"

She didn't know.

I asked if she was finished.

"No, there's more to do."

And so Mother continues to be productive, if only in her dreams.

Thursday, May 25

"Why did Dad leave?" Mother asked me at dinner.

Her out-of-the-blue question startled me for a second. I answered that he'd had a heart attack and inquired what she was thinking about.

"Oh, I just wondered where Dad was and when he was coming back," she responded.

When I told her Dad had died twenty-five years ago, she looked at me in wide-eyed surprise. "Why, I didn't know that."

A minute later, she wanted to know if I'd brought his body back here. I assured her that everything had been taken care of. I never know what Mother is thinking or where she's coming from.

Monday, May 29

When Mother awakened from her after-dinner rest, I jokingly said she'd better get up because the dishes were crying for her to wash them!

"Oh, let them cry." she said, unswayed by my not-too-subtle, manipulative technique.

I laughed, but continued the charade. While she was slowly making her way into the kitchen, I told her that the dishes were *so* happy she was going to wash them.

"Ha!" she laughed. "You're the one who's happy!"

Mother is so sharp at times.

Thursday, June 1

"We're off to get you beautiful!" I sang to a tune from the *Wizard of OZ* musical while driving Mother to the beauty salon to get her hair permed.

"Yes," she laughed, "the the top of my head!"

Her sense of humor still comes through.

The two-hour procedure took its toll, but Mother was able to eat a good dinner tonight—and feed herself, too. Maybe the new "do" perked her up.

When she awakened from a three-hour rest after dinner, she said she'd do the dishes so "they wouldn't cry!" However, instead of going into the kitchen, she went into her bedroom and began undressing.

"What are you doing?" I asked.

"I'm going to get dressed," she said, totally unaware that she was.

Saturday, June 3

What a wonderful afternoon I enjoyed with Cris! I looked at the pictures and listened to the stories about her recent trip to China. For a little while I was taken away from my caregiving responsibilities—a delightful respite, indeed.

Cris saw Mother's decline and the extent of the care she requires now. Several times, she shook her head saying that she couldn't do it. Frankly, I never thought I'd be doing it, either, but you do what you have to do.

Sunday, June 4

Mother stunned me today when she asked how Evelyn liked the cake she'd baked for her. Quickly recalling a dream she'd had the other day, I played along.

"Oh, what kind was it?" I asked. "I've forgotten."

"A white one," Mother responded without hesitation. (That was true in her dream, too.)

I said that Evelyn didn't mention it, reminding her how forgetful her friend is sometimes. She agreed, and that was the end of that conversation.

Mother was going to climb into bed tonight without undressing. She is becoming more and more confused. She didn't remember upchucking her dinner tonight, either. When I asked if she was hungry, she looked perplexed. "Why should I be hungry?" she asked.

Monday, June 5

I've had many thoughts lately about Mother's transition. She seems to be losing ground faster: more memory loss, no appetite, so tired all the time.

During breakfast, Mother told me she'd had the nicest dream last night. "I saw Dad and the boys (my brothers)," she told me smiling. "They were waiting at the gate and were so happy to see me!"

"What were they wearing?" I asked, trying to glimpse further into the details of her dream.

"Oh," she said, her face beaming, "They were all dressed in white and were so happy! They asked about you, too."

It gave me a warm feeling that I was a part of this beautiful dream.

LATER

Mother couldn't eat dinner tonight. I don't know what I'm going to do. I'm concerned about her loss of appetite.

Thursday, June 8

Did I have ambition today! I baked the most delicious rhubarb pie, as well as a dozen butter tarts and three dozen muffins! Mother saw the pie and nodded her approval, but she didn't want any, even though she loves rhubarb. What was I going to do? I had this whole pie that looked picture-perfect with its toasted meringue top, but there was no one to eat it.

Friday, June 9

Found some pie-eaters! I gave half of it to the maintenance fellows. Did they ever enjoy the treat, saying I should enter it in a baking contest! Eleanor had a piece, too, and declared it to be "just right." I was pleased.

Wednesday, June 14

When Mother got up at noon, she was all smiles. "This is going to be a big day!" she informed me.

"Oh, why is that?" I asked.

"Don't you remember? Today is the day I renew my driver's license!" she said with a bounce of delight.

"I think you're a little early," I cautioned her.

Mother looked at me in surprise and asked why.

"Because you do that on your birthday."

She asked what month this was, and then remembered her birthday is in August.

Sunday, June 18

This past week, Mother's appetite has diminished significantly. She is able to eat her usual bowl of oatmeal, loaded with brown sugar, but I feed most of it to her. She hasn't been able to eat dinner all week. I've relied on a nutritional drink for her nourishment, supplemented with a scrambled egg, muffin, or Jell-o with fruit. Eleanor made some rice pudding which Mother enjoyed. It's difficult to come up with a variety of soft foods.

I'm back to cooking for myself now.

Monday, June 19

As I looked out of the window over the parking lot this morning, I noticed Irma's daughter's car. Irma, one of our neighbors, has emphysema. Her daughter, Karen, has just retired and plans to be here to take care of her mother who will continue to need more and more help. She is just beginning this journey; I'm nearing the end.

Watching my mother's body slowly begin to shut down, I know that it will soon be her time to leave. When I see her body, all I see is just that: a body, an appearance. Beyond is a beautiful soul that is nearing the end of its purpose on this planet.

LATER

I took Mother to the doctor this afternoon. I showed him the newspaper article I had saved regarding a "do not resuscitate" form.

"You know," he said, "the best way around all this is through Hospice."

I hadn't given Hospice a thought since two years ago.

I told him Mother wasn't a Hospice patient.

"She could be," he responded kindly. "She certainly qualifies. And you could receive some help."

All I had to do was to make the contact, he assured me, and Hospice would take care of the rest. It sounded too good to be true.

Later, I shared the good news with Eleanor. What a relief to know that we're going to get some help—finally. The right people are coming into our lives at the right time.

Tuesday, June 20

I talked with Marlene, the receptionist at the Hospice office in Plymouth this morning. She took the necessary information and said that Cindy, the nurse coordinator, would call me very soon to set up an appointment.

Cindy called within thirty minutes! She had already talked with Mother's doctor and could be at our apartment immediately.

Is this really happening or is it just a dream I'm having?

There were numerous papers to sign, much to talk about—and many tears to be released. All was completed by noon. Mother was happy to meet Cindy, especially when I introduced her as the nurse the doctor sent.

LATER

I can't believe the peaceful relief I'm feeling. Mother's name will be sent to the Plymouth Township Police and Fire Departments today. There will be no resuscitation efforts. Now, she'll be able to make her transition with peace, with dignity, and in the familiar surroundings and love of her home. It is so reassuring to know that I have help as we journey into this unknown territory ahead.

Wednesday, June 21

Was yesterday real? Do we really have Hospice services now? Do I really have someone to call?

I see the magnetized card on the refrigerator listing, in large boldface type, the Hospice phone numbers for twenty-four hour help.

Yes, it is true and I'm no longer alone.

I've cried so much these past two days. The tears just continue to flow. I don't know why. Maybe it's the relief of finally having help. The burden of Mother's care was weighing so heavily on me. I didn't know how heavy it really was. I just had to keep going. That's all I knew to do. Now we have help.

My reading this morning was about nonresistance. **To resist something is to empower it.** When I resist tears, or other signs of emotion, I empower them—but I want the opposite! I'll just let the tears flow now, as they will, and not try to hold them back. They will lose their power and gradually subside.

LATER

The tears flowed at unexpected times all day.

Marian, it's okay. Don't resist. Let the tears flow. They have no power over you. Don't give them power. Just let them flow. It's okay, Marian. It's okay.

Within a few seconds, I was in control once again—until next time.

Thursday, June 22

Jackie, our Hospice nurse, spent two hours with us this morning. What a wonderful person! She is so kind, so caring, and very competent. Mother liked her immediately and seemed pleased to know that she would be coming each week.

Jackie told me that with the decreased appetite, Mother would become weaker and may not be strong enough to have a shower. When, and if, that time comes, she will send an aide to help me bathe Mother in bed. Whatever the need may be, Hospice will be there to help. I can't begin to describe the peace of mind that gave me.

Tuesday, June 27

I'm thinking about a recent dream Mother had about work. She was crocheting something, not sure what. "I worked all night on it," she told me. I asked if she finished it. "Sure!" she answered definitely. There was no question about it. When Mother starts something, she finishes it!

I wonder if that was symbolic of resolution for her life, that she has finished all her projects and is ready to go on.

LATER

After Jackie checked Mother today, we sat at the dining room table and talked. She said Mother's pressure was the best today, although she was picking up a heart irregularity. She went on to say that as her diminished appetite gradually weakens her, she may not be able to walk. When that time comes, Hospice will provide a wheelchair. Later, I may have to feed her in bed. Jackie believes Mother's death will be very peaceful, that she'll just sleep away. I know she is preparing me for what may be ahead.

Wednesday, June 28

Pat, the social worker from Hospice, came out to see us this afternoon. Actually, she was more interested in talking with me than Mother, who was sleeping, anyway. I enjoyed our conversation, especially the sharing of common experiences we'd had in working with emotionally impaired children in the public schools. It was comforting to know that Pat will make weekly visits. I'll certainly look forward to those two hours of conversation!

Thursday, June 29

I awakened this morning thinking about the social worker's visit yesterday and my feeling of slight discomfort afterwards. Pat had suggested having volunteers come in to give me some respite. I'm not ready for that. Now that we have Hospice, I'm doing fine. I want to remain in this new comfort zone for a while. After the emotion of last week, I need rest and quiet time to regain my sense of equilibrium.

Perhaps this is what happens as death nears and acceptance takes place. I feel the need for privacy. What is happening now is so deep, so very personal, and so awesomely beautiful that I can't explain it to anyone. Unless someone has seen me through the agony and pain of the past five years, they don't know. And it's too much for me to try to explain.

Monday, July 3

While enjoying the peacefulness of the evening on the patio this evening, I closed my eyes and was still. I was aware of a soft glow all around me. Then, in the distance I saw a beautiful garden. Yearning to see more, I tried to move closer.

I heard a childlike voice say, *If I only knew when Mother was going to leave.*

Do you really want to know, Marian? a compassionate Voice responded.

No, I guess I don't, my child voice answered.

The Voice continued. ***I will let you know. Trust me. I have led you this far, and I'll lead you further. Just trust me. I haven't let you down, and I won't.***

There is absolutely no doubt in my mind. I know now that I will know. I can relax. God is in charge!

Tuesday, July 4

I cried a lot while Jackie was here today. The lack of sleep last night may have caused me to be so emotionally vulnerable. I couldn't control the tears. Jackie understood.

Later, Mother had an accident which required a big clean up job. I was angry because she'd refused to take the medicine Jackie had suggested to control that problem. She'd tried to clean it up herself, resulting in a bigger mess. That was upsetting, although I did recognize her effort to help. It took almost an hour to get everything clean. I was so emotionally distraught that it was difficult to calm down long enough to do it.

LATER

The toll of five years of caregiving and having to clean up accidents for the past year appears to have added up today. The pain of it all is like nothing I've ever experienced.

It's so difficult watching my mother—the one who gave me birth, who nurtured and raised me, who protected me from danger until I learned to protect myself—become the one who now needs nurturing and protection.

It's painful watching this person who was once so strong, so independent, so dependable, so capable—become weak and dependent, with no control over bodily functions. Her life is completing its cycle, returning to where it began. My mother needs me now to feed her, to bathe her, to wipe her, to "mother" her—to protect her.

It's *so difficult*—and *so very painful.*

Thursday, July 6

Mother has lost five pounds in the past ten days. She's down to one hundred twenty-nine pounds now. I'm concerned.

I'm beginning to feel isolated. So much is happening to me and no one comes around now, or so it appears. The letters and phone calls are less frequent, too, although I continue writing five letters a week. People shy away from sadness, especially death. This is a lonely time.

I mentioned this to Jackie. She said this happens, that impending death frightens people because it causes them to face their own mortality—something they don't want to do.

Yet, this is the time when the support of friends and family is needed the most. I didn't realize that before, at least not in the same way I know it now. I'm learning there are times in life that one must face alone—all alone. Evidently, this is one of those times for me.

LATER

While showering Mother today, I was aware of how very tired I was. I cupped my hands around my mouth and talked very softly to myself: *Marian, you are going to do only this one task today. There is nothing else you need to do. You will be very patient, knowing how much slower Mother is now—and you*

thought she was slow before! Remaining very kind, compassion-
ate, and calm, you will do what needs to be done by you—one
step at a time.

It worked! I was even more patient than usual.

It's 7:30 in the evening and the bathroom still hasn't been cleaned.
It's okay.

Saturday, July 8

Marcia and Dave stopped by. Company! Mother enjoyed their visit,
too, even though she rested most of the time. As they were leaving, she got
up, stood in the dining area with her walker, and really talked with them.
This was so unusual that I stepped back to observe and listen. I was
momentarily removed in thought: *I want to remember this beautiful*
moment. Mother is so alert, so responsive. I don't want to forget, It may never
come again.

Monday, July 10

We are in our fourth week with Hospice. The caring, compassionate,
and competent professional services they are providing just keep getting
better and better and better! Jackie assured me that is was okay to call at
any time, day or night, if only with a question. I'm not alone.

I'm discovering I'm able to do only one thing each day. Tomorrow it
will be Flint. Wednesday will be laundry day. I'm very tired.

Lost myself tonight in the "Boston Pops" telecast. Getting caught up in
the music for a few minutes revived me.

Tuesday, July 11

Mother's minister plans to come out tomorrow afternoon. I have
updated the computer notes I'd written about her life. I'll give the pastor
a copy when I ask if he would do the funeral service for Mother.

I took two naps today. I'm really weary. Perhaps the relief I'm feeling, since Hospice has come in, is allowing all the accumulated tiredness from the past five years to surface.

Wednesday, July 12

Mother is noticeably weaker, but she keeps pushing herself. She was exhausted after slowly walking her route inside the apartment twice today. She wanted to wash the dishes. Reluctantly, she took my suggestion not to do them because of her back. That ingrained value of perseverance will never leave—not until she takes her last breath.

Thursday, July 13

While running errands yesterday, I saw my life in thirds. The first thirty years were the growing-up years. During the second thirty, I buried my family, and spiritual growth began. The final thirty or so years are unknown, but I know there will be new experiences, challenges, and many learning opportunities.

Friday, July 14

Jackie loaned me two books[10,11] from the Hospice library on caring for aged parents. The words touched on everything I have experienced in the last five years, assuring me I was not alone, that I belonged to a fellowship of thousands of other caregivers who shared the same feelings. The reading lifted that darkening cloud from my mind and offered me a measure of peace.

Why do I feel guilty when, in my lowest moments, I resent my mother's helplessness, her dependency upon me? My outbursts show my own deep concern, my capacity to feel emotion. I have wept oceans of

10 Grollman, Earl A. *When Your Loved One is Dying*. Boston: Beacon Press, 1980.
11 Grollman, Earl A. *Caring for Your Aged Parents*. Boston: Beacon Press, 1978.

tears. They've unlocked and released my pent-up emotional tensions as nothing else could. Afterwards, I've been able to continue on.

Resentment? Oh, yes. Just when I thought Mother was slipping away and that death would release both of us, she improved. It deepened my despair. It weakened my resolve to hang on.

I was angry. At times, I beat the air with my fists and cried out in the privacy of the basement or bathroom. How could I possibly face one more mess that spread over her clothes, the floor, the bed, the bathroom?

I wondered if the day might dawn when I would lose complete control. If so, who would take care of her? There's no one left but me.

I am so exhausted. My sleep is broken with uneasy dreams. More often now I experience headaches, dizziness, weakness. There have been moments of panic when I thought I was losing it all. I have always been so strong, but now it seems I've succumbed to weakness.

I made funeral arrangements, contacted Hospice, talked with the minister, wishing inwardly that Mother's passing could be tomorrow. Then I could rest. Then I could be at peace.

When is all this going to end?

Sunday, July 16

What I miss the most, and desperately need, has been good conversation. Hospice is providing that. I don't need anyone to come in and relieve me so I can go out. I just need someone to come in and talk with me. Jackie and Pat do that, and it's working wonders.

As usual, I kissed Mother good night saying, "See you in the morning!"

"Hope so," she replied.

This was different from her usual affirmative response. It left me wondering.

Tuesday, July 18

I'm getting fleeting glimpses now—nothing specific, just a global brightness and sense of happiness—of what is there for me in the not-too-far future. Maybe that's the proverbial "light at the end of the tunnel." The tunnel isn't completely dark, neither is it scary or claustrophobic, but it is confining. I sense I am slowly moving through it. I'm not afraid.

LATER

When I called to make an appointment today for maintenance service on my house, I told the receptionist that I was caring for my elderly mother who was dying and needed to schedule my time very carefully. That's the first time I have actually verbalized that Mother was dying.

Mother's dementia is worsening. Tonight, she told me she was going to give up bowling.

"Oh?" I responded.

"Yes," she said. "It takes too much out of me."

I agreed that was a good idea.

She hasn't bowled in five years.

She is letting go.

The Sixth Year

Wednesday, July 19, 1995

My journals have been my most trusted friends during these past five years. Absolutely everything—my hopes, my frustrations, my happiness—has been recorded, sometimes scribbled with angry jabs of the pen, sometimes blurred with tears, but more often scripted with a legibility that showed I still "had it together" and hadn't completely lost my mind or my control. Writing has been my safe harbor. It has allowed me to release feelings, to discover and unwrap new ideas, to find solutions to challenges and answers to needs—needs I didn't know I had!

Thursday, July 20

Mother had a dream in which all her friends came to visit her. She couldn't remember who they were, but she was so happy they came. I asked if she had a good time. "Oh, a grand time!" she said, her face glowing. She told me this was a birthday party. About a hundred people were there including her doctor, Jackie, Dad, Bob, Jack—everyone who had been important in her life. She wasn't sure where the party was held, but thought it was here. Oh my, a hundred people in this apartment!

Friday, July 21

I shared Mother's latest dream with Jackie when she visited today. She was fascinated.

Jackie has observed a steady decline in Mother during the month she has been with us. She said it's too early to put a "time" on it, but death is coming.

Saturday, July 22

I got up before dawn to check on Mother. I couldn't believe my eyes. Her bed was empty! I checked the living room, the bathroom. She wasn't there. I returned to her bedroom and cautiously looked on the other side of the bed. There she was on the floor, huddled between the bed and the closet—with her head on her pillow!

Immediately, I checked for broken bones. Nothing was hurting. The next challenge was how to get her up and out of that narrow space. I couldn't lift her and knew I desperately needed help. *Hospice!*

The on-call nurse was here within thirty minutes. With the exception of two abrasions on her forehead, Mother was okay. We managed to move her from the floor to a sitting position, then to a standing position, and finally back into bed. She went to sleep immediately, none the worse for the experience.

"I guess we need the hospital bed now," I said, recalling what Jackie had told me a couple of weeks ago. The nurse agreed and said she would place the order.

After the nurse left, I starting shaking. My knees felt like gelatin, and my heart was doing double time. I was the one who was worse for the experience. Mother was sleeping peacefully, and I felt like I had climbed the Matterhorn!

It was only 8:30 a.m.

Sunday, July 23

A notable thought from this morning's telecast: **Problems age you, but projects engage you—and keep you young!** I'll have to think about that after this last experience.

Monday, July 24

What a day! Jackie called this morning to say the hospital bed would be delivered today. I went into action immediately to prepare the room, finishing just as the delivery truck pulled up. Jackie arrived minutes later to help. She pitches right in, doing whatever needs to be done at the moment.

Mother asked Jackie if all her patients were like her. Jackie laughed. "No, but I wish they were, and I wish all caregivers were as good as Marian!"

Mother likes her bedroom, but she's not too sure about the new bed. It is much narrower than her own. She will adjust to it, eventually.

I'm looking forward to sleeping in a *real* bed tonight. It happens to be the one I had growing up. I've come full circle in my sleeping arrangements.

Tuesday, July 25

Mother seemed to have slept well. I certainly feel more relaxed. With the side rail up on her bed, I know she's safe and won't fall out.

Pat, our Hospice social worker, visited this afternoon. She brought an interesting article about caregivers. I can understand why some folks would shy away from a caregiving situation. It is not easy, believe me. Not knowing how long the care will have to be given, the extent of it, whether one can maintain and endure what needs to be done for the long term, and whether one is *willing* to make the commitment—are extremely important issues.

LATER

Eleanor brought us a piece of fresh raspberry pie she'd just baked. It was so good—my very most favorite pie!

I'm definitely bridging my way back to a single life. For the past two months, I've been eating alone. Also, moving into a larger bedroom and a real bed is preparatory to moving back to my home. The process is gradual.

Wednesday, July 26

Mother was passive tonight. When we said our usual good night, her response to "see you in the morning" was "perhaps." She's never said that. She is ready to leave. I think the hospital bed has had a "giving up" effect on her. I have no regrets about ordering it, however.

She drank eleven ounces of water today. That's her lowest intake.

Saturday, July 29

Joanna, another hospice caregiver, called. In sharing our mutual experiences of caring for our mothers, we talked about what I call the "yo-yo effect" and she labeled "the marathon." When our mothers have seemingly been at death's door, we would psyche ourselves for it, emotionally and mentally. Then they would rally—but not for long. I felt anger being put through that emotional pain, only to know I'd have to go through it again. Joanna had the same experience. It was a relief to know I wasn't alone with that feeling.

Sunday, July 30

Marcia dropped by tonight. Mother had that distant look in her eyes, as if she wasn't really here, although she seemed to enjoy playing solitaire with Marcia.

After Mother was settled in bed, Marcia and I sat on the patio and talked. I shared some of Mother's recent dreams (the undertaker, the party, and the one about Dad and the boys dressed in white) to show her how ready Mother was to leave. I shared her dreams of doing things to explain that "unfinished business" sometimes causes a person to hang on until "whatever" is completed. Marcia listened intently.

Monday, July 31

I mentioned to Mother that she had a birthday coming in a couple of weeks. She looked at me in surprise. "Yes," I continued, "you'll be ninety-seven. Wow! That's a lot of years!"

She didn't say anything, just smiled and shook her head.

"Not many people spend ninety-seven years on this planet." I put my arm around her shoulders and whispered, "You're planning to be here for it, aren't you?"

She didn't say anything.

"Don't check out on us yet," I gently admonished.

She was unresponsive.

Mother's water intake dropped to a mere ten ounces today. She is losing ground right before my eyes.

Tuesday, August 1

Mother was noticeably weaker when she got up today and very slowly made her way to the bathroom to wash her face. She could hardly walk. I put her face cloth and towel on the vanity, so she wouldn't have to reach for it, and positioned her walker beside her at the sink. "Little things," but they help conserve the scant energy she has. I noticed an indentation in her back caused by pressing against the side rail of the bed. I hung a piece of sheepskin over the rail to protect her fragile skin from the pressure.

A storm was gathering while I fed Mother her breakfast. The thunder rolls and strong wind were beginning to make me feel anxious. I mentioned it. "I'm here!" Mother whispered reassuringly.

The maternal instinct to protect and comfort her child is still there. I smiled.

LATER

When Jackie visited this afternoon, we talked about how "the end" might look. She told me to call Hospice immediately if there was any change in Mother.

My feelings of ambivalence seem so strange. I know "the end" is coming and fairly soon. I know it is inevitable, but the reality of it gives me a frightening feeling. Yes, it's fear. Fear of the finality...fear of my emotional reaction...fear of all that I'll need to do...fear of the future...fear of being alone.

Wednesday, August 2

While grocery shopping, I indulged in buying two cinnamon rolls to go with my mid-morning coffee. Have to be good to myself!

Mother was awake when I returned. As I bent down to speak into her ear, she put her hand up and lovingly stroked the side of my face.

I won't have much longer to feel those loving caresses that only a mother can give. It prompted another flood of tears. Yes, I'm grieving. But as I flow with the feeling, it rolls on by like a wave on the lake. There may be other waves, but if I ride them out, as I did as a child at our Lake Huron summer cottage, there's no hurt. They will pass.

LATER

Mother and I set a record tonight. We won three games of solitaire! Our victorious feat brought a smile to Mother's face and a nod of "that's the way to do it!" Even in her weakened condition, she's still a true competitor.

Her voice was barely above a whisper tonight. She's noticeably weaker. I hope we get through this weekend without a need to call the Hospice emergency number. I'm beginning to dread the weekends.

I opened a new bottle of Mother's blood thinner medication today. I dated the bottle and wondered if that would be the last one.

Saturday, August 5

I treated myself with a trip to the rubber stamp store this morning for their annual Customer Appreciation Day Sale. It was such fun selecting scrumptiously colored ink pads, as well as new rubber stamps. Because I had an "X" on the bottom of my ice cream dish, I won a door prize! (Yes, at 10:30 in the morning, I enjoyed a strawberry sundae!) I was only there for an hour, but it felt like I'd been on a vacation. "Mini-vacations" like that help to keep me balanced during these challenging days.

LATER

I never thought I'd say it, but I did. Mother got out the dishpan and was going to do the dishes—all of one plate and one knife. (I had washed the others earlier.) "No, Mother," I told her, unable to believe she had the strength to lift the dishpan.

"Why?" she asked like a child.

"Because I said so," I answered in exasperation.

I never thought I would say that to my mother. Have I crossed over the line? Am I now the parent?

Sunday, August 6

Sitting on the patio this evening in the peaceful quiet of the warm summer air, I closed my eyes. It was only seconds before I was aware of a soft glow surrounding me. I relaxed, immersed in that warm glow which became brighter and brighter. It was so comforting. I felt my body relax deeper and deeper as I allowed myself to become more enveloped by that penetrating, yet gentle, glow.

Faintly but clearly, I heard the words: *I am with you!*

I strained to hear more.

The words were repeated—softly, tenderly: *I am with you!*

That was all I needed to know

I am not alone.

I don't need to see beyond the moment.

All I need to do is trust.

Monday, August 7

I had a couple of crying jags this morning. The tears come so unexpectedly. They pass by, though, just like waves—like those little ripples I used to watch in the lake. Some would begin building up to become breakers, but if there was no energy force behind them, they'd lose momentum and quietly dissipate. Others, fueled by the force of the wind and current, would continue rising to a crest and then come crashing on the shore.

Tears are like that, too.

LATER

Mother strives to keep going. She walked four times around the living room tonight without resting. It took her five minutes to walk each round, a distance of twenty-two steps that would take me less than thirty seconds. I can only imagine the amount of energy she expended—and she has so little now. Bless her heart, though, she perseveres to keep those legs moving.

Friday, August 11

A large leaf on the African violet plant is dying. My first inclination was to remove it. I tugged it very gently, but it was still secure, not ready to let go yet.

I see the lesson to be learned. The plant is a microcosm of life. The blooms are gorgeous, evidence that the plant is flourishing. The young leaves are healthy, vibrant, standing upright on their own. But the aged leaf is drooping and has separated itself from the plant, the center of life. A new leaf is ready to take its place.

I think of Mother.

Monday, August 14

Mother was so pleased with the many birthday cards she received today! I taped them on the mirror in the living room. She liked that.

While helping Mother get ready for bed tonight, I mentioned that she'd be ninety-seven in the morning. She looked at me with mocked suspicion.

"How do you know if I was born in the morning?" she countered. Her sense of humor is still there!

I wish tomorrow was here. I so desperately want Mother to celebrate her ninety-seventh birthday. She is only seventeen hours away now. She'll make it.

Tuesday, August 15

Mother made it! She has lived longer than any member of her family. I wished her *HAPPY BIRTHDAY* with a big kiss and hug at 6:30 this morning. She smiled and then returned to sleep.

I busied myself in the kitchen, baking the favorite Coca Cola birthday cake. I cut out large numerals for ninety-seven, covered them with foil, and inserted a few candles in each to raise it off the cake. That added just enough sparkle and "specialness."

Dave and Marcia came in the evening for the quiet celebration. Mother was able to stay up for a half-hour, just long enough to blow out the candles while we sang "Happy Birthday." She couldn't eat the cake, but was pleased to see the rest of us enjoying it. She was exhausted and asked to be helped back to bed.

Thursday, August 17

Driving back from Flint this morning, I realized it would be much better to have a Hospice volunteer stay with Mother on the days I make that trip. I called Doreen, the Director of Hospice Volunteers, when I returned. She was glad I called and will work on getting someone to come one day a week for four hours. Also, I put in a request for the Hospice beautician to cut Mother's hair.

Pat brought a birthday card signed by everyone at Hospice. Mother was so pleased that *fifteen* people remembered her!

Friday, August 18

I was up and down with Mother every five minutes from 3:00 until 4:30 this morning. She said she was restless. I hope the aspirin I gave her helps. I'm so tired.

The aspirin did relax Mother enough to allow her to sleep for four hours. During the past twenty minutes, however, she has been up to her commode three times. I must tell Jackie. Something is happening, I'm sure. This is unusual behavior. It was a wise decision to request a volunteer for the mornings I'm in Flint. I'd be a nervous wreck, more so than I am now.

LATER

Jackie came this afternoon and ordered a sedative for Mother. She said the restlessness may be due to low fluid intake.

Sunday, August 20

The half-tab of sedative didn't do the trick last night. Twenty minutes later, Mother was still restless. I gave her a full pill and that worked.

When I awoke at dawn to check on her, she was awake. She said she'd just made a bank deposit!

"Oh, how much was it?" I asked out of curiosity.

"Twenty-four dollars!" she immediately responded, so proud of her accomplishment!

Yes, Mother is still "taking care of business!"

Monday, August 21

Mother was extremely restless tonight. She would get out of bed, turn around, and crawl right back in. Up and down, up and down—for the next three hours. Finally, I gave her one of the tranquilizers.

It had no effect.

I slipped another one of the small pills under her tongue, but she still kept popping up and down like a jack-in-the box.

Before I gave her the third one, I called the Hospice emergency number. Serita, the on-call nurse, said to give her the third pill and she'd call back in a half-hour to check on the result.

Mother was still restless, continuing to get up, turn around, and then go back to bed...repeatedly. Serita said to give her another pill, assuring me it was perfectly safe and that I could give her up to five.

The fourth didn't have any effect, so I popped the fifth.

That did it. Mother is finally asleep.

How long will this go on?

Tuesday, August 22, 1995

What a night! About 1:00 this morning I was awakened by a *THUD*. I shot out of bed and into Mother's bedroom where I found her sitting on the floor with her back against the side of the bed. I managed to get behind her to put some leverage under her arms. Then, with one big thrust, I was able to get her up on her feet—but only for a second. Her knees buckled, and she slumped back into my arms. Immediately, I knew it was the medication.

Somehow, I was able to get her back into bed. I put up the side rail and told her to push the button for the flasher signal when she needed to get up again. She was so groggy, though, I knew she didn't hear me. I stayed awake the rest of the night listening for her to stir.

Needless to say, I feel like a zombie this morning. Mother is still sleeping soundly. That's good.

Restlessness is an indication of the beginning of the end. It even has a name: terminal restlessness. Both Serita and Jackie explained that they often see it a few days prior to death, but it can continue longer. That information elicited a flood of tears. In spite of expecting and accepting, there is nothing that totally prepares one for the impact of that final moment.

LATER

Pat and I had a nice visit this afternoon for two hours. I really appreciate the time she spends with me each week, as well as her calls in between to hear how we're doing. Pat is so perceptive. She knows my "emotional barometer" reading immediately by the tone of my voice and the words I don't say. I was tearful today, but Pat understood. I'm so tired from lack of sleep that I'm very vulnerable. Mother can't get up at all now without my help. I'm even more confined.

This evening, Mother and I talked about my birthday which is tomorrow. I told her that Cris was coming. "I wish I could give you something," she said.

With tears streaming down my face, I kissed her. "You have given me the most precious gift I could ever have."

"What's that?" she asked.

"You gave me life. Without you, I wouldn't be here." I helped her recall the event sixty years ago and how happy she and Dad were that I was the girl they'd hoped for.

"And I'm still happy I got my girl!" Mother said.

I hugged her and told her that she's the best mother I could have had. She gave me her signature smile of pleasure.

I'm so glad I had that opportunity to express my feelings to Mother while she could still hear and understand.

LATER

It took twenty-two hours for that tranquilizer to work out of Mother's system. She was very relaxed tonight. I didn't give her any sedative.

Wednesday, August 23

HAPPY BIRTHDAY to me! It's number sixty!

The day began with an urgent call to Hospice. Somehow, Mother had twisted herself around to the *opposite end* of her bed and was unable to move. My efforts to turn her were futile. Serita came to our rescue once again. Thank God for Hospice!

LATER

Cris arrived around noon, bringing a gorgeous bouquet of pastel gladioli and all the trimmings for a birthday celebration. Jackie came to check Mother and teasingly chastised me for not telling her it was my birthday! The Hospice beautician arrived to cut Mother's hair. Plants, flowers, and cards arrived all day. It was like Grand Central Station around here!

It was mid-afternoon before Cris and I had time to enjoy the pizza and salad she'd ordered and the birthday cake she'd brought. The best gift, however, was our conversation. As usual, the time went by much too quickly. I'm so grateful for our beautiful friendship.

Thursday, August 24

Bill, our neighbor, died this afternoon. He would have been ninety-five on Saturday. Another man in our building died in March. If death comes in threes, will Mother be next?

Friday, August 25

I slept sporadically last night, not sure if Mother would use her flasher signal. When I tucked her in, I mentioned that the bed rail was up for her safety. "I'll climb right over it!" she informed me. I don't believe she could. She certainly would injure herself if she tried. That's something more to worry me.

Saturday, August 26

Karen, Irma's daughter, wants to talk with me about caregiving. She is just beginning this journey full-time. I don't know what I can tell her. The most important thing I've done is allow my mother to do whatever she can for herself. That was difficult at times, especially when I could do the task so much faster. I put myself in her place, though, and realized what it would do to my self-esteem if someone started doing everything for me, even those tasks I could do for myself. I recalled how I worked with children in the classroom. Many times, I would have to sit on my hands and allow them the time they needed to learn by doing. In Mother's case, if I hadn't allowed her to do what she could, I would have taken a very important "something" away from her.

LATER

One of Mother's friends visited this afternoon. What I thought was going to be a nice reprieve turned out to be an emotionally disastrous time for me. I resented her questions. I'm very sensitive right now and so vulnerable. To make matters worse, Mother upchucked while the friend was here and had an accident later.

No one knows.

Sunday, August 27

Another nerve-wracking night. Around midnight, I heard a *CRASH* and bolted out of bed into Mother's room. There she was, standing between the door and the night stand, facing the wall. The lamp was on the floor. I was in utter disbelief! *How could she have gotten out of bed with the rails up?* I looked. Yes, the rails were still up.

Mother clung to the wall, afraid of falling. When I took hold of her, she collapsed in my arms. Somehow, I managed to maneuver her to the commode. I sat beside her and tried to calm my rattled nerves. I tried to be controlled, but, in my panicked state, I scolded her for getting out of bed alone.

She said nothing.

A few minutes later, she crawled back into bed.

I returned to bed but couldn't sleep, fearful of what might happen next. I toyed with the idea of sleeping in a chair beside Mother's bed in order to keep watch, but quickly dismissed that idea, realizing it was not a viable long-term solution. *How could I make sure Mother would be safe?* I thought the side rails would be the answer. After tonight's episode they obviously are not.

As dawn came, I heard Mother getting up to use her commode. I went into her room and offered my arm for assistance. She refused it. Miss Independence!

I sat beside her and put my arm around her shoulder. "I love you so much," I told her quietly.

"Marian scolded me," she said petulantly.

I was aghast. *Doesn't she know who I am?*

"Who am I, Mother?" I asked gently.

"You are Marian," she answered, still looking down at her feet.

Whew!

"Marian scolded me," she repeated.

"Where is Marian?"

"Sleeping."

It was then that I knew I had two persona: the one who scolds and the one who is loving and compassionate.

"Why did Marian scold you?" I asked.

"Because I didn't call her," Mother answered, pointing to the button on the flasher unit.

I asked how she got out of bed with the rail up. She said she crawled out the foot! I looked. Yes, there was enough room. As the Hospice on-call nurse told me when I called earlier, she wishes she had a video camera to show how people, who have no strength during the day, do seemingly impossible feats at night. The power of the mind!

I've felt the pages of these last journal entries, gliding the tips of my fingers over them. They are like *BRAILLE!*

My emotions are very intense, to say the least.

Monday, August 28

Pat visited this morning. She mentioned the nursery monitor that Mary Jo, the nurse covering for Jackie, had suggested to me yesterday. I told her that I was interested and wanted to know how it would work.

Those were the magic words. She just happened to have one in the car that I could use. Hospice folks are incredible!

The monitor is really super-sensitive, even picking up Mother's breathing. It's going to work just fine. I'll continue to have Mother use the flasher signal, but if she doesn't, like the other night, the monitor will alert me.

Thursday, August 31

Thank goodness for the monitor! Mother had the same restless behavior she demonstrated a week ago—crawling in and out of bed repeatedly every ten minutes. I hoped it wouldn't last long, that she would just tire herself out and fall asleep from exhaustion. That didn't happen. I continued to listen on the monitor to the squeaks and creaks of the bed as she crawled in and out, but I didn't get up until I knew the restlessness wasn't going to stop. This time it took only one tranquilizer to settle her.

Mother awakened this morning just before Sarah, our Hospice volunteer, arrived. "I'm very easy to take care of," she told Sarah when I introduced them. That's true except for nights like last night. I kissed her goodbye and said I would be back from Flint in three hours. Then the tears started flowing. I hated to leave Mother. I'm not sure if the tears were because of the "trying" night, Mother's significant decline, my lack of sleep, or the fact that this was the first time I would be leaving her in the care of a stranger.

Maybe all of the above.

Friday, September 1

Mother was restless again last night. She even said she was. It was the same routine of getting up and going back to bed, over...and over...and over. The tranquilizer settled her for about an hour, and I got some much-needed sleep. The monitor alerted me as she continued to crawl in and out of bed several more times before morning, but I didn't get up. Finally, she exhausted herself and went to sleep.

Sunday, September 3

Another restless night. Mother was up and down every ten minutes during the hour before I went to bed. I gave her a tranquilizer, but she was up again within twenty minutes. I slipped another one under her tongue. That zonked her out for an hour and a half, but then it was up and down every half-hour until 4:00 a.m. I'm glad I was with her because she would have fallen three times. Just before dawn, both of us finally got a little rest.

LATER

The restlessness began again late this afternoon. I called Hospice. Allison, the on-call nurse, heard Mother's agitation over the phone and said she'd come right out. She suggested a sleeping pill in place of the tranquilizer which makes Mother so groggy.

I rested a couple of times today and felt revived momentarily. I'm in desperate need of sustained sleep.

Monday, September 4

I'm experiencing, perhaps, the toughest challenge of my life. It's scary, downright frightening at times. I see a change in Mother. She is noticeably thinner and ever so much weaker. She's getting closer to making her transition.

Thursday, September 7

I was able to get Mother in the shower today and took the opportunity to shampoo her hair. I'm always so relieved when I can get that done. If I couldn't, Jackie would have an aide come out. I would rather do it myself. It's good, though, to know there's an alternative.

Friday, September 8

I told Jackie I wasn't going to give Mother any more of the tranquilizer unless it was absolutely necessary. I don't like the way she reacts to it. One of the many reasons I'm caring for her at home is so she can live comfortably. What was I doing by giving her the tranquilizer? I was trying to make her conform to a schedule that was not in accordance or harmony with her changing body. Jackie listened.

I felt depressed today, partly because Jackie said she'd be on medical leave for six weeks, beginning October 1st. I have such trust and confidence in her.

Doreen called to say that she has scheduled a Hospice volunteer to stay with Mother for six hours on September 20th. Now I will be able to accept the invitation to have lunch with Joanne and Lois, my friends from the University of Michigan-Flint. I haven't seen them in four years, so we'll have a lot of "catching up" to do. I'm looking forward to that date and the respite it will give me. Imagine six hours without worry! It's been a long time since I've had that much time for myself.

Saturday, September 9

It's amazing how Mother's mind works. The other night, her face glowed when she announced, "I had a dream!"

"Was it a good one?" I asked, eager to hear more.

"Oh yes!" she answered enthusiastically. "I was with Mrs. Petrie and we went to a show."

Recalling that Mrs. Petrie always used public transportation, I asked how they got there.

Mother thought for a moment. "We took the car, then the bus."

I couldn't encourage her to elaborate any further, but was happy that she'd had such a pleasant dream.

Sunday, September 10

Carolyn called this morning. She'll be coming to Michigan in two weeks and staying overnight. I invited her to stay here if she didn't mind sleeping on an air mattress. She accepted that offer enthusiastically!

Marcia came down this evening. She and Grandma played cards, giving me a break and Mother a new partner. Marcia was given firsthand experience of her grandma's decline when she saw Mother's confusion in dealing the cards. Her skills had obviously diminished since Marcia last saw her.

Tuesday, September 12

I've resumed my walking routine. Twenty minutes of physical exercise in the fresh air does wonders to clear the mind and lift the spirits.

LATER

During a break from our card game this evening, Mother walked her inside route while I stretched out on the couch. I dozed off. When I opened my eyes, Mother was slumped over her walker. I jumped up and grabbed her just as her legs crumpled, and she dropped to the floor.

At first I thought she'd died.

Then, I thought she'd had a stroke because her speech was incoherent. I covered her with an afghan, put a pillow under her head, and ran upstairs to get Eleanor.

After we lifted Mother to a chair, I called Hospice. Mary, the on-call nurse, came out immediately. Mother's vitals were fine. The walking had exhausted her to the point of collapse. Mary stayed and talked with me for a little while. Gradually, my rattled nerves calmed.

Thursday, September 14

Sarah came this morning and I drove up to Flint. I trimmed the shrubs and forsythia. Doing those simple tasks was very healing. I need to fertilize the lawn and weed the gardens on the next trips.

Jackie visited this afternoon. She thinks Mother had a slight stroke the other night. All her vital signs remain good.

As I helped Mother dress today, I asked, "How's that ol' ear?" referring to the ear that had the beginning of a pressure sore. "Not as good as a new one," she answered. What a sense of humor!

Tuesday, September 19

I slept off and on last night with the monitor next to my ear, alerting me of Mother's ups and downs, in and out of bed. When I got up with her at midnight, she looked at me in surprise. "I didn't call you. You must have good ears!"

Little does she know! She hasn't asked about the monitor on her night stand—and I haven't told her. I'll just let her continue to think that I have "good ears."

Wednesday, September 20

What a wonderful day! The volunteers and Jackie took excellent care of Mother. I had no concerns, whatsoever. The luncheon with Lois and Joanne was so enjoyable, especially our stimulating conversation. The University of Michigan-Flint campus has expanded to such an extent since my last visit that a tour was on the afternoon agenda. The new state-of-the-art library was awesome! The best, of course, was saved for the last: the Computer Writing Classroom—a project in which I am involved. That will be a dream come true when it's completed next month.

This day made me realize how relative everything is. I had six whole hours for me—something I haven't had in over a year. And it would not have been possible without Hospice. Thank you! Thank you!

Saturday, September 23

Carolyn is a very amenable guest, making herself comfortable immediately. She said she felt she'd "come home." Mother, always the hostess, asked if her bed was comfortable. "Oh, yes!" Carolyn answered enthusiastically.

"Don't tell anyone you had to sleep on the floor," Mother cautioned her. We had a good laugh about that.

It was a great weekend! The time went much too quickly, of course.

This may have been the last time Carolyn would see her grandmother.

Monday, September 25

Mother just told me something funny, even though she was serious.

"Marian," she said seriously, "I want you to go out to the store and get a dress."

I laughed. "Why should I buy a dress?"

"For Easter," she answered.

"What kind should I get? A fancy one? What color?"

"Oh, I don't know. Get what looks good on you."

I wonder what she's thinking.

Tuesday, September 26

I slept well last night. Mother did, too. I got up once to cover her, and it wasn't long before I heard her snoring. That relieved me. Her snoring used to irritate me. I'd try to block it out by turning on my "good" ear. Not so last night. The deep rhythmic sound told me she was sleeping peacefully.

Ever since I decided not to give Mother any more of the tranquilizer, I've been more relaxed, more understanding and loving with her. I know her time is short. I want to make it as pleasant and comfortable as possible.

Now and then, the question arises: Why do others lose their parents so quickly while my responsibility continues? Two friends of mine lost their parents recently. Their burden has been lifted; mine continues. Why? I know the answer. I have more to learn.

Thursday, September 28

Mother is so childlike now. She has absolute trust in me. Jackie made me aware of that. I see myself doing more "motherly" things, such as tucking her in at night, feeding her, and kissing her forehead for no other reason than I love her.

When Sarah came this morning, I drove up to Flint. I fertilized the lawn, weeded the gardens and spread newspapers on them for mulch. In another three weeks it will be time to rake the leaves. Odd, I used to measure time by the season. Now I measure it by the week. All too soon, it may be by the day—then the hour.

LATER

Jackie came just as I had finished sponge bathing Mother. She noticed how tired I was and suggested having a health aide come to bathe Mother. I don't know. I like the flexibility of bathing Mother when I can and she is able. Bath time is a very tender, close time for us. I'm not willing to give it up. Not yet.

Saturday, September 30

Thought for today: **Miracles come from within me, not from outside.**

September is gone. When I try to think back to Labor Day, it seems so long ago. That's why it's important to enjoy each moment. Time is fleeting. It can never be retrieved, try as we may, except with pictures or mementos—or journals!

My mind keeps returning to today's thought. If miracles come from within me, that must be why I'm able to keep going every day. It would be so easy to lie down and give up, but I would never do that. Who would care for Mother? The miracle is that I have the strength to keep going and that we now have help from Hospice.

Sunday, October 1

Mother slept all night again. I think this uninterrupted sleep is indicative of the peacefulness she's feeling as she moves closer to making her transition. Everything seems to be slowing down: her walking, her eating, her toileting. Everything is in very slow motion now.

LATER

Showered and shampooed Mother today. That was a real challenge. She is so much weaker now and can do very little to help. I was glad to get her in the shower, though. Now we can get by with sponge baths and using the dry shampoo for a week or longer.

Journal writing is so great because it helps me discover the answers to challenges—answers that are already within me. After a frustrating experience of trying to feed Mother this afternoon, I was going to nap, to cry, to feel sorry for myself. Instead, I pulled out this journal and started writing. *Voilá!* The solution to my challenge appeared on the page!

I wrote:

> *Feeding Mother is also becoming more of a task. Her head droops. She doesn't close her mouth around the spoon and the food spills down her chin. It's easier to feed her at night when she sits in the chair in the living room and I'm sitting in front of her. When she sits at the table, I feed her from the side. Hey! That could be the problem! I need to try a different technique. Hmm. I might try using the tray table that came with the hospital bed. I could roll it out into the dining room, sit across from Mother and feed her straightforward. That would be easier. That tray table has been in a corner of her bedroom as a display area for stuffed animals—and collecting dust. Now it will be used for its intended purpose.*

Oh, the magic of journaling!

Monday, October 2

The new technique worked like a charm! Mother was able to feed herself a third of her cereal without dribbling because the table was closer to her mouth. It was so much easier feeding her the rest while facing her, like one would feed a baby sitting in a high chair. It's difficult, though, to watch Mother go backward from being an independent adult to a dependent child, yet in an adult body.

Tuesday, October 3

After I helped Mother dress today, I offered to bring a chair into the bathroom so she could sit at the sink and wash her face. She refused, saying, "No, I don't want to be babied." Her body may be weak, but her sense of pride and independence remains strong.

Wednesday, October 4

Mother is now aware of how weak she has become. She accepted the chair today, agreeing to sit while washing her face and brushing her teeth. That helped to conserve the little energy she has. We have another challenge, though. She is so bent over now that she's unable to put her head back far enough to rinse her mouth. Tomorrow I'll have her use a straw to sip the mouthwash for rinsing. That should help.

Thursday, October 5

I was up only once with Mother last night. She wondered how I heard her get up, saying that she didn't make any noise. I told her I just happened to be awake, not mentioning the monitor. "I was hoping you'd come," she told me as I helped her back to bed. "And you did!"

"Why did you get up?" I asked

"I didn't know what else to do."

How limited her life and her thinking is becoming now.

LATER

I believe I witnessed the beginning of the end tonight. The signs were there. Mother could not swallow her oatmeal, the only food she's able to eat now. Her voice is so weak that I have to put my face close to hers to hear what she is saying. Her water intake was a mere nine ounces yesterday and only seven today. But, in spite of her weakness, she insisted on walking her inside route twice—very, very slowly. What remarkable will power!

I'll be relieved to see Jackie tomorrow.

Friday, October 6

Mother now has difficulty crawling back into bed. I wonder what's ahead. I cried and cried last night, asking God to please not let her suffer.

Karen, the Hospice nurse covering for Jackie, called. I told her about Mother's difficulty in swallowing. She said she'd be here shortly. After hanging up the phone, I sobbed and sobbed.

Karen was so reassuring. She explained that Mother will come and go in her ability to swallow, that stroking her throat would help. The difficulty comes because she "forgets" what to do with the food in her mouth. It is all part of the dementia. It even has a name: "chipmunking!" She told me not to worry if Mother goes three to four days without eating.

Karen has been caring for her own mother for the past six weeks. Her eyes popped wide open when I told her I was in the sixty-third month of caring for mine.

LATER

Mother got up at 7:30 this evening. She said she didn't want anything to eat, and I didn't force the issue. She had difficulty swallowing a pill; eating would have been out of the question. Her liquid intake hit an all-time low today—only six ounces. This is the fourth consecutive day that it has been under ten ounces. I don't see how her body can go on much longer.

Saturday, October 7

My thoughts are on Mother making her transition. How will I respond when well-meaning folks tell me that I should be grateful, be happy, and not feel any grief because my mother "lived such a long life?"

As I look at those words—*grateful, happy, not feeling any grief*—I think yes, I can feel all that but not because she lived ninety-seven years. I can feel it because I was able to care for her lovingly and compassionately when she needed it. Yes, there will be grief. I'm beginning that process now. My gratefulness, my happiness will come because I will have no regrets. If I had to do it again, I would do it the same way.

LATER

I just returned from a short trip to the rubber stamp store. What fun on a gloomy, rainy morning! What a welcome release for my tension! I rewarded myself by buying the stamp to make this year's Christmas cards. Not knowing what's ahead, I want to begin the cards now.

I stopped at the bakery, too. The sight and mouthwatering aroma of all those varieties of freshly baked breads was such a comforting treat. What comforts the body somehow comforts the spirit, too. I bought the Michigan cherry/walnut bread and shared some of it with Eleanor and John. It was still warm when I brought it home—and Mother was still sound asleep.

This is the third consecutive night that Mother hasn't wanted anything to eat. Her liquid intake was only five ounces today, even lower than yesterday.

Monday, October 9

Jackie's surgery date has been rescheduled. It's such a comfort to know that she'll be with us for the next two weeks. All the Hospice nurses are terrific, but Jackie has known us from the beginning. That makes a difference.

Mother's vital signs were good when Jackie checked her this afternoon. She continues to weaken so Jackie ordered a wheelchair, just in case I need it.

Jackie was ready to estimate the time Mother has left, but decided against it. "I really don't know," she told me. "Your mother is writing her own book."

Mother was awake for only two hours today.

Tuesday, October 10

Received an early Christmas card from Elaine, my niece in Idaho, and her family. Enclosed were two tickets to the Red Wing hockey game on Saturday, November 4th. I was overwhelmed. I would love to go, but I didn't see how it would be possible. In her note, Elaine suggested that Marcia or a Hospice volunteer could stay with Mother. *But who would I ask to go with me?* I thought about Dave. He seemed pleased. Yes, he'll take the day off, and Marcia will stay with Mother. Things do work out. There's always a way.

Mother is very restless tonight. She's been up and down, in and out of bed every ten or fifteen minutes. Finally, I was able to encourage her to come out to the living room for a little while. She whispered that she wanted me to talk to her. Sitting beside her and holding her hand, I reminisced about Carolyn's visit, the family pictures that Elaine had sent, just anything I could think of to talk about. I don't know if she understood my words, but I think that hearing my voice and feeling my love, as I stroked her hands, was comforting. Before helping her back to bed, I gave her an aspirin, hoping that would relax her enough to sleep.

Wednesday, October 11

The aspirin had no effect. Mother was up and down until 1:15 this morning. She'd get up, turn around, crawl back in bed, and within seconds repeat the routine. I listened on the monitor. Finally, I got up and asked what she was doing. "Getting up and turning around," she said as if it was the most normal thing to do. I helped her back to bed, covered her up, and lovingly stroked her arms and hands. Perhaps the warmth put her to sleep—or pure exhaustion.

She slept for just two hours before starting the up and down routine again. My soothing touches didn't work this time. The restlessness continued for two more hours. I gave her a drink of water which settled her for an hour. Then, the up and down routine began again.

Enough was enough. At 7:30 this morning, I slipped a tranquilizer under her tongue. Twenty minutes later, she was wide awake and ready to start the routine again. I gave her another tranquilizer, talked soothingly to her, and stroked her forehead. *Finally*, she fell asleep.

I'm exhausted.

This sounds terrible. But after no sleep last night and knowing that Mother is dying, I'm very ready for it all to be all over. That, I believe, is my final surrender and final acceptance.

LATER

Jackie called this morning. When I described last night's events, she emphatically told me that if Mother is restless tonight, "Don't wait!" I am to give her two tranquilizers *right away* and if that didn't zonk her out, a half-tab more.

She said that Mother might need to be sedated, and that "it" (meaning the end) probably would be in a week.

I know now this is terminal restlessness.

Mother slept most of the day and was very groggy when she awakened. It just pains me to see her like that and know that it was caused by the medication. I had no choice, though, but to give it to her—for her sake and mine.

LATER

Mother noticed the monitor and asked what it was. "Oh, that's just a room freshener," I said without skipping a beat! She nodded. If she knew I was "monitoring" her, she would have been very upset. Ignorance is bliss.

The wheelchair arrived today. Oh, my, did Mother give it a disdainful look! When I suggested trying it out tonight, she would have no part of it, insisting on using her walker. It took all the strength that she could muster to walk the distance of twenty short steps from her bedroom to her chair in the living room. She was so determined.

I suggested using the wheelchair for the return trip, but there was no way she was going to succumb to that. It was painful for me to watch her labor with each measured step, using every ounce of the meager energy she had left. I walked behind her, my arms outstretched ready to catch her at any second. I've never seen such determination and perseverance.

The restlessness returned shortly after I tucked Mother in bed tonight. I followed Jackie's instructions implicitly. Two tranquilizers had no effect whatsoever. Fifteen minutes later, Mother's body was still in a constant state of agitation. I could feel the twitching in her hands. I slipped another half pill under her tongue, gently massaged her hands, stroked her forehead, and talked soothingly. *Finally*, her body surrendered to the medication. Now I really know what terminal restlessness is.

Thursday, October 12

I didn't sleep well—or much—last night. Mother needed to get up only once to use her commode, but she was so groggy that it was difficult getting her back into bed. I felt the strain in my back from lifting her.

I didn't sleep much after that. My mind was racing, and the tears were flowing. Each time Mother goes down another notch, the grief starts all over again. All of what I'm experiencing is part of the process which I must go through. I know and understand this, but experiencing it is so difficult. Each step, however, prepares me for the next. I know that.

LATER

After checking Mother this afternoon, Jackie said that her vital signs were normal. Her electrolytes may be messed up, though, due to the low fluid intake. She told me to begin with two tranquilizer pills tonight, as I did last night, adding half-pill increments every fifteen minutes as necessary.

Two pills didn't do it…nor did another half…nor another half…nor another. By then, I was really concerned. I called the Hospice emergency number.

Mary, the on-call nurse, said to give her another half-pill and wait thirty minutes. I followed her instructions. Mother is finally sleeping and all is peaceful.

AN HOUR LATER

Thinking that Mother was zonked out for the night, I called Mary to let her know. While we were talking, I heard a *CRASH*. Dropping the phone, I ran to Mother's room. She had gotten out of bed, but her legs were so weak she fell. Somehow, I had the strength to lift her back into bed.

Mary was still there when I returned to the phone. She said to pop another half-pill under Mother's tongue.

I panicked. That's four and a half and the max is five.

I'm terrified. *She was so groggy with two. What will four and a half do?*

I'm so scared. *Am I doing the right thing?*

Mary assured me that it was okay. My body began calm.

What would I do without Hospice?

TWENTY MINUTES LATER

After all that tranquilizer, Mother was still agitated. But I didn't want to give her the last half-pill. She was so groggy. I put up the side rails, thinking she wouldn't have the strength now to get over or around them. I stroked her hands and forehead.

The medication finally took effect.

I fell into bed—totally exhausted.

Friday, October 13

I did sleep until dawn. I got up to check on Mother and was amazed to see that she had pulled the lid to the commode into bed with her! *She must have been going strong all night long, poor soul.* She was awake so I helped her up to the commode. Getting her back into bed was a struggle. She was very groggy, and her body was just dead weight.

This apartment is a mess. I haven't even washed last night's dinner dishes. Who cares? Mother should sleep all day. I'll have time to get everything cleaned up.

Mother's minister is coming by this evening. I doubt that Mother will be awake, but that's okay. I need him.

In her tranquilized stupor yesterday, Mother still wanted to get up "to do some work." She said she had figured out what to fix for dinner. She couldn't tell me what it was, except that it had "lots of things" in it. I assured her that since it was only noon, she had plenty of time to prepare it and could go back to sleep for a little while. She agreed.

Last night, in her grogginess, she asked if I had locked the doors. She told me that she'd locked the front door. I checked. The door was locked! I'm still trying to figure out that one.

LATER

By 10:00 this morning, the dishes were done, I'd finished breakfast and was in the midst of paying bills when *whammo!* All the emotion from the last strenuous hours hit and I was knocked for a loop. My legs were as wobbly as jelly, I was shaking uncontrollably, and I couldn't stop crying. I knew I needed help.

I called Hospice and asked for Pat. She wasn't in, and I started crying again, totally out of control. Sue, the receptionist, said she'd page Pat. She was so kind. Two minutes later, Jackie called to tell me she'd be right out. Pat arrived a few minutes later. Hospice is so responsive, so sensitive to needs.

The three of us sat at the dining room table and talked. Jackie and Pat told me that I needed help, and this time I agreed. I'm so tired. I told them to do whatever they thought we needed. I no longer knew.

Jackie set up a schedule for me to give Mother the tranquilizing medication throughout the day in order to keep it in her system. She bathed Mother and called in the order for a health aide to come out Monday, Wednesday, Friday. Pat stayed to talk and reassure me.

My gratitude for Hospice knows no bounds!

Saturday, October 14

What a peaceful night we had! It was heavenly. Keeping the tranquilizer in Mother's system worked. What a relief to see her sleeping so peacefully! I'm no longer fearful of the medication.

LATER

I called my cousin Doug in London, Ontario to let him know the latest turn of events. He said he'd call the other cousins in the area, and, yes, he would check into restaurants where our family could gather following the graveside service. It was comforting to talk with him. I'm so relieved, so grateful to have his help.

All was well until late afternoon. Mother fell as I transferring her from the wheelchair to the commode. It happened so suddenly, I couldn't believe it. There was no way I could lift her. Making certain she had no broken bones, I made her comfortable on the floor and ran upstairs to ask Eleanor for help. Thank goodness, Russ, her son, was there. He picked Mother up like a teddy bear in his strong arms and gently put her into bed. How thankful I was! The right person is always there when needed.

Later, my nieces, Marcia and Kathy, came to visit. Mother didn't know them. After they left, she asked, "Who were those people here?"

Inwardly, I grieved.

Sunday, October 15

It took four tranquilizer pills to settle Mother last night. I remained by her bedside for that hour or so, gently stroking her arms and hands. I kissed and kissed her, telling her how very much I loved her, that I would miss her when she leaves, but my love for her would always be there. Twenty minutes after the fourth pill, she dropped off to sleep. She slept all night and is still sleeping at 8:30 this morning.

I was able to get Mother up to the commode and back into bed this morning using the technique that Marcia had shown me last night. Jackie had put a draw sheet on the bed and had shown me how to use it to turn Mother. That is easier on both of us.

I'm glad tomorrow is Monday. Jackie will be back, as well as an aide to bathe and shampoo Mother.

LATER

A couple of hours of sleep does wonders! I feel so much better.

I just finished writing to Pat, my loyal friend in New Mexico. Writing helps to put my thoughts in perspective.

> *My mother is close to leaving her body behind....She will make her exit very peacefully, very quietly—just as she has lived her life. I have all of the arrangements in place now and am designing a memorial brochure to give to family and friends....I am very fatigued, more so than I can allow myself to realize right now....*

STILL LATER

I'm waiting for Allison, the on-call nurse. I gave Mother four and a half tranquilizer pills tonight. She was still so agitated, but I was afraid to give her any more. I called Hospice.

Allison arrived at midnight with the new medication. We got Mother settled, but Allison was concerned about me, telling me to go to bed and get some sleep. No one had to tell me that.

Monday, October 16

When I checked on Mother just before dawn, her head was off the pillow, and she was whispering my name. I gently kissed her several times and talked to her, assuring her I was there. She fell back to sleep.

Two hours later, she was agitated. Using a warm, moist face cloth, I wiped her face with gentle strokes, placed the cloth on her forehead, held and stroked her hands. I know how soothing and comforting that is. Mother did it for me many times when I was sick during my growing-up years. I did it for Bob several times, too, when he was in the hospital so ill with cancer. I'll never forget Bob telling me how good it felt. "You do it just like Mother," he told me.

Mother has just drifted back to sleep.

Tuesday, October 17

Last night was very difficult. Four tranquilizers did nothing. Mother was so restless. For three hours I was beside myself with worry. She kept trying to get up in spite of all my efforts to soothe and calm her. I wanted so desperately to comfort her, but nothing I did helped.

It was tearing me up. I called Hospice. The on-call nurse said I could give Mother more of the tranquilizer or just wait it out. I opted to wait it out. All night long, I heard Mother's heavy breathing on the monitor and got up several times to check on her.

When I went into her room early this morning, her opened mouth was so parched. She was too weak to sip any water, so I soaked a clean face cloth for her to suck. Mother held my hand so tightly. She was trying to say something, but all I could distinguish was my name. I was so frightened. Finally, I was able to release her grip on my hands long enough to call Hospice.

Cindy, the care coordinator nurse, talked with me. I was crying help-lessly. "What have I done to my mother? What have I done to her?" I kept asking. I was so afraid that I had given her too much of the tranquilizer. Cindy kept assuring me that I had done nothing except give her excellent care. She paged Jackie. Within minutes, both Jackie and Pat were with me.

Pat heard Mother whisper that she wanted to tell me she loved me. I put my face to Mother's ear. I told her I knew she loved me and yes, I'd miss her very much, but I knew how happy she'd be to see Dad, Bob, and Jack. I assured her that I'd be able to take care of myself, and that she'd always be with me, too. I told her it was all right to leave whenever she was ready. I thanked her for being my mother.

My face was drenched with tears when I stood up. So was Pat's. "That was beautiful," she told me. "You said the right words." We hugged each other. I truly thought my mother was going to die within the next few moments.

With Jackie's competent nursing skills, Mother revived. When she was resting comfortably, Jackie, Pat, and I sat down at the dining room table to talk. I totally surrendered Mother's care to them—again.

Jackie told me that a health aide would be out every day for two hours, beginning tomorrow afternoon. Pat said she was going to schedule volun-teers so I'd have company during the evenings, my most difficult time of the day. Jackie showed me how to liquefy the tranquilizer and give it to Mother with a spoon—definitely an easier and more effective technique.

Pat stayed with me the remainder of the morning. I needed someone and truly appreciated her comforting presence.

After Pat left, I took a short nap. I realized I need rest. The hardest time may be yet to come. I dread being alone this evening. I have done every-thing. Now, the only priorities are taking care of Mother and coloring the memorial brochures I designed.

Since Mother's vital signs remain so steady, Jackie can't give me a sev-enty-two hour time frame of when death will occur. That can change any-time, though. The dehydration she experienced this morning is an indicator of more changes to come.

Mother knows she's slipping. We can keep her as comfortable as possible, but the journey she is on is one she has to take alone. Bob, Dad, and Jack are waiting to help her to a new beginning. God is in charge.

Marcia came to spend the evening. My, how I appreciated that! She said she would come tomorrow night, too. I'm glad. It really helps to have someone with me in the evening.

Wednesday, October 18

This is the hardest experience I have ever had. I keep asking God to take Mother, even though I know that is just my human need to get this over with.

"What stop do I get off at?" Mother whispered to me today.

I smiled. "Heaven!"

Yes, she's on a journey. I have no idea how much farther she needs to go. Only God does. At the end of her journey, there is nothing but a divine love and happiness that surpasses anything I could ever imagine.

I feel very peaceful at the moment. I am sitting at the dining room table so I can watch Mother and be aware of any need she might have. The tears come and go as I write. I just let them flow.

Thursday, October 19

I was just too exhausted last night to journal.

Mother's restlessness started again late yesterday afternoon. She wanted to get out of bed, but I couldn't help her by myself. I tried to keep her occupied and as content as possible while waiting for Marcia to arrive. I filed her fingernails, massaged her feet and legs, fussed with her hair—just anything I could think of that was body contact. I was so thankful to see Marcia! Mother recognized her tonight and even asked about Dave. I was happy and relieved about that. It must have hurt Marcia when her grandma didn't know her two nights ago.

We got Mother out of bed and wheeled her around the apartment for "entertainment time." She soon tired. Before putting her back to bed, I gave her four tranquilizer pills at once, as Jackie had directed. In just a few minutes, the medication worked its magic. She relaxed and went to sleep.

I was elated about the effect of that massive dose. I can't describe how relieved I was to have Mother finally relax, all that terrible restlessness gone.

As Marcia was leaving, she said she sensed the peacefulness in the apartment. It wasn't there, she said, when she first arrived.

I got out of bed several times during the night to add moisture to Mother's mouth and lips. She seemed comforted by that. I only catnapped, listening all night to her heavy breathing on the monitor.

I'm scared. I'm afraid I'm not doing all that I should be doing, but I don't know what else to do.

Now it's shortly after 8:00 a.m. Mother is so restless. She has succeeded in getting her pajama top off and is trying her best to get out of bed, grabbing the side rail to pull herself up. It's all for naught. Since she doesn't have the strength to lift herself, she simply keeps moving her hand up and down the rail.

I called Hospice and talked with Cindy, the nursing coordinator. She said I should go to bed and sleep when Sarah comes this morning. I told her how hard this is and how I wish Mother could just go peacefully and not be so uncomfortable. She listened compassionately.

LATER

When Sarah arrived, I took Cindy's suggestion. I rested, but was unable to sleep.

Jackie made her visit later in the morning. All Mother's vital signs are right on. She said Mother may go on for weeks. She is not actively dying at this point. Jackie is prescribing a different tranquilizer, however.

LATER

This may be a difficult night. In order to determine the correct dosage of the new tranquilizer, we need to begin with a small amount, giving more at hourly intervals if Mother continues to be restless.

I wanted someone with me. I called Shirley, Mother's friend from her church. Shirley even canceled a dinner engagement to spend the evening with us. I was very touched by her kindness. She sat by Mother's bedside all evening, trying to soothe her and keeping a vigil while Mother tried to get up, over and over and over. I don't know how Shirley could stay there and watch—but she did. The restlessness was tearing me up. I couldn't stay in the room. I went to the basement and did the laundry.

Finally, after thirteen mg. of the new tranquilizer, Mother dropped off to sleep four hours later. I'm so grateful to Shirley. I would have been beside myself had I been alone.

Allison explained that the physical condition of the brain deterioration is the reason so much more tranquilizer is needed. That amount would have knocked me out for a week! As the brain further deteriorates, the medication will need to be increased.

AROUND MIDNIGHT

I'm reading the letter I received from Cris today. She enclosed a beautiful piece of poetry she'd written to me. As I read it, the tears flowed. I was so touched. Cris said she had every intention of writing a letter, but this poem appeared instead.

OF MARIAN
Another day, another night,
Each more demanding than the other,
Giving love and dignity to this being,
Aged, fulfilled, and dying
Before my eyes.
Her pain and discomfort
Are mine. But mine is more,
For she is a part of me
And I of her,
And when she is gone,
I shall stand alone.
Empty and full.

Cris Platsis Chamis

Friday, October 20

The days are becoming a blur. So much drastic change has taken place with Mother in just week. I'm in utter disbelief.

This moment is all I can handle. I keep wanting Mother to go, but there is a reason for all of this beyond my understanding. I need to relax and allow God work out the plan He has designed. Somehow I'll move through this day, one step at a time.

Mother awakened just a short while ago and greeted me with the warmest, most beautiful smile—one I'll never forget! Her eyes didn't have that awful drugged look. They were bright, and she was alert.

I changed her and offered some water. She took a few sips. "I don't want any more," she told me in the clearest speech I've heard in many days.

Yes, I am convinced that the new tranquilizer is her "drug of choice."

LATER

When Jackie arrived this afternoon, she said she sensed an aura of peacefulness in our home. She is absolutely thrilled that the new tranquilizer worked so well. Mother's vital signs remain on target.

This was Jackie's last visit. Mary Jo will be our nurse in the interim. Jackie said she'd call after she got "squared away" following her surgery. We hugged. I cried and wished her well.

Mother slept so peacefully today, not awakening until late afternoon. She wanted to get up, so I called Eleanor to help me transfer her to the wheelchair for a ride around the apartment. Mother touched the antique table that had been her mother's and fingered the lace tablecloth on the dining room table, the one she had crocheted fifty years ago. I talked about everything she looked at and touched. It was important to let her know she was still in her own home with all her things she loved.

This was such a good day! It's 10:30 now. Mother is sleeping peacefully, and I'm ready to go to bed.

Saturday, October 21

I was shocked when I awakened this morning and saw it was 8:00. Guess the nights of broken sleep caught up with me. I jumped out of bed and hurried in to check on Mother, afraid I'd been negligent in my responsibilities. She was sleeping soundly and peacefully. I was relieved.

I'm dressed, the bed is made. I'm now journaling and listening.

> *Thank you, God, for such a good rest last night for both of us…for leading Jackie to find the right tranquilizer…for the compassionate Hospice workers…for Cris whose support has given me untold strength…for Shirley who gave up a dinner engagement to sit beside Mother's bed…for ALL the people who are praying for us…for the understanding that You are answering our every need. You said You would be with me—and that's all I needed to know. I have no concerns about today, knowing that You will guide and direct me.*

LATER

When Mother awakened, she looked at me and smiled. "It's so good to be home!" she whispered. I hugged and kissed her, tears streaming down my face. I wondered if she thought she had been in some other place—like a hospital.

Marcia called to say that she'd be here tomorrow afternoon, and Eleanor said she'd help today. I won't be alone.

LATER

Theo came over this afternoon and helped me bathe Mother. I certainly appreciated that! We laughed when Mother said she didn't know why she had to be bathed so much.

Mother slept until early evening. My suggestion of coming out into the living room appealed to her. Eleanor helped me transfer her to the wheelchair, and for the next forty-five minutes I "entertained" Mother. Then, the restlessness started to return. Like one tries to comfort a fussy baby, I kept her on the move—"touring" the apartment, brushing her teeth, giving her a foot massage, fussing with her nails—until it was time for her medication. I tucked her in bed with a hug and a kiss, and ten mg. of the new tranquilizer. She was asleep almost immediately.

Peace.

Sunday, October 22

Listened to the telecast this morning.

> **Surrender the outcome; begin enjoying the experience.**
> **Attachment to the outcome causes a fight, a resistance, anger.**
> **Stay in the present, in the NOW moment. The result is serenity, peace, calmness.**

What a lesson! It was exactly what I needed to hear.

LATER

Mother whispered something to me this afternoon that I couldn't distinguish, but I did hear her say, "not very long now."

Was she was telling me it wouldn't be long before she would be leaving her body?

This evening was a sad repetition of the past two weeks. The restlessness continued for forty minutes before the tranquilizer worked its magic and sent Mother off to dreamland. Thank goodness for Marcia's help and company.

As Marcia and I put Mother into bed tonight, I saw a distant look in her eyes. It reminded me of the distant look that Bob had the night he died, a look that will be in my memory forever. Mother seemed to have a sense of resignation tonight.

Monday, October 23

Mother is sleeping peacefully this morning. I feel so much better, knowing that she's comfortable. It tears me apart when she is in distress of any kind, especially if I can't ease her discomfort.

Mother is so very precious to me. Not having her with me will be a huge loss, greater than I have ever experienced. I will never be the same.

LATER

The restlessness started again around 5:00 this afternoon. Shirley spent the evening with us. I was so thankful for her help and company. She stayed until Mother was sleeping peacefully.

Shortly after Shirley left, Mother awakened and the restlessness began again.

I slipped the medication under her tongue, hoping that would do it.

I'm exhausted.

The lesson I'm learning is this: It is impossible for me to look beyond this moment. It's as if a huge, windowless, steel door has been brought down to block my view of anything beyond where I am right now.

Yes, Mother continues to teach me—even in her present condition.

Tuesday, October 24

Mother was more peaceful this evening. As has become the routine now, I wheeled her around the apartment…filed her nails…massaged her feet and legs…brushed her teeth. Then it was time for bed. I gave her twelve mg. of tranquilizer. It is now two and a half hours later and she's still sleeping. I hope that'll hold her through the night.

Wednesday, October 25

I'm not sure Mother recognizes me this morning. She looks at me, responds to my voice, but there is no verbal communication—not even a whisper.

Yesterday, Pat told me there may be a leveling off period, like a plateau. How long it will last, of course, is unknown. After that, there'll be another period of rapid decline, but it will be fast—and probably the last one.

There have been so many times during the past two weeks that I have not wanted to go into Mother's room, especially during those agonizing periods of restlessness. Seeing her so agitated and uncomfortable, and not being able to do anything about it, tore me apart. I didn't want to leave her alone, though.

Mother is significantly weaker this morning. Her blood pressure is down to 90/60. Mary Jo said her vitals were weaker. That's the first.

My mother is still within her earthly body. Her hand still comes up to tell me "that's enough" when I give her a teaspoon of water, and she'll nod or shake her head in response to my questions. But my mother—the person I could tease, could enjoy talking with, could do things with—is no longer here. I have watched her slowly slip away. Yes, my mother is still in her earthly body, but that is all.

Friday, October 27

I slept well last night and feel rested this morning. Mother was awake when I got up at dawn to check on her. I turned her and gave her almost a half a cup of water, a teaspoon at a time. It's 7:30 now, and she's sound asleep. She's noticeably weaker. I gave her fifteen mg. of tranquilizer last night. The only sound I heard all night was her breathing.

When Eleanor and I transferred Mother from her bed to the commode this morning, I was very aware of how much weaker she is. I may not be able to transfer her much longer—if at all.

LATER

I accepted Theo's offer to come over tonight. Since Mother had trouble swallowing, giving her the tranquilizer was a challenge. Theo and I brainstormed and came up with the idea of a dropper. The pharmacist suggested using a pediatric dropper. It worked perfectly.

Saturday, October 28

Marcia came prepared to spend the night with us. She sat by Mother's bedside all afternoon and read beautiful passages from the Bible to her. I sat in the living room, listening and crying. It was so touching to hear her soft voice, especially when she read the 23rd Psalm, and knowing that even though Mother couldn't hear the words, she could feel Marcia's love and tenderness.

Mother didn't say anything today. She simply shook or nodded her head in response to questions, or lifted her hand or finger to indicate she didn't want any more water or pudding.

My cousin Doug called. He said he had called all our cousins in the area and checked on a restaurant where the family could gather for dinner after the cemetery service. I was so grateful.

It took twenty mg. of tranquilizer to put Mother to sleep tonight.

Monday, October 30

Mother was significantly weaker this morning. After checking her, Mary Jo said, "Marian, we need to talk."

She began by telling me that Mother would not be here when Jackie returns from her medical leave. I knew that. She told me that Mother's hands were turning blue, and there was mottling on one of her legs. *I thought those were bruises.* The significant change, though, was the cyanosis in her hands—a definite sign that death is near, perhaps in one to two weeks. She explained that Mother's extremities will be cold, but the trunk of her body will be very warm with a temperature of 101 or higher.

I cried when Mary Jo told me the timeline. Even though I knew it was coming soon, to hear the confirmation made it real. Mary Jo comforted me, massaging my shoulders and allowing me to cry. I was shaking. I felt I had a huge, gaping wound in the center of my body—and it kept getting larger and deeper.

I called Shirley to find out if she could come over this evening. "I was planning on it," she told me. I need someone with me this evening—definitely.

LATER

It took eighteen mg. of tranquilizer again tonight. Mary Jo explained that as Mother declines further, her body will begin producing a natural sedative and she'll require less medication. But we don't know when that'll be.

Called Cris tonight. We talked about the awesomeness of this, how the natural cycle is being completed and a return to the womb is being made. I feel privileged to have not only witnessed it, but to have lived with and cared for Mother as she makes this journey.

Called Carolyn, my niece in California. She'll call Elaine and Bob, her sister and brother. She is recuperating from major surgery, but will ask her doctor for permission to travel. She wants to be here.

Tuesday, October 31

Mother is now up to twenty-two mg. of tranquilizer. After checking with Hospice about giving her the last dosage, I sat beside her. Her hands were in constant motion around mine for forty minutes. This time, however, it didn't bother me. I wanted to be there with her. Knowing that her time with me is so short, I want to give her all the comfort, love, and care I can.

Mother is too weak to be transferred to the commode. She is totally bedbound now. Her vital signs are still good, but weakening. Mary Jo noticed a dramatic weight loss since yesterday. With the lack of food and increased weight loss, the vital signs will continue to weaken.

Mary Jo said she couldn't do what I'm doing. I'm glad I never knew what I'd be doing. I would have thought I couldn't. But here I am.

There was a special closeness between Mother and me today, a tenderness both of us felt. At one time, she very lovingly put her hands on my hair. That was her way of telling me she loved me and, perhaps, thanking me for taking care of her. She tried to whisper something to me, but it was indistinguishable. We communicate mainly through our eyes and touch.

I'm going to bed now.

I'm so tired, so very tired.

Wednesday, November 1

In my reading this morning, I came across this thought:

"A new role in life with new responsibilities can leave us feeling overwhelmed. Yet, it is during such times that we discover our true strength, capabilities, and faith...."[12]

The right words are always there when I need them.

LATER

Pat, our Hospice health aide, bathed Mother, shampooed her hair, and changed her bed linen today. Knowing I enjoy watching ice hockey, she told me about her son, who is an avid Detroit Red Wing fan, too. I asked if he'd like tickets to Saturday's game. Pat was delighted and will ask him tonight. There's no way I could leave Mother now to attend that game. I hope Pat's son will want the tickets. I know Elaine and Jim will understand.

Carolyn called this morning. She can't travel for a month while she recuperates from her surgery. She's very disappointed about not being here, but both of us understand.

Thursday, November 2

Didn't sleep much last night, except for two hours between 5:00 and 7:00 this morning. That's okay. It's difficult for me to rest comfortably

---

12 *Daily Word,* 133, 11 (December 1995): 65. Unity Village, MO: Unity School of Christianity. Reprinted with permission.

with the sound of Mother's raspy breathing coming through the monitor, not to mention my intense concern.

As Mother has declined, so has everything she used to do.

She declined from bathing
 in a tub by herself,
  to using a shower chair,
   to a sponge bath,
    to a bath in bed.
She declined from washing her face
 while standing at the bathroom basin,
  to sitting in a chair by the basin,
   to using a basin in her bedroom,
    to having someone wash her face.
She declined from eating
 at the table unassisted,
  to being fed at the table,
   to using a tray table,
    to being fed in bed.
She declined from being fully dressed
 to wearing just pajamas,
  to wearing just a pajama top,
   to wearing a hospital gown so nothing
    would bruise her delicate skin.

Yes, we do come full circle.

LATER

While Mother was awake for a few minutes tonight, I told her again how very much I loved her…assured her she was in her own home…that I will always be here with her. I sensed an aura of peacefulness. A serene smile came over her face. Nodding her head ever so slightly, she closed her eyes as if to say, "Now I can rest."

Later, I awakened Mother to get her ready for the night. I talked teasingly about finally becoming a nurse to care just for her. Again, I thanked her for being my mother. I told her that soon she would see Dad, Bob, Jack…that I will always love her…that I am a part of her and she is a part of me…that she has my permission to leave whenever she's ready.

At that point, Mother raised her hand to mine. I held it and knew that she had heard me. She placed her hand on her chest, and I kissed her several times. It was a beautiful moment!

Friday, November 3

I got up at 3:00 this morning to give Mother some water and turn her. From then until dawn, I listened to her weak, shallow breathing and counted her respiration cycles. All was okay—for that moment.

Mother's diaper was practically dry this morning, meaning her kidneys are shutting down. After making sure she was comfortable, I busied myself making Christmas cards. That was an odd choice, but I had to do something—anything—to keep myself occupied.

LATER

Mary Jo said Mother was in a "level of consciousness three" which is a semi-comatose state. No pulse. She wasn't sure if she would live through the weekend. "Get on that phone," she told me emphatically, "and get people out here to be with you. This is pay back time. You are not to be alone this weekend."

There was no need to give Mother any more of the tranquilizer.

LATER

It took a couple of hours for Mary Jo's words to penetrate my numbed mind. Then I panicked. I called Theo. No answer. I left a message and called back in an hour. She was making lasagna for dinner and would come over later.

How long does it take to bake lasagna? I was frantic. I didn't know what to do, who to call.

I called Pat in New Mexico. I had to talk with someone. I needed someone. Pat was a good listener and did her best to console me with kind, reassuring words.

I was a "bag of nerves."

You are not to be alone this weekend.

Mary Jo's words kept reverberating in my head. What was going to happen? Why was it so important that I not be alone? I didn't doubt her words. Hospice nurses definitely know whereof they speak.

Two minutes later, the phone rang.

"This is Mary Meyers, the Hospice on-call nurse. I'm coming right over."

The phone rang again.

It was Theo calling back to let me know that she was coming over right away and bringing her sleeping bag to stay overnight.

I was so grateful!

Mary came first, then Theo. My niece, Kathy, and her husband came, too.

Mary talked with them and answered all their questions.

I was numb.

They went into Mother's bedroom to say their goodbyes.

I couldn't go in.

Mary gave me an angel pin to wear. Her kindness touched me and the tears flowed.

Marcia called to say she'd be here tomorrow and stay all night.

LATER

I'm relieved to have Theo here tonight. Yes, I do need someone to be with me. I have never taken care of anyone who was so sick, let alone dying—albeit my mother.

Poor Mother. She's comfortable, peaceful, but that raspy breathing sound is awful. Mary Jo said it may get worse.

Saturday, November 4

I slept off and on for four hours with my ear to the monitor. I jumped up a few times during the night thinking Mother had stopped breathing. She was okay, though—whatever that means.

Mother has such a peaceful countenance this morning. Her face is so beautiful, so smooth and relaxed. It appears that all the wrinkles have been erased. She looks very young, like she did in that photograph taken when she was twenty-four, just before she and Dad were married. She was beautiful!

Calling people for help this weekend was not asking too much because it will be Mother's last. Now is the time I'll let others "do" for us. My goal of caring for Mother in her own home has almost been accomplished. Everything is in readiness for the tasks that are ahead.

All our Hospice nurses called today: Allison, Mary Jo, and Mary. Yes, we are being well taken care of—very well, indeed.

Pat called from New Mexico. She is ready to hop the next flight whenever I call her to come. Such a good friend! And, yes, I accepted. Pat's presence will be exactly what I need. She's quiet, an excellent listener, and will be a sturdy anchor for me.

Sunday, November 5

It's 6:00 a.m. Time is nothing but a blur.

I didn't go to bed until 2:30 this morning. At midnight, bile began coming out of Mother's mouth. Marcia and I had no idea what was happening. I was so frightened. I called Hospice, and Allison came out immediately. She assured me that sometimes happens as the body shuts down.

Mother is extremely weak. Her thin arms just flop over when I turn her. She has gone deeper into a comatose state. She's allowing her body to do whatever it needs to do in preparation. All we can do is tend to her needs, talk to her, and let her know how loved she is.

The tears are flowing now. I am engulfed with grief…waiting as Mother makes the final leg of her journey.

LATER

At 9:40 this morning, Mother's beautiful spirit left her body and made its transition. It was an incredible experience for me.

During that last hour, I sat at her bedside, holding her hand and telling her how much I loved her, thanking her for being my mother…repeating everything I had said so many times.

At 9:30, I noticed long pauses between each weak breath. I called Marcia into the room. "Grandma's going," I quietly told her. At that moment, a huge amount of bile spewed from Mother's mouth. Marcia and I bathed her and changed the bed linen. We put on a fresh diaper and changed her gown.

Then, just as we were preparing to change the top sheet, Marcia said, "Look! Grandma's wide awake now!"

I looked at Mother's open eyes and saw they were glazed over. "Oh, Marcia, Grandma's in a deep coma now."

I looked again and knew the eyes were looking right through me, not focusing. She had stopped breathing. My mother was gone.

Gently, I closed her eyelids.

They stayed closed.

I called Hospice. Allison said she'd be here, but needed to call Mary Jo and Mary Meyers, our other Hospice nurses. I suggested that she might want to wait before making those calls—until she confirmed that Mother had died. "I don't want any false alarms," I recall saying to her.

Gently, Allison suggested that I walk back in Mother's bedroom and just take another look.

I did.

I felt Mother's forehead. It was cooling.

I noticed the gray look her face now had.

Yes, Mother was beyond us now. She was standing in a Light that we could not see, in a Place that we could not share. She was with her family she had long awaited to join, going from my arms to theirs. Could I possibly wish any more for my gentle mother who had given me so much?

LATER

Allison took care of everything in an efficient, quiet, and dignified manner. I had Mother's blue suit and lace-collared blouse ready for the morticians, just as she wanted. I watched them take my mother's body and carefully place it in the hearse. There were no tears, only a very deep sense of sadness.

My mother was gone.

The minister returned my call. We had made all the arrangements earlier, needing only to confirm the day and time for the service.

I called Pat and Cris. Cris told me about a vision she'd had earlier in the morning of Dad extending his hand to Mother. It was so beautiful! Mother had said several months ago that she was waiting for Dad to come for her. He did!

There were many calls today. Our Hospice nurses called: Mary, Mary Jo, and Jackie. Sarah, our volunteer, called, too. Alma, one of my good friends from Flint phoned, unaware, of course, that Mother had died. She graciously offered to let my Flint friends know.

Yes, I had tears. They just flowed. I didn't try to hold any back. As the day progressed, I felt myself becoming stronger, more confident. Then, there came a feeling of extreme happiness.

"Mother is *safe!* Mother is *safe!* "I said repeatedly. I was so happy because my mother was finally *safe.*

I was at peace, too, because I had fulfilled my commitment to care for my mother in her own home until she made her transition. With God's guidance and the help and support of family, friends, and Hospice, I had successfully accomplished my greatest goal, my most important task—the most challenging experience of my life.

STILL LATER

It's been a long day. Everyone has left now. The apartment is very quiet. I worked on the final details of the tribute brochure.

Now I'm ready for bed.

The monitor has been returned to Hospice.

I will have a peaceful rest.

Monday, November 6

Mother is safe! That was my awakening thought.

Mother is safe! I didn't realized the burden and responsibility I had been carrying for the past twenty-five years since Dad died.

Now it's over. *Mother is safe!*

I feel no sadness at the moment. Yes, I'll miss Mother—whose body gave me birth and whose heart and soul gave me unconditional love for over sixty years. Now that she is truly safe, I can only feel *happiness* and joy.

Mother is safe!

I am at peace.

Almost Three Years Later

Journaling continues to be the way I open and close each day. My journey through the grief process is all recorded as I lived it. That may be another book some day. I know that others would benefit by reading what that process was like for one individual.

Writing this book has taken more than two years. It has been a major part of my healing process. As I transcribed the journals, I relived all those months, days, and moments with tears...with laughter...with sadness...with joy. I saw how each experience prepared me for the next, how each was necessary, and how all were part of a greater plan.

I am not the same person who began that journey almost eight years ago. I have grown. I continue to evolve into becoming who I truly am— a child of God, dedicated to the purpose for which I am here: to learn, to love, and to serve with love.

About the Author

A graduate of the University of Michigan-Ann Arbor, Marian Wright has experienced a varied career in public education as a classroom teacher, a speech therapist, a teacher for learning disabled and emotionally impaired children, and a language arts curriculum consultant. Now retired, she actively supports the writing programs at the University of Michigan-Flint, specifically, the Marian E. Wright Computer Writing Classroom and Writing Center. She resides in Flint, Michigan.

Printed in the United States
21387LVS00001B/91-168